Public Expenditure Management and Public Policy in India

About the Author:

A. Premchand retired as Assistant Director, International Monetary Fund, Washington D.C. He has authored/edited more than fifteen books. Several of his books have been translated into Arabic, Chinese, Russian and Spanish. Six of his books, all published by the IMF, are now available as e–books. A. Premchand has earlier been a guest lecturer at the John F. Kennedy School of Government at Harvard University, USA. The author is now based in Hyderabad, Andhra Pradesh, India.

Public Expenditure Management and Public Policy in India

Crises and Renewal

A. PREMCHAND

ACADEMIC FOUNDATION
NEW DELHI

www.academicfoundation.org

First published in 2016
by

ACADEMIC FOUNDATION
4772-73 / 23 Bharat Ram Road, (23 Ansari Road),
Darya Ganj, New Delhi - 110 002 (India).
Phones : 23245001 / 02 / 03 / 04.
Fax : +91-11-23245005.
E-mail : books@academicfoundation.com
www.academicfoundation.org

Cataloging in Publication Data--DK
Courtesy: D.K. Agencies (P) Ltd. <docinfo@dkagencies.com>

Premchand, A., 1933- **author.**
Public expenditure management and public policy in India : crises and renewal /A. Premchand.
pages cm
Includes index.
ISBN 9789332703308

1. India--Appropriations and expenditures. 2. Government spending policy--India. 3. India--Economic policy--1991- I. Title.

HJ2157.P74 2016 DDC 336.390954 23

Typeset, printed and bound by The Book Mint, New Delhi.
www.thebookmint.in

To

Venu

CONTENTS

Acknowledgements 9

Introduction 11

1. **A Framework of Public Expenditure Management System** 17

2. **Tasks of Public Expenditure Management: A Review of the Status** 37

3. **Changing Economic Mandates and Other Aspects** 71

4. **Some Lessons from the Corporate Sector** 99

5. **Partnerships, Contractorisation and Procurement: Selected Issues** 119

6. **Delivery of Services: New Stalemate in a Hollow State** 143

7. **Use and Abuse of Tool Kits** 155

8. **Praxis of Federalism: Dominance and Dependence** . . . 223

9. **Crises and Renewal** 251

Appendix: Corporate Sector and Ethics 303

Index 311

Acknowledgements

After 2010, owing to several developments, all of which were beyond my control it was decided not to take up any new writing projects. In 2012, we moved from California to Hyderabad so that we could avail of more domestic help to assist my ailing wife. The decision not to take up any new writing remained however, at least up to 2014. During 2014, Prof Gayithri of the Bangalore based Institute for Social and Economic Change, requested me to contribute a chapter for a book edited by her. I agreed to her request with great reluctance. I knew that my own physical abilities were declining fast and that more effort was needed to produce even a single page. Having agreed, however to the request, I began to write notes that were to form the basis of the chapter. Very soon, however the notes began to grow in size, coverage and content and exceeded more than 100 pages—much beyond the scope of a chapter.

It appeared that they were becoming notes for a book. A second opinion appeared wiser. So the notes were given in a manuscript form to my friend Dr Y.V. Reddy for his advice. Despite his own growing commitments, he read those notes and came up with a strong recommendation that the book be completed at the earliest. That is how the book came to be written. My grateful thanks are to Dr Reddy for going through the 400 page manuscript and offering many suggestions for improvement. My daughter Padma and son-in-law Bhogesh offered me a room in their office where I could complete the book in comfort.

They also provided me with the needed logistical support to take me to the office on alternate days and bring me back home in time for Lunch. Their help is much appreciated. The manuscript was typed and given an electronic form by Arthur Monteiro, who rose to the occasion despite his own poor health. To him I owe a special debt. The processing of the book for publication was entrusted to Dr Y.V. Reddy who readily came to my rescue. Rituraj Kapila and his associates at the Academic Foundation were very helpful at every stage of the production of the book.

Introduction

The fundamental principles of public expenditure management are so simple that, it is said, even a child develops his own understanding of it and alters his own behaviour accordingly. He knows that he has to provide an account of how he has utilised the money given him; that he has to be prudent in spending the money and may wish to save a little for the rainy day; and that he has to be wise in organising his spending needs and choices as the resources are limited (in the jargon of economists, the "hard budget constraint"). He knows the "happiness-misery" calculus that was so elegantly described by Charles Dickens. These principles continue to be applicable as the analysis moves from a child to an individual, to a family to an enterprise and to a government, with the difference that when it is applied to a corporation and to a government, particularly one working in a democracy, there is an administrative and institutional infrastructure to support the processing of various transactions. In the corporate world, there is a Chief Financial Officer or a Comptroller who oversees the financial management of the corporation, while in the case of governments that task is entrusted to a "Treasury", as it was known in old times, or its modern version, the Ministry of Finance, and the administrative agencies.

The principles and objectives to be kept in view while managing public expenditure, particularly in a democratic setup, have become more numerous and far more complex. The discussion in the following chapters is an account of these developments. Experience shows that the application of the accepted canons of expenditure management has become somewhat comic and, paradoxically, tragic. Why this is so is the subject-matter of this book.

The subject, and its application to government, have gone through major changes in course of time. The first set of principles and the process of their application were delineated, if Kautilya's classic work *Arthasastra* is kept aside for a moment, by the writers and bureaucrats of the East India Company. Those were the times when all decisions were made by the Board of Directors in London and were transmitted to officers in Calcutta for implementation. To all intents and purposes, the Company headquarters in Calcutta had no independent sphere of action. In that context, they wanted to organise a department, later known as the Finance Department, in which all financial matters were centralised and without whose permission no expenditure could be incurred nor revenues raised.

Thus the Finance Department became the first among equals. This principle and related management reflected the importance given to the management of finances. The bottom line always was the profit the Company made from its Indian operations. These arrangements went through some minor and major changes as progress was made in developing greater power for the Indian administration after India became a part of the British Empire. Notwithstanding the administrative changes made within India, and in the relationships with Whitehall, the basic foundations laid during the Company rule continued to operate save a few cosmetic changes.

After Independence too, despite the emphasis on serving the people and government servants being viewed as serving the community in such a manner that the end needs of the people became the dominant theme, the immediate emphasis was on continuity except that the designations were changed from Governor General to President after the Constitution became operational. The Constitution provided the legitimacy for the fund structure that regulated the payments into and by the government. Thus, a Consolidated Fund, a Public Account, and a Contingency Fund (which was more notional than substantive) were organised to facilitate credit of money into the government accounts and withdrawals from them.

Beyond these accounting provisions, the only provision of substance was that the power held by the Finance Department during the Company rule was shifted to Parliament, in that no moneys could be spent without an appropriation which signified the approval of the legislature. The policy framework relevant for the purpose is provided in the "Directive Principles of State Policy", which also provided that the "State should secure a social order"—or as the first Prime Minister explained in a different context, the effort should be aimed at "creating a just state by just means"—"for the promotion of the welfare of the people" (Art. 38) "in which justice, social, economic and political shall inform all the institutions of life". This and other provisions included in this section of the Constitution (Part V) are entirely aspiring and are not enforceable by any court of law. These changes did not reflect any major change in the prevailing practice, save the creation of a social order, which was more implicit since the 1935 Act.

Changes were, however, made in the later years in the structure of budget through the introduction of a revised format that was based on performance budgeting but fell short of the exacting standards specified in that system, and measures were taken to provide enhanced delegation of powers so that the spending agencies could be empowered to transact their delegated tasks without excessive dependence on the Finance Ministry. More recently, an outcome budget was also introduced. Prior to that, a budget law in the form of a "Fiscal Responsibility and Budget Management" legislation was also enacted, providing an overall fiscal policy framework for the formulation of the annual budget. Notwithstanding these seemingly structural measures, in essence the practice of expenditure management reflects the palimpsest phenomenon. Added to that is a behavioural trait of management which is characterised by an exercise of power by the senior levels on the junior levels. Meanwhile, there have been major changes in the systems of governance in the country.

Right from the announcement of the First Five-Year Plan, many measures were taken aimed at stimulating economic growth and improvement of the standard of living of the people. These included emphasis on village development through community development projects (a programme that was abandoned within a few years after introduction) and development of small and cottage industries which are mostly rural based and reflect the traditional occupational patterns. Later, by the beginning of the Second Plan, the emphasis shifted to industrialisation and expanded state ownership and management of manufacturing and industrial enterprises. Interrupted by the India-China War, the focus shifted to a policy of augmented defence capacity and development. In lieu of export promotion, import substitution became a major policy focus.

Later, while struggling with shortages of industrial materials and foreign exchange, reliance was placed on sourcing adequate foreign exchange from donors and IFIs (international financial institutions).

Once the country moved into the orbit of the IFIs, the sponsoring and implementation of policies advocated and funded by these institutions became the focus. Thus, attention moved, echoing the periodic announcements from the IFIs, to the provision of basic needs, which later morphed into an attack on poverty and introduction of poverty reduction measures. This led, not too long after, to structural adjustment programmes. It is not that the previous programmes announced by the IFIs proved a failure. Rather, these measures were not adequate, with the consequence that the needed growth rates could not be achieved and the tired masses needed to be assured that more measures, stronger and with greater potential, were on the way.

The people did not have to wait for long. A series of developments took place that shifted the emphasis from the government programmes to the government itself. The point of departure was the recognition that government was the source of most of the problems, with their inevitable impact on economic growth. What followed was the introduction of structural adjustment programmes that laid emphasis on opening the trade channels and maintaining a proper exchange rate as well as ensuring fiscal prudence so that higher deficits and related higher public borrowing did not crowd out the private sector investment. Pointed references were made to the Ricardian theory of equivalence and the prospect of higher taxation to pay off the debt. These tenets found warm support in the form of what was then called Washington consensus. This one-size-fits-all approach became the packages offered by the IFIs to the countries drawn from the developing and industrialised world.

The new set of policies, it was emphasised by the IFIs, needed the support and participation of the stakeholders; they should start owning the new set of policies and projects. In addition, with a view to drawing up a broader and self-consistent design of development, attention was paid to the strengthening of transparency and accountability. The concerns for the citizens' grievances, as well as measures aimed at curbing corruption were also given the requisite support. Since the goal was improved governance, the need for decentralisation and extended application of the subsidairity principle was also stressed. In between, the international agencies found ample time to consider the inherent ethnic conflicts in multi-ethnic, multi-cultural societies, and attention was paid to the triggers that spark them and not infrequently exacerbate them, leading to greater damage to society.

Over the years, several management techniques were claimed to have been introduced in the ministries, their attached offices and other implementation agencies. These include investment appraisal, programme evaluation and review, performance budgeting (supplementing the main budget system but not supplanting it), outcome budgeting, performance measurement and monitoring, introduction of incentive schemes to enhance productivity, capacity building measures, and improving the interface between society and government. A good deal of management jargon has crept into the operation of the government, its daily announcements, reports to Parliament and the public, and other activities.

If these innovations, which as claims go, have been in operation for some time and have been implemented in the manner in which they are supposed to be implemented, then India would be having one of the most advanced and effective governance systems. But from the point of view of the people who are in daily touch with the street-level bureaucracy and who would experience the fruits of innovation, if there were any, directly, these benefits still remain to be reaped. It is not a problem with the people at all, who continue to depend on the government for a variety of services. They point out, on the other hand, that at every level there is need for recourse to political intermediation to get their requirements, be it potable water, removal of garbage from the streets, or provision of health and related benefits. As the middle class grows in size, there is more demand for economical and efficient services. They do not find any reduction in paperwork even after the introduction of e-governance in matters that are of greater concern to them. They find that the retail cartels have taken over the market, while the government keeps on studying the situation, as it has been doing for all these years. The people are waiting for results that, like a mirage, keep receding further. They also see a discord between what is intended and what is happening.

There have also been dramatic changes in the patterns of governance. Now, PPP (public-private partnerships) are viewed as a panacea for all the problems of governance. There is no recognition in government that in many areas its approaches have to change, particularly in regulation and expenditure management. Government continues to rely on an antiquated, uneconomical tool kit to deal with the new situation. As a consequence, the private partner cartels are having the better of the deal and at a high cost to people. The partnerships have become another layer of bureaucracy and a high-priced machinery. The promises of economy and efficiency have receded into the background.

In addressing the tasks of governance of today and tomorrow, it is important that the present state of affairs is examined and evaluated in some detail. Superficially, there are three questions regarding the system of governance currently in practice that need to be answered. First, is it better than what it was before? Second, is it capable of addressing the embedded conflicts in society? And third, is it capable of providing the just means for creating a just society? The discussion in the following pages seeks to present a picture of the system of public expenditure management now in practice and examines the limitations faced as well as the approaches aimed at resolving some of the issues. It aims at presenting a graphic picture of the elephant in the room, which those serving in government and those who claim to lead the people have so far missed either by intent or by default.

A few words about the style of the book. It avoids the typical academic style of extended footnotes and catechisms. Deliberately, these have been kept to a minimum. The intent is to tell the story in a simple and direct way. It is a modest attempt at explaining how the system evolved and where it stands now—poised for a breakdown or breakthrough.

—A.P.

1

A Framework of Public Expenditure Management System

William Faulkner, who was awarded the Nobel Prize in Literature in 1949, famously said, "I say money has no value; it's just the way you spend it." His epigrammatic sentence encapsulates several dimensions of fiscal policy.

The objective of fiscal policy is to provide goods and services that society needs. To provide them, governments use their coercive power to levy taxes and collect them. The people's willingness to pay taxes, in turn, depends partly on how the money is spent by their government. A government may also borrow from society when it believes that raising more resources may not be feasible, either or both for political and economic reasons, and therefore borrow from domestic or external sources. Borrowing involves payment of a price to the lenders. Here again, the community's participation in the government's borrowing programme depends upon how the money raised is proposed to be spent. Governments have the delicate task of managing their expenditure in such a way that there are visible and tangible benefits flowing to the people. They also have the task of achieving a balance between what is being taken from society and the benefits accruing to it in return. Provision of goods and services to the people is not merely a technical exercise: it involves, in fact, constant consultation with the representative institutions that form a pivotal part of a functioning democracy.

Such consultation is at the heart of democratic governmental processes. In this process, major roles are assigned to the three domains of a democracy, namely, the Executive, the Legislature, and the Judiciary. Together, they ensure that proper magnitudes of resources are allocated for those services; and even more important, that the resources are effectively utilised. The final results achieved go beyond what may be perceived as a mere technical exercise, concerned primarily with numbers.

It may safely be asserted that anything—and everything—in government goes beyond numbers. Fiscal policy is about people, their needs and requirements. The requirements include maintenance of financial stability so that an acceptable path may be specified for the community's prosperity. If the government's spending programmes are such that they lead to excessive borrowing from the domestic or external sectors or both, or engage in disproportionate deficit financing, the first casualty is the value of the local currency. When the value of the currency depreciates, the people get hurt: and that damages the national economy. In sum, addressing the community's needs is fraught with many possible invidious adverse consequences, which strongly advise prudence.

Above all, expenditure management has the main task, not as yet fully addressed, of managing the people's expectations. It needs to be remembered that behind each rupee collected there is a tale of blood, sweat, insecurity, and disappointment about what the government could have done with their earning for them, and they feel bilked as the bulk of what is spent is devoted to administrative expenses, at the expense of actual provision of services. Moreover, economic cycles would appear to have, in periods of recession, more adverse effect on population that belongs to the lower economic class. In periods of severe shortage, there are major interruptions in services; and rationing is frequently introduced, which seems to affect only the people in the lower-income group. The affluent appear to be exempt from all shortages and interruptions. Even where services are available, the poor are frequently called upon to accept below par services: and even so, may require extensive political intermediation, which has a price of its own in terms and may involve commitment of voting loyalty for a prolonged future. The so-called political choice is available only for a few. The public is called upon to face volatility in price as well as in the supply of services.

Even as these experiences have become the people's day-to-day routine, they remain unclear about how they should react to the periodic pronouncements made by their government about the reforms made in their system of governance and, more particularly, how a new era is about to dawn. The irony is that many of the expenditure management reforms carried out by governments are not intended to reach the people they are supposed to benefit. Consider, for example, the case of improved internal financial management in the administrative ministries. Their impact, even at the best of times, is not discernible to the common person. It is simply like a movement of furniture within one's house. Where it is supposed to have an impact, as in the case of outcome budgeting, the reaction of the common person is that it is an embellished account of what is, in fact, a failure. Tall claims, mostly unfounded, and frequent resort to lying, leave the public befuddled. Claims about improved accountability, for example, sound hollow. The public continues simply to ask why, against the government claims of blamelessness, how it explains the periodic scams that burst on the scene. In the view of the public, there has been a fundamental change in the value system, in that public virtue has yielded place to personal greed. While the government has expanded in numbers, including employees working on contracts, more and more services are being entrusted to the corporate sector, contributing to a hollow State that is becoming weaker by the hour. It has been said that the State started becoming more corrupt after Independence, and that it also became soft later on. The soft and corrupt State could not address the problems of corruption. In fact, the inexorable growth of expenditure contributed to a Hollow State. The State, in its present form, is viewed as corrupt, soft and hollow. The exploitation of public resources for personal use is viewed both as a legal and a moral failure: and any further decline would lead to even more severe problems. These, and a million other questions, on the adequacy of the expenditure management system need to be probed, evaluated, reformed and answered if the people's faith in democratic functioning is to be sustained.

A convenient starting point is a consideration of the annual budget, which is both an instrument and an outcome. It is an instrument in that it is intended to be a mechanism for the allocation and utilisation of public resources, while achieving a modicum of financial stability. It is also an outcome inasmuch as it is the result of a good preparatory work, and represents the best plan of action for the next year and beyond.

Public Expectations of Desirable Standards

The desire for order is ancient. In its pursuit, aims, and short-, medium- and long-term goals are formulated and given a shape and structure. The features common to most countries that have democratic institutions governing their finances are summarised below.

1. No expenditure may be incurred without the approval of the legislature.
2. The responsibility for managing the money so appropriated is vested with a designated official in an agency. The focal point is an agency.
3. The appropriation is intended to meet the needs of the agency for a specified period, usually a fiscal year. To enable the legislature to have a better appreciation of the expenditure proposals, the future requirements of current policies as well as new policies may be planned ahead for the next three or four years and submitted to the legislature. The legislature may approve the provision of funds for the next year or for the period for which the policy is to hold sway. Alternatively, this may be used as background information.
4. The requests for money for the next year(s) are contained in what is conventionally known as a budget or, more specifically, the Annual Financial Statement. (The Constitution of India does not use the term budget at all. Legal purists or fundamentalists who believe in the word and not the intent may insist on avoiding the use of the term budget. With due apologies to them, in this chapter the term budget continues to be the preferred term primarily for the reason that it conveys the meaning better.) The budget should be comprehensive and thus include all transactions of the government unless otherwise specifically and legally excluded. Usually, however, with a view to reducing overzealous legislative control, governments may organise earmarked funds with their own sources of revenue and with their own regulations regarding the exercise of authority in the management of these funds. It should be noted that budgets were primarily evolved to meet the requirements of legislative oversight. Over the years, however, the relationships between legislatures and executives have deteriorated and have contributed to several tensions.
5. The funds appropriated are valid for a period of one year. The authority for spending or for raising money lapses at the end of the year. The process of appropriations has a few exceptions in that some categories of expenditure are not subject to voting by the legislature; rather, they are charged or spent without formal

appropriation authority from the legislature. This type of outlays comprises the salaries of the President and the salaries of judges of the Supreme Court and other institutions whose work is of a continuing nature and which essentially reflect the continuation of the State. Public transactions, including interest paid, are among those that are charged expenditures. They reflect, for the most part, liabilities incurred and therefore have to be liquidated. Default in these payments could cause extensive damage to the creditworthiness of the country.

6. Financial transactions of the government comprise three groups: (i) taxing and spending, (ii) lending and borrowing, and (iii) selling and buying. Estimates relating to these transactions are provided in the annual budget. Together they have an enormous impact on the economy of the country.

   Budget outlays are incurred in terms of three object groups: (i) expenses on human resources, (ii) expenses on materials, and (iii) monetary transactions in the form of transfers or grants, to other levels of government, autonomous agencies, non-governmental bodies and others.

7. Budgets cover, in principle, all the agencies and their financial transactions. Mere enumeration of them could cause an information overload without any meaningful insight into the purposes of spending amounts on various objects of expenditure, and the nature of the work sought to be performed. The purpose is to be adequately transparent so that members of the public as well as those who work in government could have a comprehensive understanding of what is involved. To facilitate this purpose, a system of budget classification that is also linked to collection of data by international institutions but within the overall framework of the system of national accounts has been in use for a couple of decades.

   A budget classification system has several objectives. It is expected to facilitate the compilation of accounts; government accounts compile data in terms of the budget classification in use. As an extension of this approach it is also expected to facilitate legislative control in that budget appropriations follow the structure of the budget. In addition, it is the basic framework for the internal financial management of the agency. All legal controls follow the budget classification. Accordingly, the classification has four dimensions. The transactions are classified in terms of object categories, showing the object on which money is spent. Examples of this classification are wages and salaries, allowances, etc., office expenditure and other categories including outlays on materials and transfers to individuals, organisations or other levels of government in the form of grants-in-aid. A second dimension seeks to portray the transactions of each agency in terms of its work, which is classified in terms of programmes and activities. A third dimension relates to the work measurement or output measurement, or outcome assessment. Output refers to the production of measurable results, while outcome refers to the policy results or the impact of the outlays. A fourth dimension reflects the accounting needs in that all activities and their accounting nomenclature, follow a sort of a numbering system to facilitate quick identification. Accordingly, each agency is given the number of the grant under which the legislature provides money to defray the expenses, and the number of the major head (which broadly, but not always, corresponds to the function, i.e., one which has a distinct objective (examples, agriculture, education, etc.) which is subdivided into minor heads and units of appropriation that correspond to the objectives of expenditure. Budgets, like computers, have a language of their own and the above referred dimensions provide, like *Aadhar* cards, a unique system of identification to facilitate legislative action and internal management of the agencies.

In India, there is an additional requirement specified in the Constitution itself: this requirement is that financial transactions be presented to the legislature in terms of current and capital receipts and outlays. There is no other country which has a similar legal requirement. Parenthetically, it should be noted that the basis of current and capital classification followed in the Indian budget is different from the approach of the system of National Accounts.

As government activities grew in size, complexity and scope, the objectives of classification tended to grow. Although the primary purpose of a budget is to serve as a window on the goals, activities and finances of government so that the legislature could exercise its control, in course of time, the public has also become very actively engaged in analysing the budget so that its own actions could be determined in the light of the disclosure of government's financial intentions; and as a consequence, the system of classification tended to be dynamic in updating itself to meet the changing requirements. But as the potential readers come from several fields—policy makers, investors, speculators and other members of the financial market community, finance managers in government, legislators, the academic community and others—the main difficulty is to achieve a degree of transparency that does not throw too much light and provide excessive detail, but throws adequate light to facilitate a reasonable understanding of the government's financial intentions and plans. This has never been satisfactorily resolved.

8. The financial statement of the government as envisaged (mostly by implication than by specification) in the Constitution of India is not the same as a conventional balance sheet. Government budgets in general were and continue to be cash based, whereas a balance sheet is accrual based. A balance sheet reflects the financial status of the organisation. A budget reflects the financial requirements of the organisation—what it gets in terms of receipts and what it spends. The former reveals the stock, while the latter shows the flows to and from the community to the government. Accrual basis refers to the point at which the claim has arisen or liability incurred. Cash basis refers to the point when a payment is made to or by the government. A cash-based budget serves as an ally of monetary policy in that the cash flows of the government indicate the period when it might enter the market to borrow or even to extinguish part of the existing debt. An accrual-based system reveals the total assets and liabilities of the organisation. The accrual-based budget shows or is expected to show the full financial requirements of a project until its completion,

while a cash-based budget shows only the annual financial requirements. Accrual systems reflect the use of resources, while the cash system shows the annual flows without revealing the costs.

For a number of years, governments have relied on the cash-based system primarily because it is fairly simple and easy to operate and therefore within the reach of the common person as well as deep thinkers. Each system has its own strengths and limitations. During the British rule, accounts for commercial and quasi-commercial departments were also provided in the form of a balance sheet and on an accrual basis. Irrigation (commercial), information and broadcasting (there was no commercial broadcasting then) and railways were among the agencies that furnished annual accounts in the form of balance sheets. Following the reforms in New Zealand during the late 1980s and early 1990s, many governments have taken up the publication of half-yearly balance sheets, which are also available on their websites.

From the point of view of internal financial management, however, the accrual system has some distinct advantages. It permits the computation of costs of each activity and thus facilitates a more meaningful control of the use of resources. Thus it permits a shift of control from inputs to the use of resources. As an extension, it also enables the agency to streamline its stores and related inventory management. Moreover, it facilitates the monitoring of commitments, leads and lags in delivery, and the payment schedules.

9. After the approval of the budget by the legislature, the process of budget implementation starts. In reality, this phase reflects the actual implementation of the approved policies and the budget only reflects the financial dimension. Unlike budget formulation, which is a task that is managed by fewer officials, implementation involves thousands of officials. During this phase, it is essential that congruence is maintained between functionaries, functions, and finances. This is also the phase where two distinct approaches come into play. Administrative implementation is the responsibility of the administrative agencies as it is only natural that their primary concern is with

the achievement of the programme goals and any targets that may be specified by the policy-making levels. The viewpoint of the Finance Ministry tends to be different from those of the administrative agencies and exclusive emphasis tends to be on the financial flows only. If the resource situation does not permit it, the Finance Ministry may not hesitate to stop the release of resources to the spending agencies. It is for this reason that expenditure management is viewed as a hurdle in the implementation of development programmes. With a view to minimising the potential or actual friction between these divergent points of view, several administrative instruments have been evolved over the years. These include: (i) The administrative agencies are delegated higher financial powers so that the agencies can move ahead with the implementation process without waiting for approvals from the Ministry of Finance. The extent of delegated powers varies with the range of projects that a Ministry has; and those that have mega projects are delegated higher powers. (ii) Administrative agencies are also given an advance indication of the phasing of the releases of money from the approved budget. These releases are made either for a project or mostly on a quarterly basis. The need for such a time-sliced authority was primarily felt to avoid a rush of expenditure during the last month of the fiscal year with a view to avoiding lapsing of funds. Moreover, the release system also facilitated quarterly cash management and related debt management. These measures reduced the uncertainty about the availability of funds and thus pave the way for orderly fiscal management.

Procedures governing budget implementation are such that they specify that funds provided for a specified purpose should not be diverted for other purposes. The intent was to protect the sanctity of legislative approval. At the same time, it was recognised that owing to a variety of factors the progress in the utilisation of funds might be too slow and there could be avoidable immobilisation of funds. Such immobilisation implied that programmes which otherwise would have made some progress would not be able to do so in view of the non-availability of funds. In any event, the executive wing of the government is often engaged in re-appropriation of funds to other areas that might have a higher political priority.

The rules also specify that there should not be excess expenditure, i.e., in excess of the approved appropriation. At the same time, a total prohibition of excess expenditure could contribute to situations when some important programmes might be held up for want of funds. Therefore, in the Whitehall system, excess expenditures are permitted which are then regularised *ex-post* on the basis of the recommendations of the Public Accounts Committee, a legislative committee.

It is also recognised that several urgent needs may arise in the course of the fiscal year for which funds have to be provided. The Indian system provides for submission of supplementary estimates thrice a year. To the extent that there is extensive or routine use of supplementary estimates, it means that the original budget itself was based on optimistic assumptions and was therefore misleading. But this is an area where tradition and habit have triumphed over the original intent.

The slippages and deviations imply that adequate attention was not given to the risks inherent in budgetary estimates due either to an optimistic frame of mind or a deliberate intent to be economical with truth. These aspects get revealed at the end of the year when the accounts of the year are subjected to audit.

10. The phase of budget implementation is important for a variety of other reasons. The budget as presented to Parliament is an expression of intent and is mostly aspiring. In general, a major part of every budget represents the continuation of existing policies and the element of new expenditures may not be more than 5 per cent of the total budget. New projects included in the budget often take several years before they are completed and to that extent a budgetary provision represents only an annual segment. The provision so made may be substantial or may be relatively small, depending on the importance of the budget and the leads and lags embedded in its implementation. The nature of budget implementation reflects the type of the system selected by the government. In the traditional State, much of the implementation is done by contractors and there are specified procedures for tendering and the selection of

the contractor. These procedures also specify the schedule of payments to be made by the government to the contractor. In numerous cases, the contracted cost or outlay is often different from the estimated cost. (A notable exception in this regard is the Delhi Metro which, reportedly, was completed within the original estimated cost and time frame.) This in turn has several contributory factors. First, the initial estimate may have been prepared a few years ago before it has been subjected to the "due process" prescribed for the purpose in the government and a good deal of time would have elapsed by the stage it was finally approved by the government. Meanwhile, the actual rate of inflation would have contributed to an increase in the estimated cost. Also, there is a good deal of rigging of the contractual process itself in that contractors would have colluded to anticipate a substantial increase in the estimated cost. Moreover, the design of the project itself could have been altered to reflect the changing goals of the project and the changes in technology of the project (A case in point, if only for the reason that it is still fresh in the minds of policy makers and the public alike, is the extensively refurbished aircraft carrier acquired from Russia). These factors contribute to cost escalation, for which contractors have to be suitably compensated. The next result is the perception that there are many leakages in the system and that it is not as effective as it should be. At every step of the system, the system is expected to be looking for economies and efficiency, but then it is the same system which is contributing its own quota of anomalies and errors.

It should be noted, however, that despite the best intentions, the path of the pursuit of economy and efficiency is never smooth, and there are pressures, mostly political and other vested interests, that hamper progress at regular intervals. As a consequence, there are excess outlays, i.e., more than what is approved by Parliament, and in some cases, many cases of under-expenditure too. Both slippages reflect the poor quality of estimation, and the failure of the expenditure management system. More important, they reflect a failure of legislative control. Both aspects have an enormous impact on the allocative and technical efficiency of public expenditure. Excess and unauthorised expenditure implies that some other needy projects may have been deprived of resources. Alternatively, if the excess outlays have been financed from the proceeds of borrowing, the size of the budget deficit would have gone up, with attendant consequences.

If, on the other hand, it is a case of under-expenditure, it could very well mean that a stream of benefits, that were expected to be created, were not created, leading to an adverse impact on some sections of the community. It could very well mean the lack of a much-needed incubator in the children's ward of a hospital, lack of a bridge, or lack of a pipeline to bring water into a poor household (the rich get them anyway, either because they have resources to pay for the service or the requisite political clout) or an unattended leak in the roof of a much-neglected school building and similar other regrettable experiences that characterise financial governance in most countries. It is not as though these aspects are not known to the public authorities. On the contrary, they are fully aware of it and most of them spend their days explaining away why this could not be done and how the slippage occurred despite the best efforts. These aspects illustrate how the system itself could end up as its own worst enemy.

In recent years, there has been a change in the nature of the State itself. Unlike the traditional State, which directly managed its affairs, now it is entering into public-private partnerships. These partnerships imply that many projects would now be undertaken by the private parties from their own budgets rather than from the government budget. The role of government in these arrangements is that the services or goods are properly supplied by the private party. To that extent the management responsibility has shifted to the private party, although arrangements for the risks vary from sector to sector. In this process, the State has been hollowed. What is not yet clear, however, are the adjustments made in the expenditure management system to tackle the responsibilities and tasks inherent in a PPP arrangement.

11. The penultimate task in the annual cycle of budgeting and expenditure management relates to the rendition of annual accounts of the government. In view of the extensive computerisation of financial transactions in the banking system and by the government treasuries, the task of compilation of daily and annual accounts has become considerably easier. Traditionally, however, the treasuries send and post daily transactions, following the sequence of the payments received and made, i.e., raw data, to the office of the State Accountant General, an office which is managed by the Comptroller & Auditor General of India, but attached to each state government. A similar practice was followed in regard to the central government too until the Audit and Accounts Department was split during the 1970s, and each central ministry was provided with a Pay and Accounts Officer, and one of the nationalised banks was designated as that ministry's bank so that all transactions relating to that ministry are carried out through that bank. These organisational changes have undoubtedly contributed to faster compilation of accounting data. However, there are problems. The government accounting system has two other additional features—suspense accounts and settlement accounts.. The former relates to an arrangement under which a financial transaction is either credited or debited first to a suspense account pending final adjustment. The settlement accounts refer to arrangements under which a transaction occurring in one area, i.e., a state, is first managed by the Accountant General of that state and later transferred to the relevant level of government, *viz.*, another state or the central government. These accounts are formally settled before the end of the financial year. Transactions of this type, which tend to be large, reduce the utility of the monthly reports in that a major segment of transaction may relate to these suspense and exchange accounts. This matter was reviewed by the First Administrative Reforms Commission (1966-1968). It recommended that these accounts should be abolished and in lieu thereof a system of issue of payment orders be introduced. Be that as it may, the system continues as before.

The annual reports prepared for each level of government, centre and states, known as appropriation accounts, are expected to follow the format of the budget, and are submitted to the respective legislatures with reports of appropriation audit. The term "audit" originally referred to an oral presentation of accounts to the senate or at community gatherings. Later, it came to be understood as a process of verification. These reports, following the Whitehall system, are reviewed by the Public Accounts Committee (a committee that came into being during the sixteenth century in England and is now found in most Commonwealth countries) and later submitted to the whole legislature.

The appropriation accounts as prepared by the Accountant General or the corresponding official have undergone some changes in terms of detail. Earlier, they used to provide considerable detail but in recent years, data are limited in most cases to the major head and in some cases to Demand (an accounting term for the appropriation structure) and thus the extent of detail has been radically rationalised. But this does not appear to have any adverse impact on the overall tenor of legislative control.

12. The final step in the cycle of operations of the government relates to the preparation and submission of an annual audit report by the Comptroller & Auditor General of India and the legislative action on that. It may be noted in this connection that the office of the Comptroller & Auditor General as envisaged in the Constitution of India was endowed with a dual function—as a Comptroller of issues (release of funds at specified intervals) and as an Auditor General. In the event, however, the first part of the title never became operational and the issue of exchequer control is not even raised in public debate anymore. The second part of the title is, however, fulfilled and the Auditor General submits audit reports on the working of both the central and state governments. As an independent constitutional authority, the Auditor General carries a heavy responsibility.

The range of his audit is extensive and includes a supplementary commercial audit of commercial enterprises owned by governments and has the remit to follow the trail of the rupee and audit the working of agencies receiving amounts/grants from the Consolidated Fund of India. In theory, the audit agency is not expected to audit the policies of government. In practice, it is difficult to escape an audit of policies as an audit of transactions and the use of funds inevitably leads to an enquiry into the objective of the funds and the actual use which they have been put to. An enquiry into the objectives of the allotment leads to a detailed investigation into the policies and thus into an evaluation of the effectiveness of operations. In addition, in India, there was an agreement between the Union Ministry of Finance (during the 1990s) and the Comptroller & Auditor General, enabling the latter to undertake a performance audit of selected departments and agencies. For reasons that have never been made clear, this informal covenant between the two was never included in any legislation relating to the duties and functions of the Auditor General. Technically, audit of policies is inevitably a part of performance audit. There is a Chinese proverb to the effect that iron becomes, with effort and time, steel. In much the same way, performance audit too becomes an audit of policies in all aspects except in name. But when the audit reports become too revealing (and thus believed to be more critical than necessary), the government becomes too self-defensive and accuses the Auditor General of exceeding his remit. This is equivalent to straining at the gnats after swallowing the camel. The distinction between performance audit and policy audit is almost invisible and as such does not lend itself to any substantive discussion, although misguided lawyers in government tend to make a lot of noise.

It has also to be recognised that when both government and the Auditor General are engaged in a long-drawn-out futile effort to lend clarity to the latter's operations there are others who cast a critical eye on the financial aspects of policies and their impact on the community and the social good that emerges out of government operations. Civic groups have been engaged in taking up major and minor cases. These range from the Commonwealth Games 2010, where authorities are alleged to have swindled substantial funds for personal gain (reportedly they paid $80 for a roll of toilet paper), to a rendition of "muster roll payments" (payroll for a casual labourer), thus revealing large number of ghost employees, to the Narmada River Valley project (the protests and the informal social audit have contributed to the World Bank pulling out of the project).[1] These experiences may appear rather few and far between, but they have demonstrated the significant and the growing utility of social audit. It is a new and powerful technique that is gaining acceptance. Although the idea is by no means new, it is now a part of the "jugaad"[2] deployed by the powerless masses.

Necessity is, it is said, the mother of invention. So it is that the inadequacies of the audit system have become the springboard for informal but effective systems of social audit. Some contend that social audit is not conducted by professionals, but that is its primary attraction. It is an exercise in participatory democracy, and it is direct action by the people. It provides ample opportunities for training people. Moreover, for the type of audit undertaken by social groups, there is not much of a need for specialised training or skill. For that matter, even government auditors do not have any specialised professional expertise: all that they have is experience gained on the job.

What needs to be recognised is that audit is an in-house critic endowed with requisite legal backing that gives it the needed legitimacy, and an independent attitude. It has, by law, access to all the records and it has the avenues through which its findings reach the people. These features have enabled it to detect all the scams, save a few, and bring them to the notice of the public and the legislature. But recognition of these strengths has to be tempered by the fact that there are obvious weaknesses too. Audit undertaken by any agency, be it governmental or corporate, is selective and not comprehensive. As such, there is

1. For a recent discussion of some of the well-known cases brought out by social audit, see Denyer, Simon (2014). *Rogue Elephant, Harnessing the Power of India's Unruly Democracy.* New Delhi: Bloomsbury.

2. Jugaad, a word of mixed parentage, refers to flexible ways of thinking and a whole range of innovative ideas. For an extended discussion of the extensive prevalence of jugaad in Indian civic life, see Elliott, John (2014). *Implosion: India's Tryst with Reality.* NOIDA (India): Harper Collins India.

a distinct possibility that some matters fall through the holes and escape the notice of audit. Moreover, audit takes place after the transactions have taken place and therefore could take some time. As a consequence, audit findings reach the people long after the event, and the whole endeavour has the appearance of closing the gates long after the horses have fled. Also, audit tends to examine transactions from a legal point of view and not from the efficiency angle. It does not assess whether any organisation could do more to be efficient in the provision of services. But it does show where the vulnerabilities are and it is up to the organisation to address the issues. In this regard the organisations are like the horses that may be taken to a pond but it is up to the horses to drink or not. In the case of an organisation, however, public pressure may be brought to bear on it to persuade it to take action.

The preceding analysis shows the broad contours and the necessary elements of a government financial management system. What the system endeavours to do is to serve the public and protect its interests. Toward this end the organisations and their operating machinery have some common features. The machinery is often hierarchical so that each official has a defined sphere of work, which in itself is a segment of the total charter of work. The architecture of hierarchy may be different from one country to another; essentially, it consists of a command and control structure (relative to the task and the level of the government, *viz.* Centre, regional, state/provincial and local). This hierarchy delineates the division of labour. The offices that are designed as a part of this system generally function as pivot. This feature is called hierarchy.

A second feature is the fact that the organisation is also a reflection of the structure of authority and power—who exercises what, and what constitutes legitimacy. What distinguishes a government agency from any other organisation is its legitimacy, where its function and the requisite power to back it are provided through legislation enacted by the representative democratic institutions.

A third feature is continuity of the organisation. The activities described in the previous paragraphs have evolved over centuries. While the terminology and location of a task in the overall scheme may have moved from one place to another or may have been extensively revamped and shifted to another organisation (as, for example, the movement of the Budget Office from the Finance Ministry to the President's office, or as a part of the Planning agency—as it has happened in several countries; more frequently, these shifts have their roots in political and personal factors), the task in essence has remained the same. It is the continuity of a specified area of work that brings with it a tradition of approaches to policy-making in expenditure management. This feature of continuity enables the maintenance of a cadre with in-built features of a career stream. Prolonged experience in one area provides an opportunity to organise expertise in that area.

The third feature, thus, is expertise. Persons working in a selected area are there, in the first instance, because of their educational background and aptitude. These, in turn, enable an individual to gain access to knowledge and the daily process of dealing with people and their problems and the opportunity of applying one's skills, inherent and acquired, sharpen his judgment, and equip him to anticipate situations and to assess risks associated with a given approach. Every problem has thousands of options; but to an expert, the options are but few, all honed by experience. These are not solutions learnt from academic institutions but are formulated in the full knowledge that a solution has multiple collateral impacts. The expert's solution is one which will eventually be considered to have been the best in the circumstances, for the simple reason that it was viable and had a combination of least cost and maximising the benefit. In some cases, there may no benefits, and the need may be one of reducing the deadweight or ill effects. In all cases, the expertise has the potential of helping the public. This alone is the primary responsibility of an organisation.

Associated with expertise is the feature of objectivity. A person working in a bureaucracy is no different from any ordinary citizen—a common man, with no privileges but with opinions on most issues. What distinguishes the person working in a government organisation from the man on the street is the location and responsibility of the former. His view affects the lives of common people and thus of the community. It has therefore to be objective and impersonal in implementing the policies of government.

These features get institutionalised in government in several ways. In general, however, the views are conditioned by what the proposed actions imply in terms of how much money is needed. Here bureaucracies, like social organisations, develop a point of view, which then morphs, over a period of time, into a value—an opinion that gets imbedded into the day-to-day working of the organisation and is commonly shared by all those who work in that agency. Specifically in expenditure management, there is a value system that splits all the agencies into two groups—the first comprises all the spending agencies whose spending plans require prior approval of either the central Budget Agency or the Ministry of Finance (in India an informal distinction is made in daily usage—the central ministry at the Centre is known as the Union Ministry of Finance, while at the level of the state government is called a Department of Finance. In India, the Budget Divisions are a part of the Ministry and the Department of Finance respectively). The second group has a sole member, *viz.*, the Ministry of Finance or the Department of Finance, as the case may be. The general view is that the first group invariably asks for more financial resources to be allotted to them. Their view is that more resources are always better, as they enable the agency concerned to serve its public clientele groups better. As an extension of this approach, they tend to argue that any suggested reduction in the rate of growth of their budgetary allocation is bound to hurt their abilities to serve their public. The second group, on the other hand, tends to take the view, regardless of the need (however established), that less is enough. In the process, there is an adversary relationship that emerges and that is in continuous need of adjustment so that a level of harmonious working relationship is established. The difficulty in achieving this is discussed at a later stage. At this point, it is necessary to recognise this as a major internal area (the public has often no idea of these battles in allotting and managing public money) of governance.

How do the stages described so far come alive in the operations of a system of budgeting and expenditure control? What are the specific tasks and how are they performed? These aspects are considered in the ensuing chapters.

2

Tasks of Public Expenditure Management

A Review of the Status

The broad features of expenditure management in public organisations have been considered in the preceding chapter. It is now appropriate to consider the different components of PEM (public expenditure management). Broadly, government financial management, which is concerned with the overall process, is divided into three phases—resource allocation, resource mobilisation and resource utilisation. Provision of collectively needed services and goods requires money. Raising that money, in one form or another, requires the use of the coercive force endowed in government, or related instruments such as selling or borrowing from the public within the country or from abroad. All these are tasks that are inherently part of the overall task of resource mobilisation.

Resource Mobilisation

Resource mobilisation, however, is not a part of the subject considered here. Only the other two aspects, *viz.*, resource allocation and resource utilisation are considered here. Both these aspects constitute the bread and butter of PEM. That said, there are a few points of interdependence between resource allocation, resource mobilisation and resource utilisation that need to be kept in view. First, the relationship between what is raised and what is spent is different in public finance from that of personal finance. In the latter, income determines the level of expenditure. For this purpose, the term "income" may be interpreted broadly as well as narrowly. From a narrow perspective, income reflects a transfer of resources from the private sector to the public authority along with the delegated authority to spend it at its discretion, but with the broad approval of the legislature or a similar representative institution. It does not include the resources borrowed that would in due course be returned to the lender. From a broader point, income as accruing to a government may include the proceeds of borrowing too. Although a part of income is derived from the use of coercive power of the government, and the other part is dependent on the creditworthiness of the government, both have specified legal limits. Many countries have legally imposed limits on the level of budget deficits and on the amounts that can be borrowed. These limits were envisaged to encourage the pursuit of prudent fiscal behaviour. Admittedly, the fear is that in the absence of such legal limits, governments in democracies may be tempted to spend beyond their means that would also create many problems of adjustment to the community at large. Thus, the term "limit" in so far as it is applicable to public authorities, has to be taken somewhat flexibly. Consequently, income in the case of government lends itself to flexible use.

A second point to note is that while governments have, in principle, extensive powers to raise revenues, they also have to reckon with the public response to the use of such powers. The public always makes a firm distinction between what it has to pay to the government and what it has to receive from it. The latter is always welcomed with open arms, while the former is undertaken grudgingly. The rich hire expensive lawyers to minimise the taxes they have to pay. The poor, who cannot afford the luxury of hiring the services of an attorney and who are always fearful about the penalties they have to pay, tend to be less litigious and more compliant. The distinction between the two classes is in the ability to hire the tax lawyer. In addition, the lower-income groups may frequently factor in the value of the public services provided by the government. The poor are dependent on the government; while the higher-income groups have many options to meet their needs.

Nevertheless, both groups demand that PEM be conducted prudently and with utmost care in regard to the services provided by government, so that future impositions of tax may be minimised. In effect, they demand an efficient allocation of resources. This consideration alone imposes additional strains on PEM. Similar considerations may not have the same effect on personal finances. Notwithstanding external constraints in the form of limits on what one can borrow, it is finally a matter for the individual to decide whether he wants to borrow in order to meet his growing expenditure needs. Limits thus have a varying impact on an individual and on a governmental organisation. It may be noted that the approaches of both an individual and government converge; and there are more similarities between the two with the growth of financial intermediation in most economies. The growth of credit has led to an easing of budget constraints, with the result that both the individual and the public organisation are currently opting to borrow.

Resource Allocation

The allocation of resources in the public sector is far more complex than in the corporate sector, for two reasons. First, the range of activities undertaken by public agencies is far more complex than any organisation in the corporate sector. This complexity makes policy-making more difficult than in any other sphere. Second, many activities of government do not lend themselves to market tests. While the demand for some goods and services can be easily estimated, there are others that require the application of political calculus—in other words, how the political representatives view these requirements. This political dimension has no counterpart in the corporate sector.

PEM of any government comprises the determination of total expenditure magnitudes and achieving a balance in the allocation of resources among competing demands. The determination of the aggregate level of expenditure is a complex process, in which a variety of administrative, economic and political factors have a major role to play. Administratively, the magnitude takes into account what was spent during the previous year. By tradition, it sets the template for the consideration of either increase or reduction in expenditure. It has become a tradition for the reason that it is the easiest way in which the aggregate can be determined. Most governmental activities are continuing, and the additions or reductions are viewed as marginal adjustments. This implies that government policies are not subjected to *de novo* review each year. For one thing, it is a cumbersome exercise that is not feasible annually. For this reason, focus is laid on the additional resources needed for continuation of existing policies and the monies needed for the initiation of new policies. In rare cases, depending on the economic situation, reduction in expenditure may be needed even on continuing programmes. This may involve several changes in the structure of programmes with the objective of achieving a short-term reduction in outlays. Thus, the exercise involves the reconciliation of what is desirable with what is feasible.

From an economic point of view, the most important question sought to be addressed is whether the proposed new aggregate involves pumping more money into the community or taking more from it. If the new outlays are to be financed through additional taxation, it may lead to a situation where more may be taken from the community rather than giving more to it. In short, the determination of the aggregate expenditure level leads to a determination of the means of financing. But as will be shown later, this is not how expenditure planning was done earlier. Rather, the aggregate was derived as a sum total of the financial requirements of all the departments and agencies that are covered in the budget.

Aggregate outlays are determined by using multiple prisms. The administrative and economic prisms presented here in a somewhat oversimplified form (despite the abundant warning issued almost a century ago by Prof Frank H. Knight that oversimplification could be tantamount to a kind of falsification) due to length restrictions, do not exhaust the angles from which the issue is examined. Another important dimension is the political prism. Both administrative and economic prisms are in a way subsystems of what is essentially a political system. Each of these three prisms is interdependent on the other two.

The political prism is viewed both in a broad way and in a narrow way. From a broad perspective, it involves the determination of the goals of the nation and the choices that a government has to make and offer it for the approval of the representative democratic institutions, and ultimately the people themselves. For example, a major question which has not yet been satisfactorily addressed relates to the simultaneous pursuit of the twin goals—economic prosperity and military preparedness[1]—and the determination of their quantitative and financial aspects. The narrow approach is limited to the financial aspect of the policies, assumed continuities, new requirements and hidden pressures of several other factors. As a part of the latter approach, PEM seeks to reflect the policy choices already made, and on that basis, delineate the relative roles of the public sector, government

1. For a recent discussion of these and related issues, see Cohen, Stephen P. and Sunil Dasgupta (2010). *Arming without Aiming: India's Military Modernisation*. New Delhi: Penguin.

and the corporate sector and seeks to fashion instrumentalities for the achievement of various goals. The pursuit involves the specification of balance at each stage between the government and the rest of the economy.

On the face of it, this might appear to be both an essential and an inevitable step in any system of financial management. But as history shows, this obvious and simple step became an integral part of PEM only from 1966 onwards. Until then, the process was one in which the government agencies were asked to furnish their financial requirements as a first step. These were then aggregated and sought to be reconciled with the estimated resource situation. The financial year started with these tentative plans and the budget was steered during the year depending on the changes in the economy and the consequent changes in fiscal policies. The system had little stability, as ad-hocism became extensively prevalent. It was in this context that important questions came to be raised on the nature and adequacy of the then system of PEM.

It came to be recognised that the previous type of PEM was essentially carried out within the framework of one year—an imperative that came down from the ages as a part of the system of legislative control. The prevailing view then was that any long-term commitment of financial resources had the potential of diluting legislative control. But it proved to be an inflexible constraint in that it was difficult to plan and execute policies within a period of one year. Most policies bore fruit, if they were successful at all, over the medium term. It was also recognised that expenditure analysis was carried out as if it were a watertight compartment, unrelated to other activities and to the resource constraint which had a major impact in the choice of projects and programmes. If policies that were planned had significant resource requirements, then those aspects needed to be factored in. So, it was felt that expenditure planning should be envisaged over the medium term, and as a part of this analysis, it needed to be ascertained as to how much of the future resources were being committed for the continuation of the existing policies. This approach would reveal the margins of resources available for expansion of the coverage and content of existing policies as well as for the introduction of new policies. As an extension, the balance in the allocation of resources between the public and corporate sectors would be abundantly clear. These aspects enabled the determination of the aggregate outlays not merely for the next year but for the medium term as well. Another feature of this approach was that the forecasts were done for what were termed as focus years, *viz.*, three years. The forecasts were done on a rolling basis each year for the next three years, a feature that also set the process apart from the development plans formulated as an integral part of development planning that came into vogue in the 1950s and continued to be in practice in several countries. A development plan, by tradition, involved taking a look at what the future needed and how it could be organised by governments. But like many other things, such a fixed look ceased to have much operational significance as the economic situation was in continuous flux. It therefore required many changes to make itself useful as a plan of action. The medium-term expenditure was something more than a plan, as it covered all outlays. (No distinction was made between current and capital or developmental or non-developmental or plan and non-plan expenditure, as most industrialised countries had no development plans; the developing countries that distinguished between developmental and non-developmental had disparate practices in this regard.) The scope of medium-term expenditure was thus essentially co-terminous with the scope of the government itself.

Once the aggregate level is determined, the second step is to allocate funds for different functions of the government (for example, education, defence, etc.). In general, a function refers to a distinct sphere of activity that has no overlap with any other activity. (In other words, all similar or interlinked activities are included in the same cluster. This may often be different from the actual organisational layout of a government that reflects political expedience than organisational compactness.) This feature enables quick and easy reconciliation with the basic tool of economic planning, *viz.*, the system of national accounts. This second level of aggregation is then, as a third step, further split into programmes and activities which represent, as a first approximation, homogeneous segments of the work of an agency. This step is viewed as essential in view of the fact that while the first two steps illustrate the economic aspects of the allocation of resources, the third step shows what the government is endeavouring to provide, when, how and to whom, and the financial planning involved in such provision. It enables strategic and operational planning while serving as a building block in the overall matrix of an expenditure plan. The fourth step consists in achieving a balance in the allocation of resources in all the preceding strategies. An excess of resources in one and severe under-provision in another could contribute to a questionable allocation of resources. That said, it should be noted that as yet there are no proven methods to prevent misallocation of resources. The absence of a market for some of the activities such as defence makes it difficult to be accurate and foolproof.

It is inevitable then that the best judgements in the allocation of resources are necessarily political and thus are determined as part of the working of political markets. In any democracy, there are lobbies that seek to get more resources than others. They include the military-industrial complex (In India, this is as yet at a rudimentary stage: indigenous production of defence equipment is not significant enough, and more important, is not competitive. It is a base that is still struggling to get recognition), construction complex, social service complex, mineral sector complex, etc. The very existence of these lobbies poses an existential challenge to the process of PEM and to the managers engaged in that process. The process of medium-term expenditure planning facilitates a more informed discussion of all these linkages, and their impact on resource allocation. Despite these preparations, there are always surprises, both from domestic and international factors. The time taken in addressing these changing factors could in turn exacerbate the existing problem, and frequently, new problems may also arise. Thus, the time taken to identify the problem, and the time taken in preparing policies to address them have their own impact on the process. It is always dynamic and vigilance is the price that managers have to pay for the smooth functioning of the whole system. It is as strong as its weakest link and constant attention needs to be given to the vulnerabilities embedded in the system and the new ones arising periodically.

The allocation system described so far does not always guarantee a stable rate of growth in public expenditure. The rate of growth is determined by several factors, including development needs, requirements of economic stabilisation, and the prevalent political philosophy. Moreover, the persistent growth of expenditure creates its own policy choices. Also, the growth presents different sets of problems for industrial and developing countries. In the former group, there are compensatory factors such as the presence of a well-established corporate system, and to that extent, whatever is not provided by the public sector may be obtained from the corporate sector, but at a price. In the developing countries, such compensatory system may not be available, and lifestyles may be impacted more severely than in industrialised countries. The need for restraining the rate of growth of expenditure in the public sector contributed to the formulation of what has come to be known as New Public Management (NPM) philosophy in the United Kingdom and the United States. NPM has, in due course, gained both academic acceptance and political adherence at the highest levels of leadership and has changed the course of PEM both in industrial and developing countries. NPM has 10 principles, which in turn have affected the management of public policies in general and, more specifically, the management of public expenditure. These principles are:[2]

1. Separating purchasing public services from production.
2. Serving customers rather than bureaucratic, political or producer interests.
3. Using market pricing rather than taxes.
4. Where subsidising, doing this directly and transparently.
5. Extending competition.
6. Decentralising provision.
7. Empowering communities to provide services.
8. Setting looser objectives and controlling outputs rather than inputs.
9. Bringing about deregulation.
10. Prevention of problems, rather than cure, through planning.

To be sure, there are several elements that transcend the area of PEM and move into general management, which undoubtedly have an impact on the former. For purposes of discussion, those that are germane to PEM may be stated as follows:

1. PEM should be based on medium-term planning on a rolling basis and should envisage possible gains through reduced growth of expenditure.
2. The expenditure programmes should be subjected to market tests so that alternatives to public provision may be explored. Toward this end, prospects for reinventing public organisations,

2. For a more detailed discussion, see Foster, Christopher D. and Francis J. Plowden (1996). *The State under Stress.* Buckingham (UK): Open University Press. pp.45-116. For a more recent discussion, see Kamarek, Elaine C. (2007). *The End of Government... As we Know it.* Boulder and London: Lynne Rienner.

and those activities that can be conducted on a network basis, and government by market should be explored.

3. Expenditure planning should *inter alia be* carried out within a framework of fiscal responsibility management that provides guidance on the limits of public finances during the medium term. The linkages with other macroeconomic variables should be explicit, transparent and should form the basis of accountability.
4. Governments should undertake, in addition to the annual budget review, periodic comprehensive budget reviews to identify areas where economy in the use of resources could be procured.
5. Introduction of performance and outcome contracting should be explored.

These principles cover both resource allocation and resource utilisation phases, and to that extent elements of future discussion are also anticipated. These will be taken up for discussion at a later stage. The immediate issue that needs to be addressed relates to the organisational aspects of how these aspects are addressed and by which organisation. PEM comprises four types of control. The term "control" has always a hierarchical connotation in that it refers to the fact that the work done by a subsidiary official is reviewed by a senior official to make sure that what is done is in conformity with government laws and regulations and policies announced from time to time. The same principle of transaction of government business applies to PEM except that the relationship here is between a spending agency which is seeking funds from the government and whose request is processed by a central agency, usually the Ministry of Finance or the Ministry of Planning with a view to either accepting or rejecting or reworking the estimates. This structural relationship is elaborated to facilitate the transaction of business. This process has gone through an evolutionary process and now contains (with variations in approach and nuance): (i) policy controls; (ii) process controls; (iii) regulatory controls; and (iv) performance controls. The content of control in each of these stages and the manner in which control is exercised merit brief consideration as these phrases constitute the pivotal part of PEM.

Policy Controls

The annual policy of PEM involves guidance to the spending agencies regarding the considerations that they need to keep in view while formulating the budget estimates for the review of the central agencies. The guidance reflects the strategy that is proposed to be followed during the next fiscal year to address the economic situation in the country. If it is one addressing recession, there may be a pronounced need to step up the outlays so that they could generate additional activity in the economy. On the other hand, if the economy is going through a phase of inflation and to the extent that inflationary impulses are generated by the budget in general, and by expenditures more specifically, the situation may call for greater restraint in accommodating requests for additional expenditure. These aspects require prior consideration and the formulation of a strategy. Such a strategy has a twofold purpose—to inform the general public and other economic agents, and to guide the agencies in the formulation of draft budget estimates. This in turn assumes that there is regular review of the developments in the economy and the formulation of policy measures to address the changing economic situation. Hitherto, this kind of exercise was, more often than not, carried out in confidential discussions, which added a kind of mystery and mystique to the whole budget process. Now, however, the trends in public finances are available to the public on a daily basis and investors in the public react to and adjust their investments in the light of developing scenarios. To be sure, investors were trading in the market before too, but now their actions are based on more informed reactions that in turn are based on daily trends in public finances. To some extent, this change in what the investing public knows and when, has brought sunlight into an area that hitherto was marked by near darkness.

Specific policy guidance from the central agencies is also needed in regard to inflation adjustments in wages and salaries (more so where they are indexed) and contracts where there are provisions for compensation in the context of price increases. In addition to these common features that tend to have an impact on all categories of expenditure, there are specific areas when guidance has to be specific (both in terms of areas and content). Government activities have two features that are somewhat unique to government. First, all policy initiatives involve additional outlays as they imply employment of additional human resources and acquisition of office and related equipment. But these initiatives may not always yield the desired results. Governments are reluctant to admit policy failures, since such admission adversely affects their credibility and their political fortunes. Over a period of years, the debris of failed policies becomes an integral part of installed capacity. In consequence, the costs of operations keep rising in transactions, contributing to an inexorable growth in expenditure. Second, *all* government policies involve public outlays: there is not a single activity that does not require money. Thus, PEM requires a regular review of the dead wood as well as estimation of the financial requirements of new policies (including expansion of existing policies).

Under the existing procedures, all proposals for new policies are required to be submitted to the Cabinet along with an estimate of financial requirements. These proposals are reviewed by the Finance Ministry to evaluate the funds needed as well as the reasonableness of the cost estimates. These estimates, after review and eventual agreement on the scale of requirements, are included in the expenditure grants submitted to Parliament for approval and enactment of the appropriation legislation that permits implementation of the new policy. The Finance Ministry encourages (in practice this is an oxymoron as the Finance Ministry is always considered to be negative in approach) the spending ministries to submit proposals even when they are at an embryonic stage so that it is alerted to the need of financial resources.

To lend verisimilitude to the process, decision-making takes place at various levels, with each level vetting the recommendation of the previous level. As a part of this exercise, officials review the proposals. And later, depending on their importance, the proposals are further reviewed by regular committees (such as investment boards) ad hoc committees, commissions, groups of ministers, and finally by the Cabinet itself.[3] The process of involving so many high-level and medium-level members of the political and administrative classes may give the impression that every effort is being made to make it a participatory process and the intent is to reach viable policies. In practice, however, there is no guarantee that extensive participation will necessarily result in accurate and economic policies. On the other hand, what it does is that members of the coalition governing the country are consulted first

3. The new National Democratic Alliance (NDA) government that came to power at the Centre in 2014 has since abolished the Groups of Ministers as a separate layer in decision-making. The onus of decision-making now rests primarily and firmly on the ministry concerned. To a large extent, this reduces the diffusion of responsibilities in the central government.

so that a collectively agreed policy may be presented to the legislature and the possibility of divisive views are minimised there.

The pathologies of these administrative processes that are designed to facilitate bureaucratic decision-making also need recognition. In the formulation of policies, there are two distinct views that are apparent, which come into extensive play at every stage of the process. The administrative ministry, which has the primary responsibility for the formulation of policies in its area of assigned activity, has its own clientele and related vested interests. The name of the game in the administrative ministry is politics, in that it has to find the best ways to please them and continue to leverage their support for expanding their budgets, staff, etc., so that the overall role of the ministry is expanded and consolidated with each year's budget. From its point of view, the efforts should be consistently geared to expanding its claims on the budget. Toward this end, it is prepared to use all its political weight and related social capital. It also means that the interests of the ministry have become identical with the interests of the power blocs that have extended their support to the ministry. In governments, decision-making is rarely a one-way street, in which what one ministry is proposing or advocating is accepted as gospel truth. The administrative agencies have to reckon with the role of the Finance Ministry in the use of public money. Its role is to exercise control where control is interpreted as comprising the conservation of public resources and the achievement of allocative efficiency.

In playing these respective roles, both sides play administrative games. One of the approaches deployed for the purpose by the administrative ministry is to understate the financial requirements to the extent possible, in the belief that such an understatement would enable it to get more than a toehold in the process. To be sure, however, the consideration of major projects in government has moved a long way from a heuristic selection to extensive application of refined cost-benefit analysis and related feasibility studies prepared by consulting companies. The nature of these companies is not very different from the nature of a defence attorney, *viz.*, they argue the case of their client. Moreover, the assertions of consultants gather more weight in the case of projects that involve investment in complicated technology that has not as yet been fully tried. The veracity of these estimates is then reviewed by the Finance Ministry, whose level of expertise, based entirely on the basis of job experience in the ministry, is in financial matters. The finance ministry officials have to authenticate the proposed expenditure estimates, and to allot resources to the project, the magnitude being determined by the annual budget process. Neither aspect is simple or easy.

The annual reports of the administrative ministry offer ample testimony to the fact that the eventual outlay or completed cost bears little resemblance to the initial proposal. In turn, this shows that the administrative ministries win the case in that they gain initial approval, and their belief, that once it is approved, allocation of resources is only a secondary exercise with much money coming through supplementary appropriations during each financial year. The whole experience is akin to the proverbial camel and the Arab—the latter being pushed out of the tent. Neither the Finance Ministry nor the legislature (with all its investigative arms) can do much about this. In other words, the process and the available techniques of control have not been able to do much about it. This illustrates also that in some cases the financial aspects may not play a significant role in the determination of policies at all. A recent study into the nuclear energy sector points out that "favourable economics was not something that was inherent to nuclear power" and cites a conclusion reached by *The Economist* to the effect that "nuclear power, which early advocates thought would be "too cheap to meter" is more likely be remembered as too costly to matter", in support.[4] These examples are by no means atypical; on the other hand, the landscape of implemented government policies is full of debris of policy failures, stemming from incomplete analysis, wilful distortion of facts and figures, and diversion of public resources for private uses. Each policy failure, be it a scam or something else, is a result of lapses in PEM too.[5] In the ultimate analysis, society pays for every failure of the PEM system. Services are either denied, as a result of the failure of the system, or are made costly. The failures of the system end up as costs and sacrifices for the community. An awareness of these costs should be presenting an agenda for the reform of governance. This, however, is a different issue, considered later.

4. See Ramana, M.V. (2013). *The Power of Promise: Examining Nuclear Energy in India.* New Delhi: Penguin/Viking. pp.153 *et seq.* The author also points out convincingly that many elements that should have been included in the cost estimates were not included at all and that these failures were not given the attention due.

5. For a recent examination of scams in India, see Kumar, Arun (2013). *Indian Economy Since Independence,* Delhi: Vision Books.

Process Controls

Traditionally, the process controls described in this section were considered as the bread and butter parts of what was then viewed as PEM. At that time, relatively less attention was paid to the economics of expenditure or the impact of budgets on the economy. There is abundant testimony to this benign neglect of expenditure in the public finance literature. The points of departure came with two types of academic investigation—one into the politics of budget making and the other into the economics of budgets. The first part of investigations came to the inevitable conclusion that PEM is an extension of politics. The second emphasised the production, distribution and stabilisation aspects of the annual budgets. In due course, as was to be expected, the two fused into one and came to be considered as government financial management or PEM while tax policy and tax administration remained as separate segments. The financing of the budget through the issue of debt instruments, which was also linked with the conduct of monetary policy, came to be viewed as a distinct and self-contained field. This multidimensional approach was also reflected in the organisational assignment of tasks and responsibilities in the central government of India. Thus PEM, in so far as it is confined to process controls, is within the responsibilities of the Department of Expenditure, while budget making, including the analysis and determination of the economic aspects of the annual budgets (with the introduction of development planning in the country, the capital budgets received a different kind of emphasis and were jointly coordinated by the Department of Economic Affairs in the Ministry of Finance and the Planning Commission, whose own role waxed and waned over the years) were, for an extended period, with the Department of Economic Affairs. In more recent years, some of these tasks were shifted to the Department of Expenditure.[6] Tax policy and tax administration have always remained aloof and uncontaminated by other elements of government financial management. Debt management was in general handled by the Reserve Bank of India in its capacity as the fiscal agent of the government. Its remit was always

6. The allocation of subjects within the Ministry of Finance was not always based on principle, although one is articulated to justify a change. Truth be told, the allocation depended more on the personal preferences of the minister. Consequently, the organisational structure of the Ministry of Finance was buffeted by periodic changes. It is difficult to say that the changes were always beneficial. The politics of change is, however, worthy of an independent investigation.

limited to the domestic debt, while external debt was always managed by the Finance Ministry itself. The Reserve Bank of India was also responsible for the management of the domestic debt of the state governments, but following the acceptance of the recommendations of the Twelfth Finance Commission, a beginning has been made to shift the responsibility to the respective state governments. From 2015-16, public debt management at the Centre is being shifted to the Ministry of Finance from the Reserve Bank.

Within this organisational framework, the process controls have a crucial role to play in safeguarding the financial resources of the government. Thousands of years ago, government money and its treasures were kept in well-guarded places—such a place where the treasure was kept was known as the treasury (one reason why Ministers of Finance in some countries, including the UK and the USA, are known as the Treasury). Kautilya has even provided an architectural design for the construction of the Treasury (a design no longer in practice) into which revenues flowed and from which payments went out. The important function of the Treasury was to ensure that the payments into and flows going out were properly recorded and scrupulously maintained. To ensure continuing security and accuracy of the transactions, several regulations were formulated, thus laying the foundation to what goes on now in the banking institutions and the treasuries. Each transaction was to be entered into the record by one person, while another either received the amount or disbursed it, and a third person reviewed and checked the accuracy of the transaction. These three activities were carried out by them in England while seated at a desk that was covered by a chequered cloth. The person presiding over these activities throughout the country came to be known as the Chancellor of the Exchequer. Variations of this practice continue in all payment offices, regardless of the fact whether they operate in government or in a corporation.

This practice has contributed to devising an accounting system that is tailored to the needs of the government. Three basic steps involved in this process merit recognition, as they constitute the heart and soul of the process controls. The first step is the recording of the commitment made, i.e. where the government has made decision to acquire a good or service for which a payment has to be made when received (or when a "constructive delivery" is construed against works in progress: in the language of accrual accounting, this refers to the stage when a liability has been incurred). The second stage refers to verification, where the claim is examined to determine its legality. If found valid, it has to be ascertained that requisite funds are available and that appropriate budgetary provision exists. In addition, it has to be ensured that the official authorising the payment is indeed the person who is legally entitled to do so and that the signature on the document is indeed his own signature. These and other safeguards, which may appear trivial, are enshrined in the regulations and are legally to be complied with. And the third stage refers to payment or liquidation of the claim. That completes the process of settling a claim, in turn implying that a specified task or a part of a task has been completed.

This process has several implications for many related aspects. The first aspect relates to the security of funds in the treasuries. The maintenance of treasury balances was then part of the responsibilities of the Reserve Bank of India, although the administration of the treasury itself was the responsibility of the state government whose personnel manned it. The prevailing view was that no cheque or payment order issued by the government, whether at the centre or in the states, should ever be rejected for want of liquidity in the treasury. This was the golden rule to be followed even when a cheque was issued despite not having any funds to the credit of the department concerned. This view was taken primarily for the reason that the "bouncing" of a cheque reflected very adversely on the creditworthiness of the government and was bound to have an impact on the pricing of future debt issues. But this view is no longer held, on account of several changes that have taken place in the system. The payments are now handled by a nationally owned commercial bank assigned to each ministry. That bank would issue advance caution to the ministry concerned that funds were running low and that the government would be well advised to arrange an overdraft. Monitoring of the financial flows has become very easy as a result of the introduction of automatic data processing. The daily balances of each agency and the central or state governments are now available at the end of each day. Thus, the overall responsibility of payments is now jointly managed by the treasuries and the commercial banks in the nationalised sector. But the treasuries do not maintain as much cash as they used to maintain before, although their tasks in the sub-divisional offices continue as before. Consequently, the onus of maintaining the security of funds is divided between the treasury and the banks. In the former system, the opportunities and the temptation (notwithstanding all the legal deterrents) to engage in embezzlement were substantial; in the current system, that prospect is relatively less.

For a clever embezzler, however, the system is as porous as ever, as illustrated by the case of the Animal Husbandry Department in the state of Bihar, in which a number of officials, ranging from the Chief Minister of the state to the lowest clerk in the department were allegedly involved. The case involved purchase of daily consumables for the animals maintained by the department. In the event, however, the purchases were all a part of an elaborate scam, and spurious documents were submitted and were scrutinised by all the relevant officialdom and were paid to the so-called suppliers. The case has been dragging on for more than a decade. What it proves, however, is that even a well-designed system can be manipulated in the context of extensive collusion among all the numerous participants in the process. It also shows how difficult it is to root out corruption so strongly embedded at every step in the system.

A second aspect relates to the attitudes of the disbursing officers working in the treasuries and the banks. They have the unenviable task of verifying the compliance of regulations specified in the big tomes of *Central Treasury Rules*. The verification process is often tedious, and more often than not trivial (in the eyes of the supplicant), particularly when documents are rejected for various reasons. The criticisms on the payment process would appear to be justified, given the long lines of people awaiting payment. Clearly, abundant patience is necessary for anyone approaching a bank or treasury, although a connection to an insider could provide an instant breakthrough. But the perception of persistent trivialisation and vulgarisation continues despite the systemic changes.

A third aspect relates to the impact of the operations on the financial condition of the government. Experience shows that the outlays of the government have a seasonal pattern in that the highest share of expenditures (sometimes nearly up to half of the budget) are spent in the last quarter of the fiscal year, and more specifically during the last two days (and treasuries are kept open to handle the flow of paper even on weekends and on notified holidays) to avoid lapse of funds. This feature continues to figure in the annual accounts and audit reports with no visible improvement in the situation. It also provides plenty of evidence in support of the argument that notwithstanding scrutiny of claims for more funds in a rigorous manner, there is at the end of the day, considerable slack in the budget and no programme needs to be held up for want of funds. Some of the agencies, in particular the Ministry of Defence, argue that they should be provided with funds that do not lapse at the end of the year and are available on a continuing basis. The argument, however, militates against one of the fundamental features of government financial management enshrined in the constitution and as such needs to be rejected. The rush of expenditure imposes a good deal of strain on all concerned, as documents cannot be subjected to adequate scrutiny and major leakages are bound to occur, with consequential loss to the exchequer. That said, there is no denying the need for attending to substance than form and to purpose than the process.

Regulatory Controls

Regulation in and by government covers a very wide field. It primarily reflects the interests that are sought to be protected through a well-articulated, transparent and accountable regulatory framework. *Inter alia*, it may seek to serve the interests of the consumer, investor, and the producer (mostly to reflect the liability of the product) as well as interests of the community. The field covered by regulation may extend beyond the processes of production and include the licensing of the proposed manufacturing or service activity. The foremost purpose of regulation by government, which is mostly done through legislation, is to protect the community and serve its interests. Specialised, and for the most part independent agencies are set up for the purpose of implementing the legislation.

The regulatory activity in financial management is slightly different in its objectives and the manner in which these objectives are sought to be achieved. As noted earlier, financial management is primarily a system that facilitates the mobilisation and utilisation of financial resources which are placed at the disposal of each agency. The requirements of each agency are, however, different from those of others, as the activities of every agency are different from those of others; yet a common vocabulary and some procedures that are common to all are formulated to facilitate the implementation of government policies. Each agency organises its own internal systems of operations to its liking and convenience. But common elements such as a budget unit and an accounting unit are widely prevalent. Indeed, it can be said that the tasks and functions, not to mention the language they use, across the wide world, notwithstanding the number of languages spoken in various countries, is virtually the same. Yet they require a kind of standardisation so that terms like "appropriation", "sequestering",[7] "assets and liabilities", "plant and property", etc. have a common application. As an extension of this process, the regulatory framework in financial management seeks to formulate standards in each and every phase of internal management. In the absence of these standards, the public's understanding of what is happening in the government may be far from complete or inconsistent or both. Towards this end, the regulatory framework, which often is centralised and managed by the Finance Ministry, pays attention to the following elements.

Accounting Standards

The standards applicable to the corporate sector are, generally, formulated by autonomous professional bodies within the framework of generally accepted accounting principles. Each government formulates standards on the basis of recommendations made by the professional bodies or by others, and makes them applicable, with necessary variations, to the government. Although the double-entry book-keeping system is more than five hundred years old, many governments, including India, follow the single-entry system; consequently, the Government of India does not prepare any balance sheet as in the corporate sector. Needless to say, there are no depreciation accounts despite the vast range of assets or accounts of contingent liabilities. Since there is no resource-use accounting, no estimates of costs of government activities are available. All that a decision-maker relies on is the flow of money rather than the actual use. Naturally, in such context, the anchor of expenditure control is the estimate of the flow of money during a specified period rather than the cost of an activity. The usefulness of such as anchor is too obvious to need any additional emphasis.

In all these matters, the spending agencies rely on the guidance provided by the Ministry of Finance, which in turn is based on the manuals prepared and issued during the British rule.[8] In the circumstances, the need for standards may appear obvious but this an

7. The term has been incorporated into Russian. It is possible that a similar incorporation may have been taken into other languages as well.

8. The two volumes of *General Financial Rules, Central Treasury Rules, Public Works Code* and other manuals were all prepared in the pre-independence era, and have been periodically revised since then.

area where an initiative by the government, to put it mildly, is long overdue.

Internal Financial Management

One of the functions that has gone through a series of changes since independence relates to the organisation of internal financial management in various departments (there were about 96 departments in the central government at the beginning of 2014; the biggest ministry, in terms of the departments it has, is the Ministry of Home Affairs). It had come to be recognised by the late 1950s (recognition in governments moves far slower than the proverbial snail) that government had grown too big to have its expenditure controlled by a single ministry, *viz.* Ministry of Finance. As a corollary, it was further recognised that the best way to ensure an appropriate (the term "efficiency" was carefully eschewed then and now) use of public money was to decentralise financial management. It is not that the Ministry of Finance was totally averse to spreading the tentacles of its control but that the spending agencies were beginning to clamour for autonomy and a degree of enhanced responsibility (Their argument that finance and activity management should go together rather than being drawn by two horses each with its own mount was gaining currency). It may be noted in this context that such independence was already there in the Railways, which had a member (finance), who had simultaneously access to the Finance Minister, and in the case of Defence, which had a whole Finance Department attached to it. But the latter spoke a language different from the one used by the Service Chiefs but whose needs, including that required for the continuous modernisation of the fighting forces, was evaluated, among others, by the Finance Division.[9] In addition, there are other cases where the staffing patterns are different. The work involved also tends to vary. In ministries where the bulk of outlays is devoted to central transfer to states and local bodies, the role of the internal financial cell is often limited as the involvement is limited to the release of funds.

The varying nature of the terrain needs to be reviewed periodically and new patterns devised to reflect the changing technology and

---

9. It is not surprising that under these conditions, for several years the Defence Ministry could not spend its budgeted funds.

functions. This is an important element of the regulatory framework in this area.

A related element is that of the management information system. Such an information system is expected to be so designed as to meet the diverse requirements of central agencies (e.g., Ministry of Finance) and the spending agencies. In practice, however, the computerised data systems are primarily designed to show the status of funds such as amounts approved in the budget, amounts committed thus far, actual amounts disbursed, and the amounts available for disbursement for the remainder of the fiscal year. The management information system cannot be content with information in terms of the aggregates; rather, it should show the programme-wise detail so that the progress under the programme may be ascertained and corrective action taken. A management-oriented system by definition involves the setting up of a target(s) and a monitoring system to verify the progress made. It is plausible to argue that where the management information system is effective there is a distinct possibility of greater congruence between physical and financial aspects, and avoiding the last-month rush of expenditure. In practice, however, the top management of an agency (ministry), including its political leadership (e.g., a minister), rarely shows any interest in matters of detail, particularly where budgets are concerned. It would appear that a minister's interest surfaces only in a context where he is expected to mediate by providing an access to public money so as to create benefits for the constituents. At all other times, the top management wishes to be left alone as it has got other important fish to fry. It prefers that these routine matters are taken care of by the masters of procedure and arcane regulations, *viz.*, the Financial Adviser. An inevitable consequence is that there are no priorities, no internal triage and attention to vulnerable areas. A properly designed regulatory system, however, has the potential of contributing to a smoother system.

Performance Controls

Traditionally, the financial management systems did not include performance controls other than those relating to the progress of expenditures. To that extent they were uni-dimensional. With the introduction of performance budgeting, however, the scope of the system was expanded considerably and the organisational goals also increased steadily. Moreover, it was no longer a case of working toward the achievement of specified goals. It is now expected that the goals be achieved within the framework of specified efficiency criteria. Further, the game was not confined to the achievement of stipulated targets but now included the accomplishment of the outcome that was all along intended. The array of goals and their inter se priority are generally contextual and allocation of money may not be the sole determinant of the eventual outcome.

The process of the determination of the annual set of goals is a malleable one and the agencies have a self-interest in formulating them and in implementing them. Frequently, thus, the agencies may engage in formulating goals in such a way that they lend themselves to being attainable. Furthermore, the goals may be attained through means other than those specified. If these approaches become normal, then the integrity of the process will be severely tainted, and what little trust has been placed by the people will also be substantially eroded. Thus, the very objective of the introduction of performance budgeting may stand self-defeated. The more enduring damage is that a new organisational culture would become the order of the day. The controls in this regard therefore seek to introduce a measure of quality control. Such quality controls may be exercised by the spending agency (with suitable organisational checks and balances), or by the central agencies, or by autonomous bodies, or by groups of social audit or by legislative institutions.

These quality controls, except in so far as they are administered by the spending agency, are non-existent in the Indian system, as performance budgeting—or its variant outcome budgeting—have never replaced the traditional system of budget. No budget allocations are made on a programme basis (except when they coincide with Plan programmes or schemes) firmly linked to the achievement of specified goals. Even when they are specified, they are achieved in the traditional way by the administrative ministry with the usual hits and misses. In India, performance budgeting is an adjunct and is viewed as a supplementary document, but not as a supplementary administrative exercise. Outcome budgeting, even where it is applicable to national projects, proceeds in much the same way. It is important to note here that the vital ingredients of PEM such as cost, economy, efficiency and effectiveness are not found in the system of performance budgeting adopted in India. This then is an area where there is need for much improvement.

Resource Utilisation

The proof of the pudding, as the old saying goes, is in the eating. In much the same way, the use of public funds is best seen in the effective utilisation of the benefits created. The issue then is not merely the creation of benefits, but that they should be utilised by the group of consumers for whom they were intended in the first place. The phase of resource utilisation is far more complex than the allocation phase. At every stage, the policy maker has an obligation to look over his or her shoulder to ensure that the budget is being implemented properly and that the community is getting its services regularly and on time, and with the quality and cost estimates specified.

During this phase there are two distinct points of view within the bureaucracy. One relates to the availability of budgeted funds on time and that the releases and payments to the parties concerned are in full compliance with the rules and regulations in operation. This point of view may be called, for convenience, the financial view. The other view refers to that of the spending agency, which wants the release of funds as budgeted and when required. This view also holds the pervasive opinion that the financial angle is narrow and does not take into account the needs of the spending agency. In consequence, there is in practice a structural disconnect between those who are entrusted with the provision of services and those who are responsible for the funding of the services. Thus, the PEM system may, on one side be scrupulously adhering to the regulations while overlooking the immediate needs to be addressed. This may be a case of what is popularly known as triumph of process over purpose.

To some extent this is built into the system of expenditure financing. In India, available data show that more than 65 per cent of the expenditure at the state level is financed by transfers of all types from the central government. A higher percentage, often more than 80, of expenditures at the local level (including the district administration and municipalities and corporations) are similarly funded by transfers from the state and central governments. Other than the devolutionary transfers from central revenues, there are more than 160 Plan schemes under which straightforward or matching and specific (tied) transfers are made to the state and local governments.[10] In fact, much of the work of the central ministries is devoted to the formulation of these schemes and regular monitoring of their progress. This work schedule also includes the release of budgeted funds. It means that since these funds are included in the annual budget and the work schedule is pegged to the annual budget cycle, the release of funds by each spending agency should be a formality but is dependent on the green signal flag waved by the Finance Ministry. The flag is never shown on time, as the assumptions governing the formulation of the budget are quite different from those governing the operations, primarily the release of funds.

The budget is viewed as an important instrument to send an optimistic message to all the economic agents within the domestic economy and the international economy. This optimism may not be, and indeed is not, shared by the rating agencies and by the opposition parties in the legislature. The operational budget is not a public document, although the periodic reports released by the financial institutions are likely to show a different picture. When the reality is different from the window-dressing carried out earlier, the Finance Ministry is reduced to a regime of cash allocations that are much lower than the entitlements. This inevitably slows down the pace of implementation, and services are either rationed or are not provided. Thus, a school functions without textbooks until the end of the first quarter, and a hospital does not even make an attempt to hide its shortage of equipment and medicines; or when services are provided through public-private partnerships, informal and involuntary credit is extended by the private party to the government. In some cases, government employees at the local level are not even paid their monthly salaries. These problems, which are illustrative and are not intended to be exhaustive (it would be a long litany that is familiar and therefore bears no repetition here), have contributed to the phenomenon of dependency of each level of government on the next higher level, where much time and effort are devoted to getting what is legitimately their due. Thus, a pernicious, if unintended, effect of the difference between an optimistic legal budget and an operational internal budget is a steady and linear growth in dependency. What is worrisome is that a government which openly

10. This is undergoing change in the light of the recommendations of the Fourteenth Finance Commission. New ways need to be devised for the transmission of these transfers in the absence of the Planning Commission at the Centre.

advocates the subsidiarity principle does not recognise how its own day-to-day actions erode that principle, which in turn contribute to growing centralisation.

There is an additional aspect that merits recognition here. The releases by the central government or the state government, as the case may be, are not governed by any consistent principle. In some schemes funds are released at the very start of the financial year. In a few others, releases are made, depending on the availability of money for the first three quarters on a prorated basis, while the releases for the last quarter are contingent upon the submission of utilisation certificates, which are more in the nature of fulfilling an accounting formality rather than as a programme review function. The releases, in following a uniform approach much preferred by the run-of-the-mill bureaucrat, ignore the seasonality of work, and more important, the nature of the work itself. In the process, there a widening dissonance between programme and PEM approaches. As an extension, the PEM process has come to be viewed, with considerable justification as many aver, as archaic, indolent and unhelpful. The function of PEM is to mediate in these situations and make the day-to-day administration as smooth and as pro-people as it can be. In reality and without being judgmental, the question needs to be raised whether PEM has become a hurdle or bottleneck remover.

The patterns of resource utilisation may also have contributed to skewed federalism. A special feature of development plans is the facility under which some states are conferred a special status, which enables them to get funds from the Centre on lenient terms. Although there are objective criteria, such as the level of backwardness, share of tribal population in the state, extent of transport connectivity, the declaration of special status has become a much sought after privilege, conferring a new level of honour on economic backwardness. The underlying problem is the absence of balance in financial allocation despite the articulation of measurable criteria. This, however, is an area that falls in the organisational crevices between the Finance Ministry and the Planning Commission. This lack of balance in the allocations, and consequently in economic development, which most state governments push to the front door of the central government, is part of a political bargaining point. Associated with this, there are allegations within states of preferred treatment of some regions and carefully crafted negligence of some others, all eventually leading to the formation of new states and to the announcement of special status.[11] Basically, the whole issue reflects a political failure in mediation; and financial allocation is a major element of the whole episode. The situation is not without its own irony in that while the government and its political leadership keep professing their keen desire to decentralise development activities, the administrative class is too busy devising solutions that contribute to financial centralisation. A greater centralisation of financial resources makes the problem of balance more difficult than has been the case so far. This paradoxical behaviour has its own impact on the process of PEM.

Yet another feature which has gained more importance relates to the political mediation. As more and more resources are vested in the government sector, the access to those resources and related utilisation has become the main plank of political mediation, which essentially suggests that the bureaucracy is sought to be continually manipulated or goaded into action so that the benefits of government action may flow to the politically desired sections of the community, or selected areas of economic activity for receiving subsidies or tax exemptions, or to selected regions of a state. These activities, which range from the local governments to the central government, have grown steadily in line with the growth in public expenditure. They have also not shown any abatement despite the growing role of public-private partnerships. [12]

Such mediation, which unexpectedly takes the form of interventions with an added urgency, could change the ordering of expenditure budgets and their pattern of utilisation. For example, available evidence shows that when there was a massive tripping in July 2012 in north India in the supply of electric power, with related industrial stoppages and a host of other problems, the crisis was attributed to the power corporation in a major state having "had no choice but to overdraw from the grid to satisfy the elected politicians".[13] The intervention becomes

---

11. The clamour for separate states has a long history dating back to the Raj. For a recent discussion of these aspects, see Tillin, Louise (2013). *Remapping India: New States and their Political Origins.* New Delhi: Oxford University Press.

12. Political mediation in securing government benefits has not received much attention. An exception is the recent study by Ward Berenshot. See Bereshor, Ward (2011). *Riot Politics: Hindu Muslim Voilence and the Indian State.* Delhi: Rainlight/Rupa. 2011.

13. An official added, "We are powerless to enforce grid discipline ... there are political constraints. We are even afraid to name the (offending) states (that overdraw from the system). See Denyer, Simon (2014). *Rogue Elephant: Harnessing the Power of India's Unruly Democracy.* New Delhi: Bloomsbury. pp.394-95.

much stronger when the benefits relate to services or goods which are in short supply. The intervention is not limited to important services but extends from school admission to a seat in a railway compartment. The utilisation of benefits has thus conferred a new prominence on the local politician, who now has a new link and a permanent fixture in the long chain of bureaucracy that regulates the flow of benefits. The politician can change the destination of benefits.[14]

This element of political rationing in PEM has not received the attention due. Its focus was more on the bureaucratic processes and how those processes are utilised to provide benefits to the people but that language and process have, more often than not, different intent and not infrequently outcome too. It is also suggested that political mediation through the State and the provision of benefits has contributed to the spread of oligarchies and the emergence of rent-seeking classes, all leading to greater concentration of wealth in those who are endowed with or who have acquired a good deal of political leverage that is in turn used for accumulation of greater wealth in a fewer hands. A matter of great concern now is the concentration of wealth in a fewer hands and the growing inequality of incomes, most of which is, it is claimed, is the result of government expenditure programmes. It is further pointed out that democracies do not displace oligarchies but rather fuse with them.[15]

These experiences are fairly common in both industrial countries with Whitehall type of systems and in developing countries. For example, in the United Kingdom, one major study pointed out that in some cases ministers even decided, while sitting before a map of their constituencies as to which bypasses would enable them to win the next elections. The study concluded that "the actual decisions made depend as much on a minister's capricious exercise of judgment, the influence of one lobby against another or political considerations".[16] These experiences illustrate the role of politicians or other power brokers (The

14. See Boo, Katherine (2012). *Behind Beautiful Forevers.* New Delhi: Penguin India. This study shows that the benefits may not always accrue to the intended beneficiary but may stop with the politician who has big pockets.

15. For the growing inequality of wealth, see Milanovic, Branson (2011). *The Haves and the Have-nots: A Brief and Idiosyncratic History of Global Inequality.* New York: Basic Books. In regard to the growth and operations of oligarchies, see Winters, Jeffrey A. (2011). *Oligarchy*. Cambridge: Cambridge University Press.

16. See Foster, Christoper D. and Francis J. Plowden (1996). *The State under Stress.* Buckingham (UK): Open University Press. pp.197 *et seq*.

latter have become a professional class in themselves and in their own standing, offering their services in several areas, including arranging surgical procedure for needy patients) as quasi-consumers in deciding what is to be provided, to whom and when. This hidden presence has become a substitute for markets and in enabling the utilisation of benefits from public expenditure programmes. Thus, it would be wrong to believe that PEM is restricted to several employees at subordinate levels engaged in crossing the t's and dotting the i's, but there are significant other groups who have a major stake in the system and whose actions have a sway on the eventual outcome of many public expenditure programmes. Necessarily, therefore, any attempt at PEM should move beyond the technicalities and analyse the behaviour of other groups whose influence is growing by the day.

What is evident, however, is that there is a good deal of discontent about the reach of the benefits of expenditure programmes and how many of them are not reaching the intended group of consumers. The financial aspects in terms of the excess and under-expenditures in programmes are routinely captured in the annual appropriation accounts and related audit reports. Such reports, however, have had little impact in terms of improving the delivery of services. Nor have these reports been helpful in shedding more light on participatory democracy, or patronage democracy or political rationing. In fact, they are generally silent on these matters. The reports have not varied much during the last half century despite a growing demand for deep analysis. The quest for accountability has lost meaning in this context.

One compensatory feature, however, is that there are special studies carried out by independent researchers (but not sponsored research by well-known institutions, most of whom are well funded by the central government) which enable us to gain greater understanding of why there is greater and growing discontent about the benefits of expenditure programmes. Three studies that have come out recently merit attention in this regard. The first relates to the use and abuse of the Members of Parliament Local Area Development Scheme (MPLADS), a scheme that was launched, limited to members of the two Houses of Parliament. The intent of the scheme was to provide avenues for the constructive involvement of the MPs in their own constituencies. Initially, each MP was given an allocation of ₹1 crore (10 million) per annum. This was later increased and since 2011, to an amount of ₹5 crore (by no means an insignificant sum even in these days of inflation). Similar schemes are in operation at the level of state governments too. [17]

A general impression is that in a developing country, where the basic needs such as safe drinking water, sanitation, education, and health facilities are always growing along with the annual growth in population, there would be little or no problem in spending the money gainfully. But the available evidence shows that in these areas, where the MPs have been conferred the status of decision-makers, they have done very little decision-making, as is illustrated by the fact that during the period 2004-05 to 2008-09, the highest rate of utilisation has been 52.44 per cent, while in one year it was 37.43 per cent.[18] It is small consolation though, that the unspent balances were invested in bank deposits and earned interest. From the utilisation angle, however, what matters are the results and consequences. The poor in the country pay a price at every stage of their daily existence, and one of them relates to the use of allocated funds. Many MPs do not have a clear understanding of the role of funds given them, whether they are additive to the Plan outlays or substitutive to them, and the Ministry of Plan Implementation is less than forthcoming on these matters. Added to that is the mutual antagonism between the political representatives and the bureaucrats concerned. In many cases, the former tend to consider the latter as avoidable roadblocks, while the latter view the former as lacking in understanding of the basic intricacies of the whole scheme and as being eager to spend the money on their own personal needs or favourite hobby horses even when they violate the guidelines. If this is typical of implementation, one can imagine the magnitude of problems both in creating benefits and in taking the horses to the pond to induce them to drink the available water.

A second study relates to the rehabilitation of people (mostly tribals, who constitute about 10 per cent of the population of the country and about 40 per cent of the affected communities) displaced by the construction of dams on rivers big and small.[19] Long after the colonial government left the shores of the country, the acquisition and payment of compensation when lands are acquired by the government

17. See Surya Prakash, A. (2013). *Public Money: Private Agenda: The Use and Abuse of MPLADS.* Delhi: Rupa.

18. Ibid.: 205.

19. See Hardikar, Jaideep (2013). *A Village Awaits Doomsday.* New Delhi: Penguin.

for specified public purposes were governed by laws that were enacted soon after the country made the transition from Company to royal rule. This legislation was generally in favour of the government and not the seller. Moreover, in most cases, the sales were not voluntary and the coercive powers of governments came into prominent display. The compensation paid was never to the satisfaction of the landowner. The dams involved not merely the acquisition of lands that would be inundated by the reservoir but also the large-scale displacement of the local population living in widely dispersed hamlets, villages and other areas. In general, the people who were called tribals and who have been specially recognised by the Constitution, had their own self-contained, if primitive, patterns of life. For the most part, they remained untouched by the so-called modern amenities such as running water, elementary education, primary healthcare, etc. Their pattern of raising crops, called *jhum* or shifting cultivation, was not in conformity with the agricultural practices of the general population. When they needed a place for cultivation, they first assessed the water facilities (direction of the water flow), then burnt off a piece of the land, and started the agricultural cycle of operations. For what they could not grow on the land, they exploited the abundant tree wealth of the forest, which provided a canopy for their residential space. An inevitable result of this approach was the denuding of the forest, with concomitant effect on the delicate ecological balance.

These tribals had to vacate their traditional abodes wherever dams were built. The social conscience and the effort to maintain a human face in an otherwise arbitrary process of the government then came into display and endeavours began to be made to formulate plans for the rehabilitation of these people. Rehabilitation basically involved two elements—payment of compensation and provision of alternate living spaces with basic facilities. Both proved problematic. The determination of the compensation was itself a major irritant. The tribals had little orientation for money matters and were easily exploited by the mediators and unscrupulous money managers in the government. To the latter, it was a mere case of yet another avenue for disbursement of government money and the rules did not discriminate between the type of payees. The second issue related to the area where the people should be resettled. Far too frequently, the assigned lands were taken over by the eager beavers of the urban economy, and those who were sought to be resettled, quickly lost the assigned lands too. More significantly, they lost their style of life without gaining any new one. They were novices in urban life where they were settled. Their efforts to continue their traditional patterns of life were fruitless and they quickly became, courtesy the unimaginative process of settlement, exiles. The new environment did not care for them and they could not go back to their lands, which were now under deep water. The indifference of government, which always has bigger fish to catch and fry, and the systemic inertia made sure that these displaced people have lost everything, including their identity. As the writer of this study points out, these cases were good examples "of the inversion of our Constitution; these projects are supposedly *for the people but not by the people*."[20] It is not as though there are no good, bright and dedicated people in the government. In fact, the tragedy is that the government has many such people but they lost their voice in the heavy din of the wheels of the juggernaut.

The third study, like the other two, deals with the problems at the ground level in the rural areas.[21] Although the study deals with the situation in selected districts of Andhra Pradesh (now bifurcated into the states of Andhra Pradesh and Telangana; though its title gives the impression that it is concerned with one district in what is now Telangana state, the book is liberally sprinkled with experiences taken from many districts that are now part of Andhra Pradesh), it has wider applicability to many other states. Among the conclusions of the study are the following: (i) In many areas, there is no shortage of funds. There are many sources, other than those coming from the budget, including international voluntary organisations. The problem is that elected officials at the *panchayat* level are not aware of them. As a consequence, many problems remain unaddressed. (ii) The delivery of services is handicapped in most cases due to lack of coordination between the different agencies of the state government. Although there are nodal agencies to ensure coordination, rarely are they successful in achieving a modicum of a smooth operation. (iii) Most schemes, including their financing patterns, are designed by the central government, and most of them have a top-down approach. (iv) Agencies devote their energies to the achievement of specified targets. Once achieved, they show little interest in related areas despite the urgency involved. Measurement of performance and improved accountability and a greater degree of

20. Ibid.:181.

21. See Dawra, Sumita (2012). *Poor But Spirited in Karimnagar, Field Notes of a Civil Servant*. New Delhi: Harper Collins India.

decentralisation remain goals on paper, with actual progress lagging considerably behind. (v) Organisationally, there is little congruence between funds, functions and functionaries. Much time is lost in getting the functionaries and finances into the same line of action.

Fiscal Perversity: A Neglected Area in PEM

A successful fiscal policy requires continuous coordination between the federal and sub-national governments. Addressing an inflationary situation requires the scaling down of outlays at both levels, while during a recessionary phase emphasis may be placed on providing stimulus to the economy through stepped-up outlays or by accelerating the pace of expenditure during the year. Both these phases have been experienced in India several times over during the last six decades and more. In theory, achieving the needed coordination should be relatively easy as the sub-national governments are structurally dependent on the central government for a major part of their resources. In recent years, on an average, state governments have been getting more than 65 per cent of their revenues through devolution of national resources, grants released under centrally assisted and centrally sponsored programmes, and through other ad hoc programmes. Types of assistance include general grants, specific or conditional grants, matching grants, and loans from the central government as well as those made available through international financial institutions. The terms and conditions for loans vary, depending on the nature of the programme.

Fiscal perversity arises when central and sub-national governments are moving in opposite directions. Such movement may take place during the course of the fiscal year or throughout the year. For example, some central agencies release the funds to the sub-national governments at the beginning of the fiscal year as soon as the funds become available. In other cases, funds may be released at specified intervals during the year. Thus, when funds are released for the whole year in a single tranche, that too at the beginning of the year, there may be short-term surpluses that are purely monetary technicalities rather than being representative of the structural aspects of expenditure programmes. Meanwhile, however, the central government is engaged in borrowing money from the market to finance the expenditure flows. In such situations, expenditure managers have to ensure that the surpluses are not of a long-term nature.

The build-up of such long-term structural surpluses has been relatively infrequent. During 2010-2014, however, many state governments consistently built up strong cash balances, reflecting the generous transfer of resources recommended by the Thirteenth Finance Commission. Such a build-up has several implications that reveal a prevalence of a fiscal perversity situation or one where the fiscal stance of the state governments is contrary to the announced policies of the central government. First, the build-up suggests that the development effort may be lagging behind as funds are not utilised for the advancement of the economy. An additional feature of these balances is that they are being invested in the central borrowing programme. The recipient governments are thus making money at a time when the central government is endeavouring to borrow from the market to finance the transfers. Such borrowings, it may be argued, may be reduced if there is no immediate need at the recipient level. Second, the avowed policy of the central government was to provide a stimulus to the economy in view of the global recessionary trends that became obvious after the financial crisis of 2008. This clearly shows the emergence of the phenomenon of fiscal perversity.

In these situations, the coordinating mechanism between the central and state governments has to be revised and vigorously enforced to avoid the perversity syndrome. But this has not happened, for different reasons. What needs to be stressed is that resource utilisation efforts need to pay particular attention to these areas. Those who take a narrow view of PEM could argue that many of the bottlenecks in resource utilisation stem from the actions of the spending agencies. It is often suggested that the primary responsibility in resource utilisation rests firmly with the spending agencies and that PEM is working through its process controls only at the end of a transaction. But this is a case where the central achievement is very much dependent on the actions taken both at the heart and the fringes of the process. They are all symbiotic and they cannot be separated. The task of PEM is to promote a proper environment for resource utilisation through persistent efforts at steering the effort in partnership with the spending ministries, and, on occasion, participate in sourcing too. In the final analysis, the test of PEM is in the outcome, which is in turn dependent on effective resource utilisation.

3

Changing Economic Mandates and Other Aspects

A major objective of expenditure management is the pursuit and achievement of financial stability. The pursuit of this objective is context dependent in that it may involve upward or downward adjustments in public expenditures. Some other objectives are somewhat perennial in nature. These aspects are discussed below.

I

When budget calculations go awry, a critical infrastructure is needed to address the developing issues. In the past, anticipation of the gathering storm was often difficult until it landed on the doorstep: the reporting system was manual and was generally behind the schedule by a minimum of four to five weeks. Inevitably in that context, identification lags were long, as were policy formulation lags, not to mention implementation lags. As a consequence, the crisis continued for extended periods. Now, however, owing to the introduction of electronic data processing, data are available on an up-to-date basis.

The problem of policy formulation is, however, a different one. It is not technology dependent but is entirely dependent on the ability of the political class and the administrative class to face the problems, formulate a package of measures, and process them through the legislature. Often, fiscal crises need short-term adjustments or, more appropriately, reductions in outlays. Politically, this is an unpleasant task, as the spending agencies would already have prepared detailed plans for spending the budgetary allocations. In many cases, firm commitments would have been entered into, and there are costs associated with the violation of contractual obligations. The administrative class tends to be more reluctant to undertake this task, as any specific reductions are likely to be strongly resisted. For this reason, resort is taken to across-the-board cuts. But this implies that all expenditures are treated uniformly, while in fact each category of expenditure has to be treated differently. Imposition of across-the-board cuts implies a lack of coherent policy stance.

Implementation of policy measures involving reductions is a difficult task too. The spending agencies tend to escape the measures by deferring payments to a later date, thus showing a nominal compliance of economy directives. But these escape mechanisms defeat the very purpose of reduction: thus careful thought needs to be given to the planning and formulation of reduction management strategies. In turn, this raises the issue of the adequacy of the expenditure management strategy. At the minimum, this needs a well-designed reporting system, a national infrastructure responsible for formulation, and implementation of expenditure management strategies.

The Indian experience in this regard does not inspire confidence. Some of the features of this experience may be noted here. First, the reporting systems were not forward-looking and rarely provided detailed insights into the developing problems. Second, coordination among the various agencies often proved difficult, particularly when there was no machinery charged with the task. In governments, policy-making units tend to think that their task is over with the provision of necessary guidance and the remaining tasks are believed to be in the domain of the implementing agencies. In the real world the neat division between policy formulation and policy implementation does not always hold, as there is a good deal of overlap. Third, the administrative class, which is charged with the task of formulating policies, may be less than willing to take the initiative. They realise only too well that formulating policies aimed at reducing expenditure is not going to bring any encomiums from the people. Indeed, it is considered as a thankless job. It then becomes a task looking for a manager or group of managers. The preferred approach in the Government of India is to take the matter to the Cabinet in the hope that the intervention of the political class could have better results. Experience shows that the Cabinet in turn looks for input from the political party in power. Soon after independence, when the resource shortages were severe and the civilian administration did not, as yet, attain firm control over all operations, there was a clearly felt need to secure economies in expenditure. The Ministry of Finance was not too eager to bell the cat, and appointed an independent commission with members of the political and administrative classes to study the situation and submit recommendations (Kasturbhai Lalbhai Committee Report 1949). But by the time the commission completed its labours, there was a change in the nature of the problem in that the issue was no longer one of reducing outlays but of augmenting them to address the developmental needs.

A similar situation arose after the 1962 war with China. The central government decided on an approach of "defence with development", which required, in the event, a severe restraint on developmental outlays, including on infrastructure projects that were complementary to the defence effort. Much of the guidance for this effort came from the political class. But the effort at containing unproductive expenditure did not secure any tangible result.

In a later decade, particularly during the early 1980s, the fiscal situation deteriorated and, as usual, the issue that was to be addressed was to restrain the current expenditure of the central government. This matter was referred to a committee set up by the All India Congress Party (Patnaik Committee). Their recommendations mostly aimed at reducing expenditures on foreign visits, entertainment and hospitality related to visitors and others, purchase of government vehicles, air-conditioners, carpets, and related office equipment. These recommendations did not hurt any major programme and as such were quickly implemented. Where no lobby existed for specific categories of expenditure such as subsidies or capital outlays, it became easier for the government to introduce economy measures, particularly where the magnitudes of outlays were by no means significant. This illustrates that governments may not always be eager to take substantive measures, particularly in a context where the political costs are estimated to be heavy. Experience shows that where the political costs are high, governments may be engaged in a window-dressing game of appearing to do something while not altering the fundamental picture.

Adjustments in public expenditure of a short-term nature can be made in both directions. During recessionary periods, where the duration of recession is relatively short, a sharp step-up in public expenditure may be warranted and may need to be launched at very short notice. Moreover, the magnitude of the increase in outlays should have some relationship to the desired result, namely, the stimulus that is considered necessary. In principle, such a quick addition to outlays should be relatively easy, particularly in a developing country with a predetermined trajectory for the economy. The direction and the magnitude of desired investment are all specified in the five-year plan as well as in the annual development plan which reveals the time-slice of the outlays. In addition, it is presumed that in the context of planned development there are always bunches of projects and programmes awaiting implementation. In the context of anti-recessionary policies, it is expected that there are several quick-yielding projects that can be launched without undue delay (If they are delayed the planned results may not be derived). It is further expected that administrative arrangements in terms of specifying the level of the government would have already been completed and that necessary ecological clearances already obtained. Where these conditions are met, it should be possible to launch an expenditure policy appropriate for the economic situation.

The reality is always different from the above stated presumptions. India's five-year plans do contain several projects that are in queue and waiting to be launched. Furthermore, the political rhetoric being what it is, there are any number of promises awaiting fulfilment. The citizens have their own expectations and these different factors suggest that identification of a clutch of projects is not a complex task. But the problem is that they do not have separate lists for quick-yielding projects with a relatively short span of investment. So a new search is launched to identify those quick-yielding projects with enduring benefits. Also, experience shows that implementation of these projects requires sponsoring by the central government and provision of necessary funds. The projects may then be launched by the central government and with its funding they may be implemented by the state and local governments. The sub-national governments are more concerned with projects that have a good deal of visibility and political mileage ahead of them. Frequently, the priorities of the two levels of government may not move in the same direction. As a consequence, the pace of implementation may be less than expected and the fiscal slippage may prove a major problem down the time stream. Furthermore, there is a potential problem that needs to be anticipated. This relates to the ratchet effect of the new outlays on the level of public outlays. Although the new additions are planned to be provisional with a sunset limit, in fact the outlays begin to acquire their own support and lobbies. In due course they shed their short-term nature and morph into regular outlays. A short-term solution is likely to end up as a medium-term issue.

The other side of adjustment comprises reductions in the level of expenditure, or at a minimum, reducing the annual rate of growth of expenditure. The intent is to reduce the size of the budget deficit and thus reduce the borrowing from external and domestic creditors. Borrowing beyond a level contributes to an undesirable dependency on the creditors, as they in effect become the policy makers of the government. But the need for a budget constraint is a reality that has to be dealt with. The management of expenditure reduction involves a detailed analysis of the structural aspects of expenditure, techniques of expenditure reduction, and the political aspects.

It is the general experience of most countries that more than 90 per cent of governmental outlays are of a continuing nature and the net new expenditures are small. Even in cases where governments have development plans and therefore development outlays and capital budgets, most outlays are of a continuing type, reflecting the annual outlays on projects that continue to be implemented. Several of them have a construction period that goes beyond the fiscal year. The annual budget provision reflects the state of construction but the actual payment is dependent on the schedule of payments to the contractor as the schedule may include advance payment, inflation adjustment and others. In some cases the payments tend to be very substantial toward the end of the project. Given this situation, any possibility of downward adjustment may involve more effort than the removal of a tooth. In short, the basic truth is that expenditures tend to be rigid and pose several issues in making downward adjustments.

A cursory examination of the structure reveals first a category of outlays described as "uncontrollable". This suggests that they do not lend themselves to adjustment at all. Prominent in this category are the outlays on the payment of interest on outstanding debt and repayment of debt that was contracted earlier. These outlays reflect an agreement with domestic and international creditors and other institutional creditors as well as individual bondholders. A default in payment, regardless of reason, is likely to have a serious adverse impact on the debt-raising capacity of the country. Once the reputation of the country becomes questionable, all future borrowings can only be contracted at a higher price. If a country feels that it is going to have considerable strain in meeting its amortisation schedules, then it is advisable that arrangements are made with the international finance institutions for a line of credit to tide over the difficulty. This too involves a price in terms of perceived loss of sovereignty, as policy-making shifts to the creditors. Given these difficulties, the label "uncontrollable" may appear apt.

Another element of outlays that is also inflexible relates to payment of salaries and wages. In India, every government employee is paid a specific salary as per the scale assigned to him. An additional element is the annual increment in the scale that is paid invariably, except when it is withheld as a result of disciplinary action. The employee is also not retrenched from service. As a consequence, continuing employment and payment of the annual increment become inflexible elements in outlays. Fortunately for the western industrial democracies, their governments are endowed with more flexibility: employees can and in fact are retrenched at less than two weeks' notice. Such abrupt termination, however, involves the payment of contractual terminal benefits that contribute to a sharp increase in the annual outlays. A similar effect is found in India too when the central and state governments introduce voluntary retirement programmes. In these cases, public outlays ratchet up rather than registering a one-off reduction, a result that is seldom welcomed as it is contrary to the intent.

In countries like Canada and USA, the annual increment in salary is not an entitlement of the employee but a part of the discretionary action endowed in the government and is a reward for performance. Denial of an increment is an adverse reflection on the employee's performance, while grant of an increment(s) is recognition of meritorious work. Where, however, the national economic situation is considered to be dire, the compensation package may be altered and, like the rest of the community, this too will be considered as a sacrifice by the employees of governments. A related element is the payment for cost-of-living increases. In industrial countries, cost-of-living adjustment is a part of the discretionary power delegated to governments. In India, awards for cost-of-living increases are generally based on the recommendations of independent pay commissions. In general, however, governments have only a Hobson's choice, and the perceived reluctance is a make-believe and part of an elaborate ritual where the end result is never in doubt.

Yet another element that is considered in conjunction with the compensation package relates to the entitlement payments. In western industrial democracies, the share of entitlements in government outlays is very substantial and governments have no room to escape them as these are prescribed by law and the recipient has a legal right to take the government to court if it does not honour his entitlements. Entitlements confer a range of benefits on people who are below the poverty line, and those that have different requirements such as the medical benefits for the elderly and those who are unemployed or those who suffer extensive damage to their patterns of making a living, and similar other categories. Any change in the payable benefits requires changes in the original legislation, which is so difficult that few governments resort to that. The political fallout can be so severe as to lead to reversals in political fortunes.

In India too, there are notional rights, such as the right to education conferred by the Constitution, but the non-provision of education is not a matter that an individual with a perceived denial can take up with the judiciary. There are other rights for employment in the public works programme, and a host of other financial benefits such as the provision of a gas cylinder, domestic electricity use, supply of daily consumed food articles, etc. The government has full powers to vary these benefits in the light of an assessment of its own fiscal capacity and therefore these entitlements are very different from the entitlements provided in the USA. Partly, this difference arises from the fact that India follows the traditions of a common law country while the USA follows the civil law traditions where government policies have to be legislated. In principle, the former has ample flexibility in action while the later is heavily circumscribed. The arsenal of government may include several instruments that can be used for securing reductions in expenditure, but they have substantial limitations too.

Yet another category of expenditure that is amenable to regular increases but not reduction is subsidies. Subsidies cover a wide range, from daily consumables to, in a broader interpretation, the varying range of tax expenditures. Strictly speaking, subsidies refer to the losses suffered by governments when they are engaged in selling a product below its normal price. The intent is to cushion the impact on the ordinary consumer so that he continues to have access to the consumables even when their prices are moving beyond his price range. When states were initially formed, there was no intention to provide subsidised goods. Rather, the intent was that collective efforts were to be made to make available goods and services that would not otherwise be available to the ordinary consumers. That was the time when state was envisioned to be limited in its functions to ensuring reason, lawfulness and morality. In the approaches of Plato and other Greek philosophers, there was recognition that the private and public lives of a society's members are interdependent. It was recognised that if the latter is wicked and corrupt, the former cannot develop.

In the conception of the Greek philosophers, good and evil coexisted in society and in the forms of government such as timocracy, ochlocracy and tyranny. It was too early for them to go beyond the mental attitudes behind the different forms of government. Those developments came much later as the functions of the State expanded, as a part of the welfare state, to include poverty alleviation as a major element of the functions of the modern state. Not to engage in this activity was to fail in one's obligations to society. The scope of subsidies is, however, no longer limited to the service of the poor and needy. Primary and secondary education is a fundamental right of the people, as is the right to employment for a minimum period during the year. The policies of government include the provision of subsidised inputs into selected major activities. These activities would presumably have expanded further but for the growing limitations of state finances. People began to feel that subsidies were growing so fast that they were crowding out other essential expenditures. It is in this context that demands began to grow, seeking a severe curtailment of the range and volume of subsidies.

The clamour for reduction of subsidies, which in some cases took the form of a major political platform, has its roots in economic and financial factors. It was felt that subsidies, as an important factor contributing to the rapid and inexorable growth of expenditure, should be subjected to a reduction, more so in a context when the emphasis was on the reduction of government budget deficit. But subsidies are so firmly entrenched as a policy tool that their abolition is an impossibility theorem. What can be done and, indeed, what is frequently attempted, is only a minor alteration so that subsidies can be made more sustainable.

Some of the adjustments are not a matter of choice. The only questions are how much and when. The effort is more to maintain the subsidy in its original form but to make sure that the amounts are not too big. Thus adjustments are made to pass on the price increases by the supplier, as in the case of oil and other POL (petroleum, oils, and lubricants) products, while retaining the essential rationale, or the original intent of the subsidy. This leads, in the current economic situation, to a constant revision of the prices at the retail end. A frequent revision is likely to erode the credibility of the government and introduces a chain reaction. All of which would lead to a recognisable increase in the price level. If, on the other hand, no price adjustment is made, the whole burden would be shifted to the government budget, with the inevitable consequence of a bigger dose of inflationary financing. If the government acts, its credibility is likely to be severely undermined. The result is likely to be the same even if it does not act, as the effects of higher budgetary deficits would felt sooner or later (sooner than the government wishes them to be).

Another important category of expenditure, where considerations of national security, not financial factors play a very important role, relates to national defence outlays. Excluding the personnel pay and maintenance of duty stations (including food, oil and related items), the defence budget contains enormous amounts for the purchase of new and modern weapons needed by the armed forces. No army in the world accepts to fight a war with obsolete equipment, or equipment less effective than what the perceived enemy has. This lesson has been driven home since the disastrous war of 1962. Subsequent attempts, such as Operation Bluestar, or the role played in Sri Lanka, have not exactly added to the glory of the army. So the armed forces have been engaged in a substantial programme of modernisation of weapons involving huge sums that remain unspent. One reason for the slow utilisation of funds is the long lead time needed for the fabrication of the equipment. Defence equipment, excepting the ones sold in the parallel market operating in the shadows in Eastern Europe and the Middle East, is not something which can be bought off the shelf. A second factor is the process of tendering and procurement now in place in the Ministry of Defence. The process has reportedly become so corrupt that decision-making is going at a snail's pace. Oddly, no part of this domestic paralysis is secret and is widely known both to India's supporters and foes. In this situation, the feasibility of any reduction in public outlays becomes a delicate issue with emotional overtones. In fact, even a suggestion about a possible reduction in the outlays is viewed as an insult to the armed forces amounting to treason. As a consequence, defence outlays are maintained and increased every year, if only to assure the people of the government's commitment to achieve its national security goals.

The other major category of expenditure that has gained considerable visibility and attracted undue political attention (with each political party seeking a competitive edge over the others, with each one proclaiming that it is more development oriented than others) relates to capital (or development) expenditure. An impression has been created to the effect that any reduction in these outlays as an anti-inflation stance should not even be contemplated let alone implementing drastic reduction. This is an image that has been long sought and carefully cultivated with considerable tact and craft by the government regardless of the political party holding the reins of power. Given this context, governments find it hard to restrain development expenditure, as it would be taken as an anti-growth measure, although it is as clear as daylight to those monitoring the government that outlays are reduced through a sheer rationing of resources, and if necessary through the piling up of arrears in payment. The government believes that these facts come out, usually with a lag, after the completion of the fiscal year, and by that time other events would have gained precedence over the shortfalls in expenditures under the development head. The reasons for this subterfuge are purely political, as no government desires to go to the polls with an anti-development image. Despite these difficulties, there are facts that need to be taken into account to gain a proper perspective. Development outlays generally involve massive investments in mega projects, where a good deal of planning is undertaken even before the first shovel brings out the soil. Following that planning and given the long lead time for the delivery of much of the equipment needed, orders are also placed, leading to substantial commitment of financial resources. Once committed, contractual liabilities being what they are, it is not advisable to go back on the contract. In other areas, where such advance commitments are not made, governments can put those projects on hold and attempt to reduce the outlays so that the overall size of the budget deficit would be manageable. Planning is always the religion that speaks the language of priorities. But in reworking the priorities, care is needed to ensure a sectoral balance. An area which has potential adverse political impact is any effort to reduce developmental outlays while allowing the current expenditure to escape the brunt of adjustment. Similarly, if subsidies are not reduced as they might affect the corporate balance-sheets, it could mean that the economic adjustment is taking place mainly in the operations of the public sector rather than in the operations of the corporate sector.

Yet another way of adjustment, but without involving any reduction in outlay (in fact the measure is claimed to be budget-neutral in India) is to increase the efficiency of government operations. During this decade, i.e. after 2010, the central government has been managing an incentive programme to encourage greater productivity. Under this programme, those who have shown more productivity are awarded higher annual increases while those who have not shown any improvement stand to lose out in getting the increment. Thus, from a financial angle, there is no reduction in outlays, and to that extent its contribution to any fiscal adjustment programme is virtually non-existent. Whether the increased productivity has contributed to any higher benefit to the community is a question that can be answered only on the basis of anecdotal evidence. The claim of the Cabinet Secretariat notwithstanding,[1] it is moot whether the productivity gains so achieved have created any ripples in the imagination of the public. It can also be safely asserted that there is no programme of activity which has staked a claim for reduction of staff while maintaining the normal expected workload.

Reduction in outlays has become more difficult in recent years for another reason. In its effort to reduce the prospective size of the government, PPPs (public-private partnerships) have been actively encouraged by the government. These partnerships are broadly of two types—vacating a field of operations to the corporate sector which would invest in and operate those activities, and agreements under which the corporate sector would provide the benefits that are essentially funded by the government. In the former, the arrangements imply a substitution to the government capital budget. To that extent, capital or development outlays would be incurred by the corporate sector and for that reason may not be subjected to the austerity regime contemplated by the government. The latter are funded by the government and the tenets of austerity may reach them too. In principle thus, they may be susceptible to short-term reductions, though, in practice, there are difficulties in that the services offered through these arrangements are most in the social services—health and education. These services are crucially dependent on demand, and the situation is such that there is unlikely to be any reduction in demand in the foreseeable future. As a consequence, cuts have to be made in the existing level of services: any potential increases are postponed indefinitely or until the crises are overcome.

In view of these difficulties, and given the imperatives that the budget deficit has to be reduced through a containment of expenditure growth, what can the governments do? The options available to the country are dependent on its financial situation and the severity of the crisis. Equally important, the capacity to administer harsh medicine is dependent on the political climate in the country, in particular the

1. See Government of India (n.d.). *India 2013*. New Delhi: Publications Division, Ministry of Information and Broadcasting, p.42, for a discussion of this programme.

strength of the party in the legislature. In a democracy, battles are won or lost on the basis of the numbers—the relative strength of the party in power, and the strength of the party (or parties) in opposition. The game and the potential for success are also dependent on the capacity of the government to face confrontational politics, *viz.*, street demonstrations and fights. For all these reasons, governments choose the easier way out. Where, however, the country is heavily indebted to institutional creditors and bondholders from abroad, the pressure from them would determine the acceptance of the package of easier options prepared by the government. Usually, the package contains the following: (i) several promises to hold the line on subsidies; (ii) promise to freeze the outlays on wages and salaries and to hold the number of employees at the same level for the future or until the crisis blows over; (iii) immediate measures to eliminate what is considered as wasteful expenditure (In the Indian parlance it translates into elimination of outlays that usually take place in the last month of the fiscal year—e.g., purchase of air-conditioners, staff cars, electronic equipment, and other items that are deemed essential for the maintenance of offices), and (iv) elimination of outlays on some conspicuous items such as entertainment, visits and study tours to foreign countries (that are somehow so arranged as to coincide with the summer season, when stay in the capital city tends to be less comfortable). These measures impose, if properly implemented, a measure of adjustment on the part of the government sector. But policies are so designed as to contribute to a uniform degree of loss of benefits so that nobody may raise a hue and cry about discriminatory treatment. This approach, which is technically known as across-the-board cuts, has been and continues to be the favourite choice for most governments. It should be noted, however, that this approach is also considered as a sham in that it is designed primarily for the sake of appearance and not as a meaningful measure. For whatever worth it is, it usually figures on the top of corrective agenda that most governments formulate to address the deteriorating financial condition. It is also adduced as evidence that the government is taking these measures although they inflict a sacrifice on it.

The question arises whether these measures have any tangible effect on the level of public expenditure. Available evidence suggests that the measures that have a substantive effect relate to the freezing of wages and to the reduction of government employees. The latter does contribute, as previously noted, to a spike in the level, reflecting higher severance payments. On the whole, however, these measures demonstrate the willingness of the government to swallow the bitter pill, on the one hand, and they also have a dampening effect on the rate of growth of expenditure, on the other. It sends a different signal to the community as well as to the creditors that structural adjustments are being made. The magnitude of change in the level of expenditure in the immediate context may not, however, be much unless and until a coherent programme of reduction on the various components is envisaged. Moreover, care has to be taken to ensure that there is no loss of balance in the interrelationships among the various components of expenditure. A reduction in the size of the staff without any adjustment in the nature and content of programmes and activities is likely to contribute to distortions. Avoidance of these distortions requires careful planning of the proposed reductions.

The Indian experience does not, however, reveal any planning of the adjustments. More often than not, the government departments responsible for the management of expenditure do not show any initiative. Instead, they prefer to wait for the political initiatives outside the normal policy-making processes. The directions that come from the political party do not, however, focus on the programmes of expenditure but emphasise the need for reduction in items of expenditure such as travel and purchase of equipment. When these measures are deemed to be inadequate, they take a major policy decision to declare a plan holiday or freeze the plan outlays. This measure does not, however, pose any insurmountable problem to the government as it does not disturb the existing situation. So everybody's turf is maintained, while the future pattern is put on hold. Meanwhile, it has the magical effect of achieving a reduction in expenditure. This effect is achieved by deferring planned expenditure and affects only the expectations and not the existing claims. [2]

---

2. The political effect of the reduction can also be to the advantage of the government in the first round. In February 2013, for example, the Finance Minister claimed credit for raising development spending by 34 per cent. In February 2014, however, the development expenditure in the 2014-15 budget was reduced by 58 per cent, this time ostensibly for reducing the deficit. See Gurumurthy, S. (2014). "How to Handle UPA's Financial Landmines?", *The New Sunday Express*. 6 July. But these political advantages do not last long, particularly when the rate of inflation in the economy continues to be high and continues to have an adverse impact on the common man. The barometer for the common man is the retail price level and not the budget.

As noted earlier, austerity management is never an easy task and is rendered all the more difficult and even intractable in view of the fact that the sacrifices that the people have to make on that account tend to impose burdens which they never welcome. It has to be recognised, however, that the formulation and implementation of fiscal policy is like walking on the sharp edge of a blade. Politicians and administrators alike make it a point to tell the people how they are endeavouring to improve the lot of the people and how they should look forward to the next budget for the goodies that are in the offing. But when the economic situation turns adverse, sometimes beyond the control of the policy makers, remedial measures need to be taken at the earliest, as otherwise, problems become more difficult with time. The remedial measures include additional tax measures, price increases where state trading is involved, and reduction in expenditures. The reactions of the public vary, and each measure goes through the political and economic calculus, subjective as it is, before a considered judgement is arrived at. But the fact that revisions have been made and expectations have to be scaled back does not sit well with the public. The public keeps reminding itself about the promises made to it by the political leadership about creating a prosperous world for its benefit.

In reality, the question needs to be asked whether the promises made and expectations created should be considered as credible at all. But the public suspends its own judgement in matters concerning the political promises made. So the sudden change in the direction leaves it confused and bewildered, and is left to fend for itself. The reactions of the public to tax and price increases are on expected lines, all because the public does not ask how long the price increases can be resisted. In India, for example, railway fares have not been increased for more than a decade. But even the educated traveller believes that his travel should be subsidised by others. As for expenditure, the public has been raised on the belief, for more than half a century, that the growth in spending is all for its welfare, and that it would continue to be the policy of the government to strive for increased expenditures. In making these promises, two effects are generally ignored by the political class and the potential victims. The first relates to money illusion, in that people tend to believe that the higher amounts they are getting have the same value as before. The second is the prevalence of the Baumol effect in that the same services provided by the government tend to cost more with the passage of time.[3] Furthermore, it has to be noted that the reactions of the public to price increases are far more severe than their reaction to reduced expenditures. This is to be expected in the context that an increase in the price directly affects the pocket of the consumer. A reduction in the outlays affects only certain categories of people and the effect varies depending on the income of the recipient and on the service provided.

A more nuanced approach in the formulation of an expenditure management strategy would have had the effect of educating the people and making them reduce their expectation. Here a profound and a major difference is to be found in the approaches of industrial and developing countries. In the former, since the 1980s, there was recognition that expenditures were becoming unsustainable and that they were placing severe burdens on the fiscal and administrative capacities of the government. To address the former, structural changes were made and several activities that were hitherto handled by the government were now hived off to the corporate sector. The administrative capacity was sought to be improved through a process of reinventing the government. In India, however, little effort was made to educate the people about the limits of expenditure as well as the strain on the capacity of governments. In the absence of the much-needed educational effort, governments tended to be ad hoc and were completely at sea as to how to progress and which tool was to be used for what purpose. The tool box itself was half empty and the tools were also rusty, owing to disuse for long periods. Moreover, there was a spatial and mental gap between those who were responsible for the formulation of austerity packages and those working at the street level engaged in providing the much-needed services. In the final analysis it is the people, the stakeholders, who have to make all the adjustments without being fully aware as to why they were being called to make these onerous adjustments. It is this lack of knowledge that riles them and turns them hostile toward the government.

Furthermore, given that adjustment is always difficult, more so when it is imposed suddenly, there is never unanimity even among the political parties as to the validity of the policy prescriptions announced. True to form, the opposition parties would always oppose the measures

3. Named after William Baumol, a Professor at Princeton University, who was the first to bring this phenomenon to the notice of the public.

as they think that they could do better. In fact, however, measures included in an austerity package tend to be the same regardless of the political ideologies of the parties in power and in opposition. More than the legislatures of the country, the first task for the government is the approval of the international credit institutions, creditors, and bondholders, all of whom tend to take a financial view rather than a political view. Their demands tend to have uniformity in that they include many belt-tightening measures. These measures, often conceived under duress, are seen as being imposed from outside. Also, the measures tend to have differential impact on different sections of the community. As a result, the existing nexus between the three legs of the iron triangle, *viz.*, corporate interests, political class, and the administrative class, gets divided depending on the respective interests, and there is seldom any agreement between the legislature (except when a party whip is issued—and often this measure is resorted to, so as to have discipline in the legitimisation process), the public and the government on what to reduce, what to eliminate (In India there has been no elimination despite the endeavours of an Expenditure Commission at the Centre during the first decade of the 21st century) and what to augment. It is not always logic that ends up winning the game. In fact, the process becomes so chaotic that logic is not even a remote possibility. Rather, it is the creditors' wish that is transmitted to the Finance Ministry, which then becomes the nodal agency responsible for implementation. The creditor wins the game because he has all the cards in his hand, and stoppage of credit flows has the potential of choking the economy at the receiving end. It also implies a high degree of centralisation in decision-making, where the secondary effects of budget cuts hardly figure in the initial discussion, though they become too evident for anybody's comfort, soon after.

For example, during 2009-2012, in Greece, as a part of austerity management plan agreed with the IMF, the European Union, the Central Bank of EU and the group of creditors, health spending was reduced by a quarter. The result, it turned out, "was a jump in HIV infections, rising infant mortality, patients left without medicines and a malaria epidemic".[4] In part, this pattern of skewed results is due to a lack of communication between the technical people and the financial experts (read, administrative agencies and Finance Ministry respectively). It also

4. See *The Economist*, 5 July 2014, p.51, in the report titled "Laying Down the Scalpel".

reflects a situation in which there is no initial road map and one is hastily drawn up in the fervent hope that it would meet the divergent interests. More tellingly, the experience also reveals that expenditure management lacked a strategy and, not infrequently, also lacked an understanding of the core of governance. It is the task where the "tin gods" (the elite administrative class responsible for policy formulation: Lord Curzon used this felicitous description more than a century ago) have failed the political class and the people of the country. It is not merely expenditure management which has shown its lack of capacity but it is also the political class who rarely take a macro view of expenditures and are more interested in the local projects and the "big ticket items" that bring visibility to all. The political class pays a higher price when they are rejected by the voters, who cannot comprehend the rationale behind the frequent uncertainties in policies and costs.

II

Economy, Efficiency and Effectiveness

There is hardly a government which does not deploy these three phrases in the annual budget speeches and in the periodic fiscal reviews as well as in the much too common strategy papers and related policy announcements. Two reasons are adduced for this organisational pathology of the Finance Ministries. First, it is expected to reflect the government's commitment to achieve these features in the utilisation of public resources; and second, a related myth that a routine incantation of these phrases would by itself promote a culture of fiscal prudence in all public bodies. Given the importance of the budgeting concepts, it is necessary to be clear about the content of each concept and also to be aware of their history, limited as it is, in India.

The term economy, in its conventional use, was mostly applied to a reduction in the aggregate expenditure of a project or a programme. To be sure, what is provided for in the annual budget is only a slice of the total and any reduction therein does not refer to the total outlay. But the aggregate is of importance in that at the stage of the consideration of a project and its feasibility it is the total that is viewed as an important variable. If that total outlay is considered as excessive or beyond the capacity of the public body, then efforts are made to vary the design and explore the possibility of bringing the project to fruition below the initial cost estimates. This type of economising has been going on for centuries in governments at all levels, and to that extent it is a conventional method of seeking economies.[5] The design is assessed both on technical and financial merits and the former is frequently subjected to extensive revision in the light of the latter constraint. It all depends on the severity of the financial constraint. If it is severe, the constraint becomes a hard one. If, on the other hand, the design cannot be changed as changes may impose undue risks, then the financial constraint is relaxed.

In recent years, the scope of the economy has been defined in a stricter way so as to permit a discernible difference from efficiency. Economy in this context refers to completing a project or a programme at lower outlays than initially planned, but without any modifications in the design of the project. Efficiency in resource use is said to take place when a larger project or a programme is implemented with a given set of resources. In other words, this refers to cases where more is achieved or produced, or a greater number of customers or clients are served by the infrastructure in place, or within allotted resources. This is a case where more is produced per unit of inputs. Assessment of efficiency assumes that there are objective standards set up for the purpose. Effectiveness refers to the outcome from a given outlay. Typically, the issue is whether the objective set for the programme has been achieved within the time, cost framework and within the specified period.

The application of these concepts in India, particularly at the level of the central government, merits brief consideration. Even during the colonial rule, the issue of economy figured extensively, particularly after the 1920s when the Standing Financial Committee was set up in the central legislature. It was an environment in which the Indian political leadership was growing impatient with the colonial government's outlays on military and on public investment programmes. For this and other associated reasons, the Standing Financial Committee was organised and it was entrusted with the task of scrutinising new proposals for expenditure. For the most part, however, the technical aspects of these

5. It may be recalled in this connection that several modifications were made in designing the Indian railway system, particularly in the hill stations. Tunnels were considered to be very expensive and the alternative was to lay the loops. For an interesting discussion of this and related issues, see Sharma, Seema (ed.) (2014). *India Junction: A Window to the Nation.* Published on behalf of the Ministry of Railways, Government of India by Rainlight/Rupa, New Delhi. The book offers many engineering, financial and administrative insights into the early experiences in India. The same experience also holds good for irrigation projects.

proposals were beyond the professional capacities of politicians and they ended up relying on the evaluation of the Finance Department. In the end, the committee became a rubber stamp, but a much-needed one to add a dimension of legitimacy to an administrative decision. It is moot whether the efforts of the committee brought any reasonable economies although the experience enabled the members to temper their views with financial empiricism; in itself a salutary effect.

Until 1956, there was no major initiative to address the broader aspects of the three phrases, which began to be used in tandem rather than in a stand-alone fashion. The Finance Minister was concerned in 1956 that the Plan outlays were growing at a rapid pace and he felt that inevitably there would be some wasteful spending in the large public investments and other programmes. Also, there was no assurance that all the funds were being spent wisely. An imperative of the times, it was believed, was to formulate a strategy aimed at addressing these problems. Toward this end, the government established two organisations, *viz.*, Committee on Plan Projects, and a Programme Evaluation Organisation, as adjunct bodies to the Planning Commission. The former was to explore avenues so as to attain efficiency, while the latter was to evaluate completed projects and programmes so that lessons of experience could be learnt. Both these organisations opened new vistas into project management, but their impact on financial management was not even transitory, as their work was not brought into the loop of the expenditure management cycle.

It was to be expected that this theme of major operational significance would be picked up for renewed attention by the Administrative Reforms Commission, which came into being during the mid-1960s. By this time the inadequacy of the inherited budget and expenditure management system were becoming evident to the governments as well as to the people. As the amounts of public expenditure were steadily growing and as more and more diverse and complex activities were being taken up by governments at all levels, the existential question regarding the operational machinery was as to how it was securing economies and efficiency in expenditure. The academic studies that were brought out by the American academia and by the think-tanks were in the meanwhile getting increasing attention both in the press and other public fora.

Curiously, however, this issue was not raised in this form either by the Administrative Reforms Commission or by anybody else. It is not as though the policy makers were not aware of this and related issues:

rather, they appeared to be reluctant to raise an issue for which they had no immediate answers. The civil servants, who are usually very articulate and liberal in their opinions, were found to be tongue-tied. It was in this environment that performance budgeting came into being, with a strong endorsement from the Administrative Reform Commission and by the then Cabinet Secretary. But the Ministry of Finance was not too anxious to embrace the new system, not because it had any fundamental objection to that, but because it was not sure as to what it was getting into. It did not want a wholesale reform but it was not in a position to oppose proposals of reform, as the wind was against it. Performance budgeting was primarily seen as a tool of improved internal financial management and had no magic formula to procure economy and efficiency. The reaction, in the circumstances, was to introduce the suggested budget system on a supplementary basis, i.e. to prepare a performance budget, releasing the existing information provided in the budget and Plan documents as yet another document. Inevitably, it did not have any impact on the financial management temperament in the government but gave them a putative answer to silence the critics and to defend themselves against new onslaughts.[6]

The problem of securing economies and reorienting the management system toward that end remained a burning issue for which the government had no answer. There were no advocacies of any newfangled ideas nor were there any defences. (In fact, there was no way in which the inherited system could be defended.) It could not live with what it had, and it had no alternatives either. In this context, the government had a bright idea, which it never expressed before since 1858, when James Wilson presented the first budget under the new management, *viz.*, rule by the Crown. The idea was—why not ask the people? Accordingly, when the late V.P. Singh, who subsequently became the Prime Minister for a brief period in the tumultuous decade of the 1980s, was presenting the budget, a brief (too brief, in fact) paragraph was included in the annual budget, observing that expenditure control was becoming too problematic and given the urgent need for economies, suggestions were welcome from all to improve the budget. But this did not elicit any

---

6. A discussion of the saga of reform in financial management in India is provided in Premchand, A. (2008). *Trapped in the Comfort Zone of Denial: 50 Years of Expenditure Management in India*. New Delhi: National Institute of Public Finance. Every effort has been made to resist the temptation of repeating that discussion here.

response from any quarter; and if the government had any ideas of its own, it made no attempt to make them public.

So business continued as usual, and a few years later, after a few more coalition governments came and went, an Expenditure Commission was set up to secure, as a one-off measure, a reduction in expenditure through reorganisation of central ministries, improvement in operational systems, and through rationalisation of programmes and staff strengths. As usual, the commission made a slew of recommendations that had no serious impact either on the level of expenditure or on the functions and number of agencies (which continued to proliferate as in the past—presumably because, like the Bourbon kings they learnt nothing from the past or were not keen to learn) or in terms of staff strengths except those contributed by voluntary retirement schemes. So the stagnation continued until a second Administrative Reforms Commission was appointed in 2005. It was asked to make recommendations for the revamping of the public administrative system, and to "achieve a proactive, responsive, accountable, sustainable and *efficient* (emphasis added) administration for the country at all levels of the government". The addition of "efficient" was, from any point of view, a welcome change. The commission delivered 15 reports, including one on "Strengthening Financial Management System" (submitted) in 2009. Since then the reports were reviewed by ad hoc groups and Committees of Secretaries and other specified channels. Partly as a result of these endeavours, draft legislation concerning the citizens' grievances was prepared and remains to be enacted. But that does not go into efficiency (as defined in the context of expenditure management). Many other recommendations remain to be implemented.

Meanwhile, the basic problem of expenditure management continues to be addressed through ad hoc approaches, as is evident from the fact that the Fourteenth Finance Commission has been asked, among other aspects, to address the problems of expenditure management too. Even as they are struggling to come up with a meaningful framework for improvement, an Expenditure Management Commission was envisaged. An announcement to that effect has been made in the budget speech for 2014-15, presented by the new government in July 2014. This is the first time in India that an Expenditure Management Commission has been proposed. The preceding discussion illustrates the tasks and challenges that would be addressed by the commission. What the commission will do and the kind of impact that its recommendations might have on the system and its capacity to serve the people are matters that will come up in the near future. Although there is not much in experience that inspires confidence, there is also no need to be pessimistic. On the contrary, there is reason for hope in view of the commitment of the new government to make governance more effective.

The major question that needs to be considered at this stage is whether there is any incentive for the administrative agencies to economise in spending and to seek enhanced results. This, in a way, is at the heart of expenditure management. As has been repeatedly pointed out earlier, expenditure management is much more than maintenance of accounts and the related payment system, and consists in ensuring prudence at every stage of spending. It is now said that, thanks to the electronic data processing system, compilation and maintenance of accounts has become a routine, so much so, as they say in the financial district in New York, even a trained monkey can perform the tasks. They no longer require people with advanced and professional training to perform them. In this situation, there is a heightened emphasis on securing economies in outlays.

Does the system have the capacity to address this issue? Answering this question involves a brief look back into the process of formulation of policy packages and related integral parts such as programmes. It was noted earlier that proposals in this regard start in the administrative agencies, which start consulting with the Finance Ministry and the Planning Commission (where Plan outlays are involved) even from the embryonic stages of the programme. Necessarily, the proposals contain their estimates of human resources, materials, and money needed for its implementation. As an integral part of this consideration, a view is also taken whether it is to be implemented through in-house arrangements or has to be tendered or has to be out sourced including through PPPs. (PPP arrangements are becoming increasingly popular in government circles as the demands they make on the government budgets tend to be less.) Necessarily, the estimates are tentative and they are refined over time. In general, the immediate point of attention is the amount of expenditure involved. If the outlay tends to be substantial, every effort is made to underestimate the financial requirements and to hide some elements that may surface at a later stage. All types of design changes and techniques of creative accounting are resorted to in the hope that they escape the attention of the Finance Ministry.

Once the proposal is accepted and the initial battle is won, it is included in the budget with an estimate of the outlays. Once included, the proposal becomes an official policy of the government and it acquires a legitimacy of its own. The policy is subject to minor adjustments for so long as the additions and alterations do not constitute new services or new items. If they are considered as new services (in non-technical language—new policies) then the process is repeated. The budget estimates for the approved policy are, in principle, considered inviolate. In practice, they are violated every day and throughout the fiscal year. There can be excess expenditure, which is then regularised *ex post facto*. If the estimates prove insufficient or suffer from deficiency, then supplementary estimates are processed. There may also be cases where the entire budget provision may not be spent, as equipment might not be available or the needed land was not available but such under-expenditure is never due to any deliberate effort to procure economies.

The existing system of operation is such that there is no incentive for anyone to save money for the reasons given here. First, the employees are not motivated to spend less, as the future budgetary allocation could be reduced in view of the previous year's under-expenditure relative to the estimate. The pace of expenditure is viewed as a good barometer of the expenditure needs of an agency. If the amounts are not fully spent, it means that the agency does not require the money provided and therefore this could be reduced in the following year's budget. This logic holds only for under-expenditure, in that excess expenditure during one year does not constitute a claim for more money in the next year's budget. The agencies therefore always put in an extra effort to spend every rupee allotted to them, and it is for this reason that there is what is called a "spending spree" in the month of March, i.e. the end of the financial year. Second, if the programme involves tendering and choosing a contractor, the ability to spend moves from the administrative agency to the contractor. Given the long lags between budget preparation stage and actual implementation, with appropriate adjustments made for inflation, the contracted price is likely to be higher than estimated. This happens despite the obvious advantages of competitive bidding and bulk purchases. So the scope for economies, in so far as the administrative agency is concerned, is limited. Third, many programmes of the central government are implemented through the state and local governments, and their approach to secure economies is not different from the approaches of the administrative agencies at the Centre. These factors do not militate against an exploration for economies: but no such exploration has been initiated nor is any such proposal in the offing.

Similarly, there is no systematic effort to promote efficiency either. Every programme that was formulated as a part of the development plan also comes up with its own specification of targets to be achieved. These targets are invariably formulated by the central authorities and there is very little elbow room for the lower authorities. Despite frequent sermons about decentralisation, no effective decentralisation has taken place. In this context, the task of the implementation agencies is only to fulfil the targets, and to the extent that efficiency can be achieved, it is possible only if some yardsticks of efficiency are built into the programme itself. This is the case with the flagship programmes too. In fact, the prevailing culture is that there is one class which is responsible for the formulation of the programmes and another group, that is another class, which is exclusively responsible for implementation. Thus, reviewers are engaged in review and their focus is limited to the goals set up by them. The implementation class is constantly goaded into fulfilling those targets and to report to the higher authorities about the progress. This frequently leads to anomalous situations in which the implementation class spends more time preparing reports for the use of the programme formulation agencies. The focus moves invariably from implementation to reporting, in turn leading to more inspection, and more reviews by the political and administrative classes. A possible, if as yet unexpected, issue is the administrative overheads incurred on overview and reporting. In some cases, the cost incurred on these overheads may be more than what is spent on the core programme itself. These aspects could have emerged with greater clarity if there was adequate emphasis on efficiency by the radars of the Department of Expenditure at the Centre, or the financial departments in the state governments. The Department of Expenditure, which is supposed to be the exemplar in this regard, has not so far paid much attention to this subject, though claims are made, at frequent intervals, that it is constantly endeavouring to take allocative and technical efficiency to higher levels, without adducing any empirical evidence in support of its claims.

This issue could have been addressed as a part of the bill on grievances (it remains to be enacted and there is no date or schedule for making it a piece of approved legislation) but no such attempt has been made. What is regrettable about the bill is not the delay in enacting it into legislation. Delays have become a part and parcel of every sphere of government and the people have accepted that as a part of their life. But the grievance procedure, which reflects a citizens' charter, does not even invoke the term "efficiency" let alone addressing it. Its aim is only to provide a service within the time limit set by the administrative machinery, which suggests that it evaluates its performance against a yardstick set by itself. It is reasonable to raise the issue of efficiency but that is beyond the pale of the proposed legislation.

The third aspect of effectiveness too reveals a mixed picture. During the first decade of the twenty-first century, the central government introduced an outcome budget system in the form of a separate document, initially limited to plan projects and programmes providing a description of the outcomes. The idea behind this effort is to provide a bridge between the financial outlays and the impact of the resources so utilised. In effect, it seeks to answer the basic question whether the objective of the programmes for which resources have been provided, have been achieved. It is different from performance budget on the one hand, and the evaluation system, on the other. The former provides an idea of the outputs or services provided, while evaluation is more judgemental in that it seeks to answer the question whether the same result or enhanced results could have been achieved with fewer resources. The outcome budget or the goal of effectiveness is to go beyond the performance budget in that it is concerned with the impact. This approach can be used to ascertain the outcome of macro objectives as well as projects and programmes and those specified in the Fiscal Responsibility and Budget Management Act. Similarly, the Sarva Siksha Abhiyan can also be analysed in terms of the impact of the progress made. In both these cases, however, the objectives are set by the very agencies that later become responsible for their implementation. The reasonableness of such self-stipulated goals is not beyond valid doubt. Giving the benefit of doubt to the government (which requires a leap of faith to some) it can be said that if properly implemented, it has the potential of providing an achievement orientation to the agencies. Towards this end, the agencies conclude memoranda of understanding about the likely outcomes to be achieved and the effectiveness of those programmes. Much remains to be done in this regard.

A new factor that has to be noted relates to the growing number of PPPs, including in areas where quasi-social goods are being funded by the government but provided by the private partners. The primary difference between previous arrangements and the arrangements that have come into vogue in terms of partnerships with the corporate sector is that in the former all stages of the work are under the direct control of the government, while in the latter the responsibility is shifted to the corporate sector. The first feature of these arrangements is that the agreements between the two sides are made through binding legal contracts. Any failure in following the provisions of the contract may lead to extended litigation. A general limitation of the contract is the fact that it is unable to cover all possibilities, including, as a former Secretary of Defence in the United States during the second Iraq war (and it is still lingering on in Iraq with inestimable impact on the citizens, including expatriate labour from India), Donald Rumsfeld, said, there are "unknowabilities of unknowns". It is an inherent task that goes with any contract and PPPs are no exception to that rule. The government does not also know much about the internal financial management of the receiving bodies. In such a context, the receiving party has no interest to pursue the least-cost method except in so far as it earns a higher margin of profit. In reaching that goal, many corners may be cut that could eventually damage the quality of the product itself. Moreover, in regard to quasi-social goods, the quality keeps changing and regular observance of established standards requires a regimen of standards and periodic inspections. More important, the government is expected to be ready to supply the same service in the event of an unforeseen event in the corporation such as a management or technical failure.

Will this arrangement contribute to an improved pattern of resource utilisation? The short answer is—yes, but only in so far as financial flows are covered. Anecdotal evidence suggests that some arrangements have already generated fraudulent transactions, all aimed at taking advantage of the short-sightedness of the granting agency. The government itself is not in the know of many aspects as it is also traversing totally new grounds. Its experience or its abilities are not adequate to address the existing issues or those that might arise hereafter. Meanwhile, it is becoming evident that in education, many institutions that are now engaged in organising engineering, medical and other areas of advanced technology do not have regular faculties or fully equipped laboratories, with the result that quality is deteriorating. The Knowledge Commission and other bodies are regularly pointing out that with all the resources devoted to education, there is not even a single institution in India which qualifies as among the world's best. Granted that PPPs are not aimed at reaching the best levels, it may not be unreasonable to expect that India is somewhere near those world-class levels. Realism suggests, however, that when policy makers are more concerned with social justice and related progress, and pursuit of efficiency does not figure in the list of priorities, the end result cannot be very different from what it is now. It may be time to scale down the expectations.

In terms of addressing short-term exigencies, such as economic emergencies, PPP arrangements pose a formidable problem in that they are all contractual; and anything that is contractual does not lend itself to short-term adjustments except at enormous cost.

4

Some Lessons from the Corporate Sector

Quality apart, are the people and the government getting something in return for the reliance placed on the corporate sector? It will be recalled that one of the primary reasons for the introduction of the new management philosophy and reorienting the government is to pursue the reduction of public expenditure. As a part of this effort, another expectation was that the much-admired corporate management system would also, if only through a process of osmosis, have some beneficial impact on the public sector. Even the oligarchy-dominated Indian corporate sector is claimed to have made much progress in the management area.[1] Available studies attribute the success of the corporate sector to the following factors: (i) a strategic vision for the company, followed by a well-organised operational management system and the functioning of the supporting administrative infrastructure of delegation of powers and responsibility, and a system of reporting that enables tally of the results on a daily basis; (ii) importance of a properly organised accounting system and the availability of accounting skills; (iii) centralised financial control and pursuit of parsimony in expenditure; (iv) adequate recognition of the fact that the community has reposed its trust as a corporation or a brand name and that trust should always be maintained; and (v) a system of management culture that emphasises traditional public values. Importance is also attached to succession planning.

Are these practices applicable in toto to the government sector? The answer is that in regard to each of the identified special features, there are major differences, as well as some similarities between the two. A detailed consideration is provided further on. But it is first essential

1. For a recent discussion of the progress in the Indian corporate sector, see Timberg, A. Thomas (2014). *The Marwaris: From Jagat Seth to the Birlas.* New Delhi: Allen Lane & Penguin Books India. pp.102-49.

that the different institutional settings are considered. The government sector seeks to serve the whole population and as such provides goods and services that are far beyond the range of the corporate sector, let alone a single enterprise. An enterprise, by definition, is concerned with the production of a narrow group of goods and services. It may be owned by a single individual, or a joint family, or a partnership or a stockholding company where the stock is held by thousands of shareholders. The management pattern depends on the nature of the ownership.

In the case of government, the range of products is too large to lend itself to enumeration. More important, there are no limitations on the government in terms of expanding the range of services to be provided. It has no obligation to undertake a market survey to estimate the demand for the products, as may be the case with the corporate sector. The corporation is a creature of the market. Government is the creation of the people to provide such goods and services as are not usually provided by the corporate sector. The corporation draws its revenues from the sale of its products; the government has the coercive power, the most significant differentiating factor, which no other organisation, with the exception of elected public bodies, has. The corporation is run by a management, which either owns the company, or alternately elected by the shareholders. The general body of the shareholders meets infrequently, usually once a year and the corporation has some obligation to provide information, a balance-sheet and related accounts, to the regulatory authorities and to the public. The management of the firm is the body that is responsible for the day-to-day conduct of its business. It is subject to market discipline and the regulations specified by the regulatory authorities. The public, comprising the various groups of consumers, is the final arbiter of the fortunes of the company. If the products are not acceptable to the public, it ceases from buying those products, leading eventually, in the absence of other options, to the closure of operations and to exit from the market. If the operations of that company are of a strategic nature or are of critical importance in the daily lives of the people, the public authorities may intervene and may wish to save the corporation by extending its life through change of management, infusion of more capital or finding a partner. The links between the corporation and the public authorities are several and each one of them is designed for a special purpose. In day-to-day life, however, the sustainability of the firm is dependent on its capacity to please its own shareholders through a steady performance. Its relations with the consuming public are dependent on the price and quality of its products. In this respect it is in competition with other producers, where each one is vying with others to garner a greater share of the market.

The government has its own processes for ascertaining the public's needs and to determine what can be provided and when. It gauges the public opinion through the voice of the public representatives chosen periodically by the people. Although the forms of government may vary, there are varieties of ways for eliciting the view of the people. In the final analysis, a government is designed to address the needs of the people. The representative institutions impose a political discipline on the government to ensure that all important matters are approved by the representative institutions. Numerous checks and balances are devised to ensure prudent behaviour and fiscal discipline. The motives that guide the actions in the corporate sector are different from those of the public bodies. In the former, the primary motive is profit and profit alone. It has no social responsibility except to serve the interests of the consumer. In the case of governments, there is no greater motive than to serve the people. It is a privilege conferred on the elected representatives by the people who have the option of changing the elected representatives from time to time. Both types have self-specified patterns of ethical conduct. Experience conclusively shows that when people reach responsible positions, they tend to lose sight of how they got there. They end up desiring more and more power, and power alone, and at any cost, becomes the driving passion. It is observed in the *Mahabharata* that "every one is a slave to power: but power is not a slave to any one". That slavery to power corrupts the soul of the individual and that corruption soon spreads. And when that happens, organisations tend to decay unless corrective measures are taken. The decline of organisations may have its origins in many factors that may not always reveal themselves. The declining capacity and the under-achievement of the machinery is therefore a matter that should be subjected to periodic analysis.

While there are differences that set apart the privately held corporation from a government organisation (It should be remembered that the government also has its corporations and private limited companies, which are clones of the corporations in the private sector), there are also several common features that need to be recognised. For example, accounting has common functions both in the corporate sector and the government. In the corporate sector, what holds sway is double-entry accounting, on accrual basis, and cost measurement. In government, accounting is much simpler and is usually a single-entry basis, and cash is the primary medium. In recent years, following the introduction of new public management philosophy, and the financial management reforms carried out in New Zealand, governments and public sector organisations have also moved selectively to accrual accounting and preparation of half-yearly balance-sheets. Generalisations in this regard have therefore limited value. The change has to be ascribed to the introduction of electronic data processing machinery. That alone has narrowed the differences between the corporate and government sectors. This should not, however, lead to the impression that the differences have narrowed considerably. Such a conclusion would be misleading. In the application of these systems and in their day-to-day use for internal management, however, there are other differences that cannot be ignored. These are discussed below.

Most private sector organisations, particularly those who have adopted the modern management techniques, have taken to the preparation of strategic plans on a regular basis, though, for obvious reasons, these plans cannot be divulged as their competitors are usually on the alert to get this information. For internal purposes, the good old intuitive approach of an experienced manager has yielded place to the formulation of strategic plans. Formulation is only the first stage: they are regularly updated in the light of global developments and are also subjected to extensive risk analyses. The developments in the domestic and international economy are constantly overtaking the events and any corporation that has not taken the precaution of updating the strategic vision runs the serious risk of lagging behind others. More significantly, the corporate culture is now dependent on the quality and reliability of the strategic plan. That said, over-reliance on the strategic plan alone may prove a handicap and is generally avoided. The plans should not create a false sense of security: the signals may be mixed, and consequently, the end result could be a fate similar to that of the *Titanic*.

In government, however, a strategic plan for the government as a whole requires an unmatched vision and leadership. The activities are diverse, and each activity is important for those engaged in performing it, who may not be sufficiently alert to the interdependencies in the vast web of government. Some major sectors, however, have their strategic plans or some plans, which for want of any other description, are also viewed as strategic plans. Some ministries advance these plans in conjunction with other major events such as the national budget. Along with the submission of the annual budget to Parliament, the Ministry of Finance, for example, prepares a medium-term fiscal outlook or Fiscal Policy Statement, in addition to several other documents. Similarly, the defence Ministry also publishes documents about the modernisation of the armed forces and their equipment requirements. The major issue, however, is whether these documents constitute strategic plans. The short answer is "no". These documents are so general and the goals are so diffuse, and the plans are so tentative that they do not convey the impression of being a definitive road map. Nor are they operational plans that bring the middle-level management to a chosen path. The overwhelming impression is that those plans are being prepared more for the sake of form than for any functional use. The major difference between the corporate and the public sectors in this regard is that in the former, a strategic plan reflects an operational culture, while in the latter it is more an expression of an intent, intended for the purpose of fulfilling a promise made to Parliament.

In so far as the accounting system is concerned, governments have in general adopted—or attempted to adopt to be more accurate—commercial accounting systems, so that internal financial management could be more effective in the agencies. Moreover, the introduction of electronic systems has substantially reduced the long lags in reporting data. As in the corporate sector, daily reporting systems have come into operation in government.

There are fundamental differences, however, in the way in which systems work in governments. To start with, the introduction of accrual accounting in government has not been without problems. For example, if revenues are recorded on an accrual basis, a far optimistic picture emerges about the resource picture as there is no allowance for the lags in collection, the appeals against initial assessments of tax liability, and associated features. The actual collections on a cash basis, which is the basis on which money is released to the agencies and payments are regulated, is far behind the figures recorded on accrual basis. There is a similar pattern on the expenditure side too, in that there are long lags between commitments, the point on which accrual expenditures are recorded, and the actual payment. Further, some payments are bundled together. Some progress payments have little relationship to the commitments made. The accrual expenditures in the commercial sectors are recorded to ascertain the costs, which in turn are based on the actual use of resources for a product.

In government, however, there is no inventory accounting system (in some cases there is inventory of assets, or plant and equipment; most governments do not have data on the human resources provided for them) and the costs of programmes are rarely computed, let alone using them for managerial purposes. Furthermore, the governmental accounting system has several suspense accounts, exchange accounts reflecting the advances and payments made for the equipment ordered and received on behalf of the state governments, and several special accounts and personal ledger accounts managed by disbursing officers working in remote areas. Although commercial accounts too have special vehicle accounts or special purpose accounts (a feature that was also a contributory factor to the financial crisis of 2008), the other enumerated accounts here are not found in the corporate world. The issue that needs to be recognised is that in government, the spending agencies maintain a detailed set of accounts for their own management and another summary version that follows the pattern of appropriation accounts. They do not have balance-sheets, and as such they tend to rely on the pattern of appropriations as approved by the legislature. Government accounts have multiple users, and multiple objectives even within the government itself, while in the corporate world everybody plays the same sheet of music. It is doubtful whether a daily balance-sheet, as in the commercial world, will be of substantial utility in the government.

In the corporate world, the top management is generally professional by training. Even the family-owned enterprises have been providing training to their own progeny so that there is a good deal of continuity in management. In many families, there are qualified chartered accountants and those who have advanced degrees such as Masters of Business Administration with specialisation in finance and accounting. Thus, the language of accounting has the virtue of cementing relationships between the top, middle, and operational tiers of management. In government, there are far more layers, comprising the political class, the administrative class, and the operational class manned by people from various services and from different academic disciplines. The political class, it can be asserted without fear of overstating a fact, has rarely any accounting orientation, nor is it expected to. Its role is to provide a much-needed political perspective. It is the political class which can claim to know the pulse of the people. For the corporate world, the market is the one which sends signals. In government, it is the political class which knows the pulse, and more important, is elected by the people and is therefore obliged to safeguard the interests of its constituents. It does have a broad idea of the general trends in finances, and there are several people in the administrative class who have the functional responsibility for keeping the political class well honed on the latest position. The political class has also the task of facing Parliament, where more than 500 people are eagerly awaiting to be briefed. Any failure on the part of the political class to live up to the expectations can only contribute to a shorter shelf life on the treasury benches—a prospect that nobody looks forward to. That said, a distinction has to be made between being informed, on the one hand, and capacity to take action, on the other. In this regard, the corporate sector, while having a distinct advantage, has also revealed that slippages are not the exclusive preserve of the public bodies.

What should be the pattern of financial control? Does centralised control, advocated and found in the corporate world, offer a viable alternative to the public bodies? Here again a detailed examination of the relative settings in which financial control is exercised is likely to be useful. In the corporate sector too, as in government, a distinction is made between corporate financial planning and the day-to-day system of management of payments. In between, there are stages of financial review of tenders, estimates and final decisions on the schedule of payments. The former task is a part of the responsibilities of the management tier, while the other, in particular the payments, are the responsibility of the financial controller. In government, particularly at the Centre, the Chief Accounting Officer of a department, who is also its administrative head and the Secretary of the department, is technically responsible for the financial management of his department. But this task is substantially in the hands of the Finance Ministry, and the Secretary of a department has every responsibility except the financial part of it.

But there is no activity in government which is devoid of financial implications. In practical terms, therefore, in earlier times, the spending agencies felt so constricted that they had to approach the Finance Ministry for approval of the budget, for approval of specific proposals of expenditure, for changes in the plans of implementation, for relaxation of rules, and for general management of finances. It was total dependence on the Finance Ministry—a prospect that no one in the administrative agencies relished. They were so severely circumscribed with established financial control that they could not think beyond their dependence.

This tradition had a long history of more than two centuries, dating back to the earlier days of the East India Company. Even after the rule shifted to the Crown, all proposals involving major outlays had to be referred, for approval, to the Finance Department, as it was then called. Very soon it became an established rule that no expenditure could be incurred except with the approval of the Finance Department. This rule was not altered even after independence, excepting that after the Constitution came into being, the power of approval was shifted from the Finance Department to the legislature. The approval of the legislature was given in the form of enactment of appropriation acts which was only the first stage of approval. Thereafter, the approval of the Finance Department or Ministry was still essential for several policies and proposals. All this meant year-long association and dependence on the Finance Ministry.

Dependence yielded an unexpected result. It is said that in cricket, if a long stop is posted on the boundary line behind the wicket keeper, the latter would have every incentive to leave a few balls so that the long stop may field them. In the absence of a long stop, however, the wicket keeper would have no option but to catch every ball that came his way. In much the same way, there was a suggestion that the spending agencies too were not unhappy with the quality of their own work even when it was, for the most part, below par, as their impression was that the Finance Department, which had the final say, would do the spadework as well as the lapidary task. Besides, the Finance Department was generally inclined to take the view that there was little or no financial conscience in the spending agencies. In making this argument, the Finance Department was oblivious that it was responsible, in one way or another, for the absence of financial conscience in the agencies. This, in turn, created an adversarial situation, which was creating its own tensions and loss of cohesion in the government. The situation would have been a lot worse if there were at the time a 24/7 media, as happens in current times, that would be reporting *ad nauseam* the lapses on the part of the governing institutions.

The growing dependence came to be resented by those who had become dependent. On the other hand, like the mythical Greek character Sisyphus, they might have even enjoyed that dependence in odd moments, particularly in vulnerable situations. Dependence on the Finance Department also meant that there was a shared responsibility in policy-making. In consequence, accountability also became diffuse and it was difficult to pinpoint the responsibility on a single official or an agency. By the time all the consultations were held with all the agencies and the final crossing of t's and dotting of i's was completed, policy-making became an indivisible exercise. Everybody's fingerprints were partly visible and partly obliterated in this exercise, and the lines blurred beyond recognition, that not even a well-trained sleuth could decipher them. More significantly, the range of activities of each agency started to experience a burgeoning growth, to such an extent that no single ministry or department had the capacity, notwithstanding the in-built human inclination to over-estimate one's own capacity, to control what the Finance Department considered to be the buccaneering proclivities of the administrative agencies.

So, the realisation dawned that the time had come to loosen the grip of the Finance Department and make the spending agencies accept a higher level of responsibility to manage their own finances. It was no longer a case of centralised financial control which comprised not only guidance but also the management of selected operations such as payments and monitoring of financial and physical developments. This meant that along with responsibilities, more financial powers were to be delegated to the agencies. But the Finance Ministry, which now swallowed that camel—the need for financial decentralisation—began to strain at the gnats and adopted a niggardly attitude toward delegation of financial powers to the agencies. The result was a system of delegation that came in the form of rations that never proved satisfactory to the agencies. The endeavour was, it appeared, to retain the important provisions for the management of the Finance Ministry, while delegating the mundane and routine matter to the administrative agencies. Thus, for appearance sake, there was delegation, even if reluctantly agreed to by the Finance Ministry, while in fact, the essential elements remained in the hands of the Finance Ministry. The delegated powers could be exercised only when supporting budget provisions were made. These provisions, i.e., allocation of funds, were subject to the approval of the Finance Ministry. The ministry also retained extraordinary powers in that it could intervene in the affairs of an agency when there was reason to do so. The administrative agencies could always take up matters with the higher authorities, *viz.*, the Cabinet, when they found that the ruling of the Finance Ministry was not to their liking. But then, few preferred to be on the wrong side of the Finance Ministry unless they had the strong backing of the Prime Minister. When the Finance Minister was stronger than the others, the spending agencies rarely sought a show of strength. In government, financial strength was partly dependent on the relationship with the Finance Minister and the Prime Minister. If that relationship was seen as a strong one, then the views of the Finance Minister were not questioned. At the same time, the other ministers had also to be kept content. Besides, as noted earlier, governments have grown to be too big to be controlled by a single agency: it is a physical impossibility.

To sum up, centralised financial control may be an asset in the corporate sector but is clearly a liability in the public bodies. The differences between the two are significant. The functions of the corporate sector are narrow, as is the range of its shareholders. Governments, on the other hand, are the biggest organisations on the surface of the earth. Their governing institutions are numerous, and at each stage they have compulsions to be transparent and inclusive.

In concluding this part of the discussion, it is important to recognise that centralised financial control is difficult to implement in government not merely because of size, but also because the essential supporting technical infrastructure may not be available therein. In particular, if the expenditure management system is anchored in a system of budgetary ceilings for each spending agency, it would be easy to implement a centralised financial control. Under a system of budgetary ceilings, each agency would be apportioned a fixed sum that is for the most part unalterable. It remains inviolate for the simple reason that no supplementary appropriations would be processed except in unusual situations. The ceiling becomes the hard budget constraint. In the Indian situation, however, the expenditure management system is not anchored in any specific area and is flexible in all areas and throughout the fiscal year. The annual budget is only one of the many steps; and even when it is supposed to be exhaustive, additions and alterations are made throughout the year and, more importantly, there is no penalty for excess expenditure; and frequently, "savings" may be induced by not providing necessary funding for approved programmes and projects. At the same time, these changes may be considered as parts of centralised financial control. But the spending agencies have enough flexibility to re-appropriate and, not infrequently, misappropriate too. In a state that is considered to be soft, centralised financial control is unlikely to be feasible.

For a corporation, yet another area that is considered very important is to acquire goodwill and trust from its consumers, who must be made to feel that they are stakeholders in its survival and success. A corporation survives and thrives on its brand name. This reputation is worth much more than all the money spent on publicity exercises. So, it is averred, the corporation's future depends on the continuing trust reposed on it by the stakeholders.

In government too, credibility is important, almost to the extent that it is indispensable. Where credibility is absent, government announcements fail to convince the governments' constituents. In the last few years, the most important problem in governance has been winning the people's trust. Here, the track record of public bodies has been wanting in several areas: it is a long litany.

First, governments have failed to maintain stable price levels in promoting employment. Each governmental announcement leads to expectations that are, by definition, hard to meet. Projects take a long time to bear fruit. Meanwhile, basic amenities like consistent supply of drinking water or power remain beyond the reach of the voter and housewives have to trek long distances to get drinking water. In agriculture, the government acts as the main supplying agency for many inputs, ranging from seeds to fertilisers, irrigation water, pesticides, and a host of other materials. Any delay in supplying them causes many interruptions in the schedule of farmers. Usually, there are any number of slippages in managing the supply of the inputs: and governments are never short of explanations for their failures.

Also, no one is ever punished for these slippages, with the farmer himself becoming entirely responsible to bear his losses and loss of his livelihood. Second, the long lags or failures made in fulfilling the promises made end up as irritants that are sought to be covered up through a persistent resort to lying. To cover up their lapses, a non-communicative language has been developed by governments. The reports are either intended for specialists or for other government employees, and not for the common person. As efforts at being economical with truth became an integral part of government management, they also began to reflect on the form of democracy, which is now known as mendocracy. Third, the range of corruption is believed to be so extensive today that no area is exempted from it. The so-called efforts that governments claim to be making to reduce corruption are treated with derisive contempt by the common person. Fourth, in particular, the expenditure management system has failed to endear itself to the ordinary citizen, who finds no instance where the services provided have been either efficient or economical. As a result, the system has ceased to appear on his/her mental radar. It is now his/her firm conviction that the usefulness of the system remains to be proved.

Given this state of affairs, governments have tended to develop a thick skin to criticism and loss of credibility. All that they can do now is to minimise the future loss of the remaining credibility rather than undertake the uphill task of rebuilding credibility. The fundamental difference between the corporate sector and government is that the former can maintain its brand name. When part of it is eroded, as happened to the Coca Cola company, it was regained with assiduous efforts. Governments too can take up the revival of their reputation by gaining the support of the people, as for example the government of Tamil Nadu did through the establishment of Amma canteens, Amma water, and Amma pharmacies. This approach of addressing one problem at a time has the potential of yielding tangible results. This should, however, be tempered with recognition of the fact that trust, like many other features in human relations, is transient and may change at any time. Precautionary efforts too might not always yield results. A strategy to gain the confidence and trust of the people cannot be replicated in other situations even if there are common features. People change their views for reasons that are clear in their private universe that no outsider can fathom. This holds good both for public bodies and the corporate sector.

Yet another area where there are similarities as well as differences between the corporate sector and government relates to the structure of authority and power. Authority refers to formal structures. Both in government and in the corporate sector these structures are specified in the relative legislation—the constitution in the case of government and Company Law in the case of corporations. More than two centuries ago, when the East India Company was granted the Royal Charter, it was approved by the government through the Regulating Act of 1778. Prior to that, there was a good deal of trade carried out with Mughal India. What enabled the beginning of the legislation that started in the seventeenth century in England was the belief that the "sovereign's" prerogative to regulate all trade with infidels, a right based on the assumption that an unbeliever was automatically an enemy of the realm."[2] To be sure, it was only an enacting approval and much was left to the Company to develop a role for itself. And it did develop a role, largely due to the enterprise shown by Sir Josiah Child of the Company. Its interpretation went much beyond the initial scope envisaged for the Company. In Child's view, the promise they made to themselves was "that they will establish such a politie of civil and military power, and create and secure such a large revenue to maintain both at that place (Madras), as may be the foundation of a large, well grounded, sure English domination in India for *all time to come*"[3] (emphasis added). What this proves is that power comes not merely from what is given and what has been legislated, but from the initiatives and daring shown by both who are working in an organisation and also those who are outside it and those who come into contact with the government and the corporation even by accident (Recent events in India show that an unfortunate accident such as widowhood, occurring in a corporation, e.g., the Birla family has the unforeseen consequence of that person being catapulted into the centre of power, with potentially enduring impact). Here the structures do not change but the form of an external unspecified power alters the pathology of an organisation in both public and private sectors.

In both government and the corporate sector, the structures of authority are elaborately stated to the point that even the oath to be taken by the specified authorities at the time or assumption of office is stated in avoidable detail. The arrangements about the finances, the functions of the executive and other domains such as the judiciary and the legislature in the case of public bodies, and similar aspects regarding the corporate sector, including the strength of the board of directors, the number of directors nominated by the government, their functions, levels of compensation and their relationship with the chairman of the board, arrangements for audit, and annual or periodic meetings of the shareholders/stakeholders and the details of the regulatory framework and the powers of the regulators, *viz.*, the government or the autonomous body authorised by it are laid down in considerable detail. Broadly, the government maintains an arm's-length relationship but may intervene any time where the regulator believes that the actions or

---

2. See Keay, John (1991). *The Honourable Company, A History of the English East India Company*. New York: Macmillan. pp.177. *et seq*.

3. Ibid.: 179.

inactions of a corporation threaten to disturb the stability in the market or violate the rights of the consumer. As a part of this intervention, the regulator may specify the actions to be taken and the reports, not to mention their frequency, to be submitted to the regulator.[4] It is important to note that though the corporation has several operational freedoms, the regulator is not simply a potted plant but is a vigorous, visible hand. The hand is intended to guide and mentor the corporation when it is in a difficulty or when its compliance of the specified levels of integrity are needed to protect the consumer. The guidance may come in the form of specification of accounting and auditing standards (In the United States, the impact of the Sarbanes and Oxley and Frank and Dodd legislation following the financial crisis was still lingering as of 2015. Similar efforts were made in the European Union and in the United Kingdom too). The real seat of power then is in the government. The most significant factor to be noted is that in both government and the corporate sector, the structures of authority reveal only a partial picture and eschew the personality factors. In both spheres, personalities change the fortunes of the organisations. It is also surprising that personality continues to have a massive influence in large organisations such as governments, as well as in small organisations such as a corporation. In both cases, administrative innovation is very much dependent on the context in which reform/innovation is undertaken, as well as on personality factors. In both cases, the spadework done by consulting companies may be found useful and the final outcome depends on the organisational culture that is sought to be changed and the content of the management culture that is proposed to be ushered in. In some cases, reasonable advice may be ignored because the powers that be are against change. In which case, a price is to be paid for resisting change or for making irrelevant changes. Committing follies is not the exclusive preserve of governments: there have been many corporations where poor decisions led to disastrous consequences for them. So, the apparent advantage of the corporations may be more imagined than real.

Another area where the corporate sector is claimed to have some advantages over the public sector relates to succession planning, but this issue requires examination. In the corporate sector, a general convention in family-owned companies is that the heirs of the owner of the company

4. For a discussion of a recent case study of this type if intervention, see Bandyopadhyaya, Tamal (2014). *Sahara*. Mumbai: Jaico.

.ake over the reins of management after the latter's demise. As in royalty, this is not always as straightforward as may appear at first sight. There are fights among the successors and each one seeks to outwit the others and claim a greater share of the family riches. In many instances, the wills are contested. In fact, these matters in pre-independence India went all the way to the Privy Council in London. Even in recent years, the division of companies between the two brothers in Reliance Industries required a kind of adjudication with the help of old trusted friends of the founders of the company. Elsewhere, a lady underwent a sex change operation in order to be considered as a male heir, while in another case, a widow who transferred all her property to her accountant became a hotly contested issue in the judiciary and is nowhere near a solution.

The situation was different a few decades ago, when issues of succession took place within the family and the successor was groomed to take over the responsibilities. There was a persistent effort to provide continuity and avoidance of uncertainty, particularly for the groups of creditors. It was recognised, however, that as corporations grew in size and became too big to be controlled by an individual or a family, alternatives had to be found. This came in the form of a study commissioned by the Ford Foundation (India), which came to the conclusion that management should be professionalised. To promote this, a pool of talent needed to be created and three institutes of management were set up. Even then, there was scepticism about the feasibility of teaching business principles, and the usefulness of the graduates for the management of the companies. The belief, which has since faded away, was that business management was in the blood veins of some communities and that no amount of academic learning could replace intuitive judgement. At present, however, there is a viable cadre available in most corporations comprising well-trained professional managers. The discipline of business management acquired a new sheen and competition for acquisition of academic degrees. But succession planning, while facilitating a smooth transition, may not always prove successful: there are any number of companies where professional managers took decisions that proved too costly for their companies.

In government, succession has to be seen in terms of two layers, with the top layer comprising the political class and the second layer comprising the administrative class. The latter has many other layers, including the middle and lower levels, as well as technical and administrative cadres. The change of the political class is generally preceded by a long period of preparation to gain the people's support, and thus change is not sudden. In India, at the central government there have been fifteen prime ministers, three of whom were members of the same family. Power passed on smoothly to the successor, except in the case of the first prime minister, whose daughter succeeded him after a brief spell, when the post was held by another person. The passage of the baton was, for the most part, bloodless, and there has not been a single occasion when the transition required the intervention of the armed forces. The position in the contiguous countries, excluding Sri Lanka, has been different. In Nepal, the succession was smooth as it was under a monarchy until recently. Even the royalty has been displaced, and the country has been endeavouring to usher in a constitutional democracy. In Bangladesh and Pakistan, the armed forces assumed power several times, and completion of the full elected term by elected representatives has been a rare event.

In so far as government financial management is concerned, the finance ministers had generally a stable stay in power. At least three of them presented more than five budgets, with one of them presenting nine budgets under two different administrations. India has been fortunate in having a large dose of political continuity. Leftist parties never gained complete control of government, though they participated in coalition governments, even holding important portfolios such as the Home Ministry. The absence of leftists was more than compensated by the Congress Party itself having radical philosophies such as abolition of privy purses to former princes, nationalisation of banks, extensive land reforms, limitation on salaries in the corporate sector, and high level of marginal rates of personal taxation that bordered on expropriation. In fact, when the leftist parties held power in states like Kerala and West Bengal, their approach to economic management in spheres that were left to the state governments was far more moderate than the approach of the Congress Party. In other words, for all practical purposes, continuous stay in power did not lead to stagnation. On the other hand, there were many discontinuities and U-turns from their traditional policy stances. Significantly, they also moved away from dirigiste state management of the economy to market liberalism, although, arguably, such pendulum swing was not caused by philosophical shifts as much as due to the steady, if avoidable deterioration in the economy and consequential approach to international financial institutions and other creditors.

As is to be expected, when power was held by one family and its descendants, succession was anticipated, though there was noticeable opposition. In this process, political options widened substantially: new partners were created, all in support of their leaders, rather than based on divergent political philosophies. The consequential political instability also contributed a series of prime ministers holding power for very short periods, creating in the process a revolving-door approach to succession. This was a situation in which there was an erosion of both personal and institutional power. When strong persons were at the helm, there was a perception of continuity and stability and all power was assumed to be held by them, whether or not it was true in fact. When the head of the government was seen as weak, institutions gained in power until a strong personality emerged.

These features are common both to government and the corporate sector. In both cases, governance is influenced substantially by the personality at the top. When that personality transcends the institutions and their processes, and imparts a much wider perspective, domains of institutional power yield their place of importance to the top person. Just as a democracy has embedded features, so also a corporation has many features that bring instability despite all precautions taken in planning the succession. This was the case with one Prime Minister who came to power with the highest legislative majority known till then, in the wake of the murder of his mother who was a Prime Minister for a very long period. Although this succession was not planned, the people voted for him with their heads, hoping that it would bring about a period of stability. But the expectations soon evaporated, as he committed all the mistakes that one could commit, and quickly lost power and his life.

The corporate sector fared no better in India and in the subcontinent in this respect. One factor that was not given much importance in succession planning is the role of trade unions. There were instances where the new head was extended only lukewarm support and some of the chief executives lost their lives at the hands of their own company workers. Workers anywhere are a fractious and emotional lot and it does not take long to ignite a fire among them, which can become uncontrollable. In such cases, succession planning moves swiftly from the boardroom to the public hall and the decisions are taken by the workers.

Succession planning in government at the second layer is different from the political level. The differences between the two are existential in that by definition, the civil services have a continuity and are unaffected by the changing political fortunes. Political continuities and discontinuities are a result of electoral choice. As regards the civil services, every department in government is headed by a (permanent) secretary, who generally reaches that position after prolonged assignments at the lower levels, remaining in the senior position for three years or so before attaining superannuation. During all the preceding years, he/she is regularly evaluated for performance. Most of these top posts are filled up by people drawn from All India Services or other central services. Lateral entry was permitted in the early decades after independence, but is now limited to the positions attached to ministers and the Prime Minister. In the armed forces, a similar system is followed, and the next army, navy or air force chiefs are known well before the present incumbents retire. So, in a way, succession planning at the second level is far more smooth and orderly than at the political level or in the corporate universe.

The situation in the state-owned enterprises is, however, different. Although enterprises both in the public and corporate sectors have several common institutional features, succession planning in the publicly owned enterprises follows more the traditions of the administrative services, partly for the reason that many of the top posts in the enterprises are held by people drawn from the administrative services and rarely an insider is appointed to the post except in the financial sector, where many of the present chiefs would have served their institutions in a different capacity. As in the civil services, here too there are many levels of screening and evaluation before making the final selection. In some cases, the Prime Minister's approval is also taken just to protect everyone's skin. An inevitable consequence of this approach of marking the boxes at every level is that quite a few posts are not filled in time. It is a reflection on the systems of governance that enterprises in which thousands of crores are invested, adequate care is not taken to ensure that they are properly staffed at the top.

The foregoing reflect the general features that are considered to be relatively in favour of the corporate sector. As the discussion illustrates, many of the perceived advantages of the corporate sector may be ascribed in part to the relative small size and narrow focus of the corporate sector. Yet another feature where the corporate sector has a relative advantage over the public bodies relates to the pursuit of economy and efficiency in operations. In the corporate sector it is obligatory, whether on the shop floor or at the top echelons, to pursue efficiency with utmost vigour.

The competitive advantage of any corporate entity lies, except when the market is protected by government legislation, in having a higher level of efficiency than the competitors. Its movement to the top lies in being conscious of efficiency in operations. The system of competition rewards those who are efficient, while within the corporation awards and career progress go to those who excel over others. Government on the other hand is a huge organisation were there are substantial transmission losses in the communication of policy decisions to the operational levels and thus a gap between intent and action, as a consequence of which pursuit of efficiency does not become a part of management orientation. If central directions are issued, they may be implemented through methods other than those specified for the purpose. If, on the other hand, implementation processes are decentralised, there is every opportunity to subvert the announced policies of the government. No amount of monitoring and reviewing by the nodal agencies set up for the purpose can prevent such subversion entirely.

In India, even when subversion is found, no action is taken on those responsible for the simple reason that it takes a long time to initiate action; and even where initiated, the results may be far from conclusive. If the issue is referred to the judiciary, it may take even longer to reach a verdict. Further, most government officials are politically connected, and influential leaders are brought in to mediate. The end result is that the presumed guilty official is never penalised. It should be noted parenthetically that political mediation takes place even in the corporate sector. No corporation likes to be on the wrong side of the powers that be: they realise only too well which side of their bread is buttered. Thus in both realms, an administrative problem morphs rapidly into a political one, and unlike in the western democracies, industrial action, *viz.*, laying down the tools and proceeding on strike, starts on the spur of the moment. These cultural factors need to be specifically incorporated into the study of management and application of its tenets. The efficacy of any tenet depends, in the final analysis, on the cultural factors.

5

Partnerships, Contractorisation and Procurement

Selected Issues

The limitations of the government sector have been recognised over the years and attempts have been made to overhaul the machinery, but with no discernible effect. (These aspects are considered further on.) Administrative Reforms Commissions (ARCs) were appointed in 1966 and 2005. Their reports were reviewed by various committees of secretaries and others. This in itself has been a time-consuming process: nearly a decade after the Second ARC was set up, its findings are still being processed, with no end in sight. Meanwhile, however, several important initiatives were taken, including announcement of a policy of PPP (public-private partnership) in the infrastructure area prominently, and other areas. It is envisaged that PPPs would also be established in the defence sector.

The idea of partnership with the corporate sector is an old one in industrial economies, and there was extensive collaboration between the two during World War II. The idea was revived in the United Kingdom in the late 1990s, primarily for two reasons. First, given the imperative of reducing the fiscal deficit, and given also the imperative of undertaking much-needed development in infrastructure and other areas, PPPs were evolved as a way out of a piquant situation. Second, the new public management philosophy emphasised the need for adapting corporate practices in the government sector, for which PPPs came to be believed as the most opportune and inexpensive means, through a process of osmosis. In India, a beginning was made in this direction in 2006. A PPP cell with its own website was established and a PPP Appraisal Committee set up in the central government. With several expectations in view, governments at both at the central and state levels have entered into various PPP agreements, and the total investment under such agreements has been growing by the day.

In concluding these agreements, a couple of protective privileges have been extended to the private sector partner. While these are not extended uniformly to all sectors, the privileges include exemption from the Right to Information Act and the purview of the Lok Pal. These exemptions are substantial and have become a part of the administrative process without consultation with the public or legislative approval. This means that the government is not permitting independent investigation into this phenomenon.

Whether the expectations about the adoption of best practices and consequent improvement in efficiency are valid is a moot question in view of the limited experience. But the experience of the expansion and modernisation of the two civil airports in Delhi and Mumbai does not offer much hope for the future. On the other hand, the contractual agreements with the private sector show the same handicaps that have so far characterised the management of contracts in India. To start with, the agreement provided large tracts of land to the private partner at highly concessional rates. More significantly, as the Airport Authority of India did not have up-to-date land records, the actual land leased out turned out, on a systematic survey, to be significantly more than what was originally included in the negotiated agreement. Secondly, the project cost went up by several times of the negotiated contract. To compensate for the increased cost, the private sector partner was allowed, without the authority of requisite legislation or legislative approval, to collect a user charge. In the case of Delhi airport, the private partner was permitted by the central government to collect a development fee. Yet another feature in the case of the Mumbai airport was that the contracting party was allowed the unilateral authority to extend its operations for a period of another three decades on the same conditions and terms as set forth in the original agreement. Many of these and other features were approved by the Committee of Ministers of the central government, and as such with the full support of the government.

These matters have been placed in the public domain courtesy the performance audit reports prepared by the office of the Comptroller & Auditor General. As usual, there was a short-lived indignation and promises to improve the situation and, as is customary, nothing has happened and presumably, very little is likely to happen in the future.

The tradition of protest, promise to make improvements, and eventually no improvement in public benefit, continues unabated. Now that a new institution called 3PIndia is proposed to be set up, as announced by the Finance Minister in his budget speech 2014-15, it is appropriate that the failures and the reasons therefor are examined here.

The purpose of PPPs is not merely to provide a benefit or a service expeditiously, but to pass on the benefits of the arrangement to the user and the consumer. The experience cited in this context shows that the Airport Authority was remiss even in the maintenance of its own land records. The Authority was also expected to be a beneficiary of the best practices of the private party. In the event, those practices did not prove beneficial: the cost escalation of the project was too exorbitant that it was in turn socialised through the levy of user charges and development fees. It may be argued, on the other hand, that the cost escalation could have been even more but for the deployment of the so-called best practices. But this is a counterfactual argument and is therefore partially fraudulent. The common citizen, who is at the receiving end, has no means of knowing which one is the real reason. All that he knows is that he has been lied to and there has been a breach of trust. What is even worse is that the arrangement between government and the private party has been extended unilaterally for an even longer period. In effect, it means that the monopoly of a public utility, which an airport is, is permitted to exact a high price from him and the rent of the monopolist is raised and extended for a longer period. This is an egregious failure of the management system, and more specifically the expenditure management system. The State allowed itself to morph into a hollow one in the belief that an improved service would be provided through the PPP. But the argument, based on the experience of the Airport Authority of India, seems to have been heavily in favour of the contracting party. These are precisely the areas that the expenditure management system should be alert to and make systemic improvements in.

There is also a broader and more important question that needs to be addressed. The whole idea in opting for PPP is the expectation that in addition to bringing additional capital and thus mitigating the fiscal crisis being or about to be faced by government, PPP has the definitive potential to serve the public interest better than government agencies. If, on the other hand, the arrangements lead to the creation of enduring monopoly or near-monopoly institutions, it remains to be answered whether the public interest is being served or whether it is being adversely affected. If it is the latter, then it may be a case of an unattractive and costly change without the benefit of improved efficiency in the delivery of services. In the light of the performance reviews carried out by the audit agency, it would appear that in the case of the modernisation of airports in Delhi and Mumbai, the gains to the public from the PPPs are not too evident, though the gains to the corporate sector from the arrangement are not in dispute.

This experience emphasises the need for a revamped expenditure management system, starting from project planning. If the experience of a steady escalation of project costs is common to both public and private sectors, particularly in the infrastructure sector, then the need for improvements in project planning is far too evident. Similarly, contracting procedures may also be in need of improvement. The matter also calls for greater involvement of the government during project implementation so that the likely problems may be anticipated. It is also necessary that the contracting agency is fully equipped with an adequate management structure. Government's involvement cannot be too intrusive, nor can it be a hands-off approach. If the relationship is to be an arm's-length approach, then the content of that approach has to be delineated fully.

Equally important in a democracy are two elements that have not so far been addressed at all. First is the issue of decentralisation of project implementation. Infrastructure projects go beyond airport expansion to roads, bridges, flyovers and so on, including the construction and expansion of major and minor projects. While the users of these projects go beyond the local people, participatory democratic oversight of these projects, now an embedded right, has to be ensured. That participation comes at various stages. During project planning, the local people would like to be assured that the take-off and landing of aircraft does not create too much of noise pollution. Thus, noise abatement techniques have to be addressed as a part of project planning and necessary clearances have to be obtained from the local government as well as from the local people. Since direct participation by all the affected denizens tends to be an unwieldy affair, a process of associating their representation has to be evolved. This will have the effect of introducing yet another layer of consultation and approval to an already lengthy process. While opinions may differ about the advantages of creating yet another layer, the choice for the government is either to associate the local people at the initial stages or to face their ire and organised opposition to the project at a later stage. In such a situation, the better option may lie in the former.

A strengthened expenditure system has also to address the issue of legislative oversight on the accounts (which reveal the patterns of utilisation of both public and private funds) through a legislative committee such as the conventional Public Accounts Committee (PAC), a tool that we have imported from the practices of the House of Commons. Over the years, the ambit of the PAC expanded slowly to reflect the growth of state ownership and management of enterprises. To address the special needs of this sector, a Commercial Audit Division was established in the Audit Department, as well as a separate Committee on Public Sector Undertakings. In a similar way, it has to be considered whether a separate Audit Division and a legislative committee to undertake an annual examination of the performance of PPP arrangements is necessary. This may necessitate the association of subject specialists (educationists, medical administrators, etc.).

Yet another area where further action is needed relates to measures to prevent fraud and protect whistle blowers. As the scope of PPPs is expanding to include the educational and medical services, the scale of fraud and abuse of delegated authority has grown so much that there are very few reliable estimates available about the leakages in the use of public resources. The imperative for stemming those leakages hardly requires any emphasis. It calls for, in conjunction with the redress of grievances, draft legislation that continues to await legislative approval, and possibly, draft legislation to deal with fraud against government (Similar legislation was enacted in the United States more than a decade ago). The litany of these issues suggests that governments may have acquired through the PPP phenomenon a whole new wide field of checks and balances that needs to be designed. It also means that each administrative innovation brings as much convenience as a new set of problems.

Surely, these could have been anticipated to a major extent, but governments were at the time enjoying the first flush of relief on the capital expenditure front. Moreover, they could always argue that the involvement of the corporate sector would bring in a new work ethic and a new management style oriented to efficient functioning. These propositions have not been empirically tested so far, and the evidence anyway is far more anecdotal than empirical. The more nuanced question is how the fundamental difference between the corporate sector, which by tradition is wedded to the principle of profit making, and government, which ostensibly claims to be far more service oriented, is being reconciled. If the way forward is more in the direction of PPP arrangements with consequent amendments to public policy, then it stands to reason that the advantages of the new arrangements with the corporate sector are conclusively demonstrated to the people in general and to the taxpaying public. Meanwhile, there are other areas where public provision of services is getting steadily replaced by other systems that have the two-way potential of providing improved services on the one hand and inviting a whole set of new problems, on the other. Two forms which are gaining new currency in this regard relate to increased resort to contractorisation and reliance on grant-aided organisations.

Contractorisation

Contractorisation is an old practice of government, and the central government has had extensive experience with this approach. Traditionally, resort to contracts was limited to the goods and services consumed by government, i.e. acquired for direct use by its staff, or acquired for providing services to the community, or in the area of construction: buildings, roads, bridges, railway lines, ports and airports, or even major multipurpose projects. Contractorisation also involved the importation of equipment used by the defence forces, i.e. equipment used by the forces but not manufactured by the ordnance factories and other public sector undertakings under the direct management of the Union Ministry of Defence. The scale of such contracts underwent major changes since World War II. The range of goods used by the government grew exponentially during the war, and two significant internal innovations were made in the government machinery to accommodate the change. One was to set up an exclusive organisation devoted to the management of procurement, staffed with engineers and procurement experts well versed in the acquisition of all kinds of goods and equipment. The second was to organise a cadre called Finance and Commerce Pool to manage the financial aspects of procurement. The organisation was later entrusted with the task, at the end of the war, of the disposal of surplus stores and all other equipment that ceased to be useful for the defence authorities. Although the Finance and Commerce Pool was abandoned at the end of the war, most of the practices relating to the review of contracts were integrated into the expenditure management machinery, which was suitably strengthened to address the massive task of economic development of the country. It may be noted, however, that both these features of procurement were present during the nineteenth century when the British government undertook the construction of a railway network from scratch.

In more recent years, there has been a move to contract out services too. Partly, it was inspired by a move to contain the pay rolls in the government. For historical reasons, employment with the government was—and continues to be—much coveted, particularly among those whose chances of alternative employment are virtually non-existent. The expenses for maintaining this category of employees (category D) are relatively high. With a view to economising on these outlays and the growing pension burden (Pension is the main attraction to seek employment with government) governments at all levels decided to contract out some services. Contracting out also became necessary in areas where specialised skills were required, such as surveys and related research, software development, as well as expertise in cyber hacking and associated attacks. In contracting out, not infrequently, contracts may be tendered on a global basis and even those whose bids are not necessarily the lowest may still be awarded the contracts if their technical skills are deemed to be too valuable to be ignored.

When medical and health or educational services are contracted out, payments to the institutions providing these services are made as a reimbursement, in an arrangement that is technically known as third-party payments. As a rule, governments have a prescribed rate schedule which is akin to the rate contract under which approved items are supplied to the government(s) at a price determined jointly by the vendor and the government. In regard to medical services, the claimant is usually a government employee or a member of the government-managed (such as for those who are below the poverty line) health insurance service or health service provided by the government or by the corporate sector. The hospitals and educational institutions for the provision of services are selected by the agencies concerned, more or less on the same principles as are applicable to a procurement contract or a construction contract. The primary emphasis in the selection process is the adequacy of the services and the capacity for doing so, with the quality of services provided being subject to periodic review.

The process of defence procurement has some added dimensions that are not found in the procurement of other items. For one thing, the tendering is on a global basis, and most bids are supported strongly by their national governments, taking the issue from the narrow confines of a tender to a delicate foreign policy issue. The tender may also include arrangements for the sharing of technology. There could also be a requirement that the company which has been awarded the contract should invest a specified percentage of the total value of the contract in the receiving country. Given the magnitudes of outlays, the whole process is expected to be transparent, although to the insiders each proverbial twist of the arm may be evident. In order to avoid the taint of corruption or decision-making under the influence of unspecified international powers, various committees are appointed to process the same proposals over and over until an agreement is reached. But the layers of review have not entirely eliminated the perception of corruption in these deals. The perception, as subsequent evidence has shown, is not entirely without foundation. Indeed, in a number of cases, the evidence of wrongdoing has been overwhelming.

Some may argue that there is no alternative to contracting out, as the government is not equipped to do all the things by itself. It therefore is not merely an expedient to contract out, but a necessity. The important issue that arises is how the expenditure management system copes with this departure from its own traditions. But as noted earlier, contracting out itself is not a total novelty: rather, the point of departure is the scale of contracting out and the complexity of operations that are addressed through this means. Nevertheless, some issues that the expenditure management system addressed in administering the departures from the traditions and their implications for the present and future governance of the democratic polity need to be considered. This consideration is intended to provide greater insight into the working of the process of contractorisation and its financial implications.

The first inherent advantage of contracting out is that it does not contribute to growing recurring outlays. The substantial element in expenditure growth generally is the growth of personnel. When services are contracted out, it is the contractor that recruits the necessary staff, who are reflected on his rolls and not that of the government. This gives the impression that there is a definitive reduction in the staff employed by the government and to that extent there is a putative reduction in the wage bill. This, however, is not how it works in practice in India. When services are entrusted (a form of contracting) to a NGO (non-governmental organisation) that organisation recruits the staff on the understanding that at a later date (the date is dependent on the political pulls of the staff) the workers would be, to use the language of the government, regularised; in other words, brought on to the rolls of the government. This creation of a deliberate illusion is common to both the central and state governments. The latter make it a point to bring on this type of contractual employees onto the government rolls around the end of the five-year period for which a new Finance Commission is undertaking a review of the expenditure financing requirements of the government. In effect, the practice involves self-deception as well as deception of the public.

Another aspect of contractorisation is the attempt to substitute market tests for administrative controls. The latter reflect the best judgement of the official or a group of officials concerned, which reflects their administrative experience. In many instances, this judgement, some contend in justification of their actions, is far better than market tests. The market is not a perfect mechanism as there are cartels, collusions, and other forms of coalition-based trade-offs that disturb the market. The market may be imperfect, as contended by Joan Robinson a long time ago, or it may simply become a monopolistic competition, as argued by Edward Chamberlain. That said, it should be pointed out that the purpose of setting up regulatory institutions is to ensure, in most cases, a fair degree of competition. On the assumption that there is competition in the market, choosing contractors on the basis of competitive bids is more advantageous than exercising administrative control. The latter often involves the selection of a few on the basis of the limited knowledge of the decision-maker. In a competitive environment, there is a self-selection in that the most reasonable bid, subject to satisfactory fulfilment of technical requirements, stands to be selected. It may also bring more economies or value for money than would be the case if an administrative decision is taken. In an administrative decision, the costs are at best putative, and in any event are not based on competitive quotations of bids. Administrative decisions are also most likely to lend themselves to politicisation of decision-making. The ministers, who represent the political class, have their own interests that may not in fact seek the lowest price. The intent of political mediation is to skim off the margins. Even more important, each administrative decision has the potential of creating a domain of patronage which, other things being equal, may wish to perpetuate itself and continue to obtain a rent. In this case, both the political class and the contractors become rentiers, and in due course acquire the mantle of oligarchs.

India's experience with coal allocations proves this likelihood; it has also cost a good deal to the government and to society.

Resort to market tests, it should be recognised, may not always work to the advantage of the government. Much depends, however, on the area in which contracts are solicited. In the defence sector, for example, it is conceded by those who are engaged in the manufacture and supply of equipment, there is nothing like fair competition. To begin with, the competition is limited to the few manufacturers in the field. Most of their clients, particularly developing countries, want cutting-edge technology but lack the supporting infrastructure and may not even have the technical expertise to evaluate the bids. Where companies are engaged in the manufacture of the equipment, they need an export licence from their own governments, which may or may not be granted, subject to purely political considerations. Sometimes, these governments themselves may behave like mercantile states in that they effectively become the salesmen for the companies. There are few better illustrations to demonstrate the extensive links between government and the corporate sector than in the military-industrial complex.

In many of the military-exporting countries, the military-industrial complex is a behemoth, backed by extraordinary lobbying effort. Its process of bidding is at best opaque and at worst mysterious. The options for additions and alterations are numerous, and each add-on contributes to a price increase that is rarely made explicit in the first bid. The cost of manufacturing is also not known. Experience shows that after all the discounts and kickbacks and explicit commissions, the manufacturing companies make sizeable profits. This raises significant questions about the level of expertise available in the military-importing countries and their capacity to make the expenditure management system far more effective than in the past, if at all there is indeed an effective expenditure management system that can address these issues. In practice, each time a country thinks that it has developed expertise to see through the games of the vendor, the latter alters the game. The advantage is always with the vendor or with the party that has adequate resources to hire more talented people who can devise more games that often prove to be impenetrable. This is somewhat akin to the problem experienced in tax collection. Those who can afford it, and there are many, hire the most effective tax lawyer that money can buy, so that their overall tax liability is reduced. All that the military buyer can do is to make an effort to reduce the price, while being fully aware that there are severe limitations to achieving that goal. The main limitation is that the vendor is only too well aware that he has near monopoly in supply and that the buyer is in dire urgency to buy his equipment.

An added complication is that on the buyer's side the financial and the technical expertise are not integrated. The financial expert has little knowledge about the equipment and is guided by the expertise of the armed forces, who suggested the purchase in the first place. Having suggested the purchase, the armed forces are unlikely to change their demand, regardless of the price quoted. This split on the buying side is fully exploited by the vendor, who takes a take-it-or-leave-it stand in the negotiations.

A complication is likely to arise if the parties involved on the purchasing side expand with the size of the order and with the outlay involved. A case in point is the import of Tatra trucks by India's Defence Ministry in 2011. Although the purchase deal was directly negotiated and settled by the Defence Ministry and Army Headquarters, it was later suggested that the trucks should be first imported by a public sector undertaking (so as to bolster its balance-sheet) and then resold to Army Headquarters. This added to the transaction costs, and the Defence Ministry ended up paying a higher price. This suggests that when there is a pie, many claimants want to share it. This may not be typical of public sector behaviour, but is not unusual. Many of these dealings come to light, however, years after the event, when the audit undertakes an investigation.

It has been pointed out earlier on that in defence purchases the first stage of negotiations represents a sort of a putative settlement. As progress is made in the fabrication of the equipment, changes are proposed by the buyer, reflecting his changing needs in terms of changing technological developments that have come to his notice. Inevitably, this contributes to an increase in the eventual price paid. No part of these developments can be expected by the buyer, and with a view to acquiring the much-needed equipment (which is always advocated on considerations of national security, the price is a secondary consideration) the higher price becomes acceptable. Questions may be raised whether some of these developments could not have been anticipated at the time of making the policy decision to acquire the equipment. In theory, the answer is "yes". In practice, however, it has not been found to be feasible even in industrialised countries. Thus, this approach to the acquisition of military hardware has become a fixed part of the negotiation landscape. The advantages of a competitive market then prove illusory. To minimise the adverse fallout, the buyer seeks other compensatory adjustments such as foreign direct investment by the vendor. Here again, the issue ends up becoming a far bigger one in that it moves from a routine acquisition of hardware to a major policy question relating to foreign investment in a strategic sector. This aspect raises a host of issues that are not a direct part of the process of contractorisation and are therefore not considered here.

Political Interference

One argument that is usually advanced in support of a competitive tendering process is that it eliminates the role of politicians and their involvement, which may result in changing the purchase decision to favour someone of their choice. This is based on the assumption that the market is entirely autonomous (a questionable assumption, given the mercantilist role played by the government of the selling country) and that it is free and fair. So far as military equipment is concerned this remains merely an assumption. As we have seen, the features of the defence equipment market do not support the validity of this argument. The opaque nature of the market permits all kinds of involvement by the political and administrative classes, and their final decisions tend invariably to be political rather than purely financial or technical.

The situation is worse when the equipment is bought in the secondary market. After the dissolution of the Soviet Union and with the establishment of independent republics, the secondary market for military hardware expanded suddenly. Many countries in the Middle East and Latin America rushed into this market to avail themselves of what they viewed as a once-in-a-lifetime opportunity.[1]

Thus, political involvement is an accepted phenomenon though every government, regardless of its ideology, publicly avows that it is not involved in such transactions. In reality, their involvement is a constant feature and their interplay with other competing forces, all of whom jostle for space, in this long scramble for public resources for personal use, is an established feature of negotiations. In this context, there is not much that the expenditure management system can do.

1. There were many transactions which were settled through questionable means and with debatable results. One such area was the issue of debt that India owed to the Soviet Union. Details of this episode have never seen daylight.

This system is designed to deal with ordinary situations where people deal with each other in good faith. Where that good faith becomes a rare commodity, the system is not equipped to deal with it until it is taken up, usually after a few years, by the audit agency and the criminal investigation department. Even then those investigations may reach a dead-end, as has been the case with the purchase of Bofors guns by the Government of India a couple of decades ago. To this day, the details of that transaction have not become available and nobody has been penalised for this transaction. Thus, those who advocate greater reliance on more effective audit and deployment of more trained procurement personnel should be made aware of the limitations of the system and the subversion that it goes through. A dose of realism is helpful in having a better understanding of the systems of governance.

The preceding discussion illustrates the complexity of the issues associated with defence management in general and with defence procurement in particular. The issues encountered cover the whole gamut of governance, including the involvement of the ministries. Any effort aimed at improving the situation should aim at covering all the issues, not simultaneously, but in a phased manner. Like other problems associated with governance, neglect will inevitably lead to additional complexity and more difficulties in addressing them. Routine incantation of the need for transparency and accountability does not and has not contributed to improvements, and it is delusional to think that the introduction of Right to Information legislation (which is now found in more than eighty countries) would have some beneficial impact. As a result of this legislation, work processes in government have been expanded to include more people, so that the responsibility may be rendered more diffused, and take decisions more on the basis of off-the-record oral transactions than on the basis of the written record.

The experience of many a country shows that when innovations are introduced, the civil services have their own way of neutralising their effect in the medium term. The moral of the experience is that the entrenched civil services do not actively embrace innovations except when they are advantageous to them. If the innovations are intended to benefit the community, it is more than likely that they will be given a pro forma welcome by those who will be entrusted with the responsibility of their implementation. Like all rational beings, they see each innovation and weigh its pros and cons, partly in terms of what that holds in store for them and for the people. If it is all loaded in favour of the people, and if the terms of implementation turn out to be adverse to them, they will turn opportunistic and self-serving. Specifically, in terms of defence management, given the enormous potential for corruption and scams, the civil and political classes would like to make sure that all the interests are addressed before a final decision is taken. That final decision would necessarily be a compromise in view of the large variety of interests involved. Each interest has a political class supporting it, and when these interests are not addressed, decisions too will be delayed, so long as there is no immediate threat of a crisis erupting suddenly. In terms of national security, such crises arise only when a contiguous country escalates tensions and threatens to conduct its foreign policy beyond the conventional peaceful means. This is one reason why, despite frequent assertions about the imperative of the modernisation of defence forces, there are many decisions pending on the actual placement of orders. Each step of delay could, regrettably, mean that one of the interested parties remains to be satisfied about the terms offered.

The parties involved in the game have remained the same over hundreds of years. In the days gone by, when the favourite pastime of royalty was to mount a raid or even an invasion over one of the many neighbouring states, the armed forces were offered many inducements, such as sharing of spoils and potentially expanded power base, to induce them to become active participants in the affair. Now there are no invasions on a regular basis, but there may be infrequent incursions aimed at inflicting damage on the next state. This may be intended to change the balance of power with competing interests. These variables continue to have an impact on the conduct of foreign policy and on defence management. There is also a new variable which was not explicit in the past but is now palpably a dominating factor in the formulation of defence strategies. This relates to the domestic rate of economic growth. When a country is experiencing a surge in its growth, the defence forces tend to demand more and more resources so that their machinery could be modernised (through substantial replacements and additions) and the balance of power is maintained. While this provides growing impetus for more purchases, the inability to arrive at an equitable distribution of resources acts as a severe restraint in finalising procurement decisions.

Inevitably, these tensions in the system contribute to a different fiscal issue of limited capacities to utilise allotted resources. Annual allocations remain unspent and the armed forces argue that their situation is different, and on that basis, they should be offered non-lapsable allocations. The problem is then deferred to a future date, when a compelling situation may arise for the government to undertake speedy procurement. Meanwhile, the fact that the process has so far been moving at a snail's pace may itself be a compelling argument in favour of the maintenance of that rate of deliberation. In matters of governance, arguments can be advanced both in support of progress and in favour of the status quo. It is for the political class to unravel these knots and push the process onto a higher momentum.

Social Services and Contractorisation

During the last two decades there has been growing contractorisation in social services too. Thus, medical services are now being provided by privately owned hospitals. Collection of garbage and treatment of waste are also being contracted out to private parties. Education too is now being provided by several privately held (either in a corporate form or by public charitable trusts) and managed institutions. This feature is not entirely new. Privately held schools and colleges were a part of the educational system even during the British period. These institutions received public assistance in the form of grants-in-aid (provided for in the budgets every year) from the government. Now, as a part of contractorisation more educational services in a large range of disciplines covering liberal arts, science and technology and professional education both at under- and post-graduate levels are being offered under private initiative. There are other services provided by NGOs (including faith-based organisations) that are either fully or substantially funded from the public exchequer.

The expansion in the range of activities undertaken by agencies other than governmental is a reflection of the times. On the demand side, the inexorable increase in population and consequent need for the provision of services, particularly in the context of the work of a paternalistic state, has made it necessary to explore other avenues in addition to government. On the supply side, it has been felt for some time that notwithstanding organisational innovations, increase in the number of government levels (supranational, national, provincial or state, zonal and local) and provision of numerous incentives to the staff, there are obvious limitations on the capacities of government to manage them effectively. It is not merely the increase in population that is adding to the strains and stresses of government: the expectations of the people and the complexity of the services to be provided are also stretching the management capabilities of government. This is not to imply that government has been standing idle, without equipping itself with the resources and the imagination to manage them. But these efforts and the pace of adjustment are found wanting. The alternatives available make the selection of contractorisation fairly easy.

Take the provision of medical services. This has two principal components, *viz.*, insurance and social assistance. The former involves payment of monthly premiums and reimbursement of expenses incurred, though the scale of reimbursement varies. Social assistance is primarily intended to serve the needs of those below the poverty line. Their needs are met by both government hospitals and privately owned hospitals. The hospitals have some eligibility requirements, and their inclusion in the service provider category organised by the government is comprehensively reviewed periodically in the same way as a contractor's eligibility to participate in a bid announced by the government. Governments too have their own insurance schemes, which vary between the defence and the civil sectors, and there are differences between the contributory health scheme and the insurance schemes organised by the Ministry of Labour and Employment of the Union Government. These differences apart, it is reassuring that the medical needs of the citizen are met in a variety of ways. The participation of corporate hospitals has vastly expanded the scope of the medical services provided. More significantly, the large-scale investments made by the corporate sector in the latest technology assure that the best services and the latest expertise that money can buy are being made available to the citizen.

The establishment of a multiplicity of schemes of insurance and multi-speciality hospitals, not to mention the ambulance services, have clearly expanded the choice available to the consumer. But if it is a case of organising an efficient service, then there are a number of issues that need to be addressed. For one thing, the services as organised now are in many states exacerbating the urban-rural divide rather than reducing it. In the state of Andhra Pradesh (before bifurcation) there were more than three hundred corporate hospitals, all located in the state capital or in big urban centres like Visakhapatnam, Vijayawada (the provisional capital of Andhra Pradesh after bifurcation), Tirupati, etc. As a result of this development, which was not envisaged by the state government but has come about based entirely on market considerations, the rural areas continue to have poorly organised medical services. Moreover, a new class of middlemen has emerged, mediating between the service provider and those seeking its services. From an expenditure management point of view, the market/contractor-provided services are coming at a higher price. The medical industry has lost no time in developing a new skill, in addition to its repertoire of medical skills, in terms of unbundling the services so that the charges collected can be higher. More demands are made for clinical tests (some with debatable essentiality) and more medicines than are needed are prescribed. All these avenues are exploited to the hilt to derive the maximum financial advantage. Purely from a financial point of view, the question is asked whether it is not more advantageous to have more hospitals established and managed by the government itself. But having made the paradigm shift it is no longer possible to turn the direction as the people have made the choice in favour of less bureaucracy and greater availability of service.

A related area which has witnessed burgeoning growth is the provision of education at all levels. Starting from kindergarten to post-doctoral education, the corporate sector has taken initiatives to set up a whole range of institutions. The corporate sector is not limited in either vision or capital and has become the chosen instrument for providing professional education in the medical and engineering sectors. As with medical services, the institutions that offer these services are first scrutinised by government and are then awarded a kind of contract to provide services for which it pays. In this system, eligible students, i.e. those from scheduled castes and tribes and other backward classes are sent to these institutions and their expenses, such as fees, are underwritten by the government. It is, however, a contract with a major departure from conventional contracts in that the fees may not always be determined by the government. Education being a state subject, the actual practices vary from one state to another. In Andhra Pradesh, the annual tuition fees payable were determined by the government. But with rising inflation, the managements of the educational institutions found it difficult to provide the services and sought an upward revision in the schedule of fees. The government on its part found its own fiscal situation too strained to permit such a revision. The corporate sector then took up the case with the judiciary, who saw a good deal of reason in its plea and awarded a new fee structure. In the process, the government lost the power to determine the fee structure and an unusual contract feature emerged, *viz.*, that the contracting agency has no power to fix or negotiate the price. This feature was not anticipated in designing the original contract structure. While in principle the adjudicating authority of the judiciary was never in question (because any of the contracting parties can approach the judiciary for justice), what was uncomfortable for the government was that it had to swallow the bitter pill of its lack of power to determine the fees to be paid to the organising committees of the educational institutions.

The fact that the administration of the educational institutions has moved into the corporate sector has also brought in a new form of corruption, many state governments contend, on a massive scale. Inspections and audit by government and independent agencies and social audit by the community have revealed that the number of students on the rolls and eligible for reimbursement was often much higher than the people actually attending the institution. This provides ample support to the contention that wherever public money is involved there is bound to be fraud and embezzlement. This theory was first propounded by Kautilya in *Arthasastra* two millennia ago. His recipe for prevention or the proclivity for expansion of fraud was to impose heavy penalties on those found guilty. In principle, the remedy for fraud and corruption is to resort to the judicial process, which takes the case away from the domain of the executive to the domain of the judiciary. But the judiciary is already over-extended, litigation is expensive, the State is the biggest litigant, and therefore any prospect of getting quick results is non-existent. Meanwhile, the greed of the corporate sector and the frequent ethical lapses keep on contributing to a new state of affairs that is not different from the past. If in the past it was the State that became corrupt, now both the State and the corporate sector are found to be colluding to switch public resources for personal use and accumulate greater wealth by the participants in the process. The competitive gains, to the extent there are any, are more than wiped off by the corrupt practices on both ends.

The issue also arises whether the corporate institutions offer better quality of education. The fact is that education is no longer a service: it is a commercial good. As a commercial proposition, the institution is expected to bring in profits and the immediate goal is to bring added value to the balance-sheet. The government has an immense stake, as has the local community, in achieving upgraded educational skills, but the instruments they have to achieve this laudable and necessary goal are frequent inspection and regular audit. The latter is more of a financial instrument and has the potential of revealing fraud but is not fully capable of assessing the quality of education imparted. Inspection too has not proved effective. To be sure, it points out, for example, that the qualifications of the teachers are not adequate, that classroom and laboratory facilities are woefully short, that sanitary facilities are below par and such other discoveries. These findings are duly passed on to the authorities who, in order to be compliant, promise immediate remedial action, which, however, remains in the same stagnant stage until the next inspection. The cycle goes on and the march of folly continues at a faster clip. This is, by and large, the experience of the state which is the biggest buyer of educational services, but that capacity does not provide any additional leverage. Inevitably, the common citizen is fed up and is unwilling to repose any more faith in the government. In his view, it is a failed, hollow giant.

In addition to the corporate sector, government also utilises other avenues to deliver much-needed public services while continuing its role as the financing principal. Prominent among these other avenues are NGOs. The range of NGOs is fairly large and includes private autonomous voluntary organisations or faith-based (quasi-religious) organisations. The latter have been there for a very long time and some Jesuit organisations were present even during the British rule. During more recent years, NGOs have sparked off new controversies, particularly about their financing sources and where their loyalties lie. In some countries, particularly in the former Soviet republics, motives have been ascribed to them, bringing them into disrepute. In some cases, their activities were also suspended. These actions were taken primarily for the reason that the governments in some of these countries tend to the view that these NGOs are working against them. These wider political questions constitute a separate enquiry. The discussion here is confined to the financial relationship between government—the provider of finances, and NGOs—the providers of services.

When a request for a grant is approved, the agency concerned processes the application for seeking provision in the budget and securing legislative approval for the appropriations. Once the budget provision is secured, it is for the administrative agency to specify, in consultation with the Finance Ministry, the time-slice of the release of funds. Such apportionment and the specification of the time schedule is intended to prevent immobilisation of funds at the receiving end. The grant-in-aid is specific in that the basic objective that is proposed to be achieved is needed to be stated explicitly. The grant is also subject to a good deal of ring fencing, depending on whether it is for budgetary support or for capital expenditure incurred for the acquisition of a capital asset or for the construction of an asset. Once an asset is recognised, its maintenance could well be the consideration for a future claim on resources. The depth of ring fencing and its effectiveness are dependent on the ingenuity of the agency as well as that of the receiving institution. The latter's effort is, in general, to ensure minimum compliance, while the granting agency seeks to erect an edifice of administrative controls so that the utilisation of public money can secure a public purpose.

The grant-in-aid is, as a matter of principle, intended for ad hoc assistance and is not meant as a conduit for annual budget support. If the support is regular and recurring, then there is little difference between a government agency and an autonomous institution usually registered under the Societies Registration legislation. A further feature of the grant-in-aid is that it is usually expected to finance only a part of the overall requirement of the receiving institution. Again, if the government is providing, say 80 per cent of the financial requirement of the grantee, then there is considerable blurring of the boundary lines between a government agency and an autonomous institution. In turn, this raises the more fundamental question why the route of an autonomous institution is preferred to that of a government agency. It is the preferred mode because the grant-in-aid liberates the receiving institution from the engulfing shackles of government bureaucracy. A hidden agenda is to carve out a separate domain of patronage, ostensibly with the purpose of providing a public service, funded by the government but outside the usual rigours associated with the government budget. In several cases, however, there is a nobility of purpose and devotion to duty, as is evident from the long history of NGOs in India. One should therefore show restraint in applying the tarring brush.

After the funds are received, the receiving institution is expected to furnish, depending on the conditionality governing the grant, a utilisation certificate to the government, which completes the budget cycle of action. Depending on the magnitude of the grant and the public purpose served, the receiving agencies may be inspected, and may be audited, on a supplementary basis, by the Audit Department. These aspects may be considered as routine if all the steps go like clockwork. Experience shows, however, that getting funds released from government is a far tougher proposition than the removal of a tooth by the dentist. In involves many hurdles and is a tapestry of enormous complexity—in fact so complex that the grant-receiving bodies frequently wonder, in moments of indignation or righteous introspection, whether it is worth all the trouble.

Consider, for example, the release of funds. This requires frequent visits to the Finance Ministry and paying obeisance to the tin gods of that ministry. Finally, when the funds are about to be released, the recognition dawns on the grantee that it is only a part of the intended grant and not the full tranche. So the cycle is repeated endlessly, though the steps in the cycle may be drastically reduced, depending on the political mediation. If the institution has a well-connected godfather, the revolving escalator moves faster. It is not the importance of the public service but the clout of the personality behind the institution that makes the procurement of results easier.

Given all the administrative limits described hitherto, why are NGOs considered as important links in the chain of public service delivery? The main reason behind the spurt in the support of NGOs is the canvassing on their behalf by the international financial institutions. From their point of view, government is already over-extended and is found to be lacking in commitment. Governments do not lack organisational skills: they recruit the best talent available in the country through competitive examinations. But governments have become so big that their day-to-day management has become problematic. The availability of an alternative makes it easy to choose proven paths. The grant-aided organisations are small, mobile, committed, and have lower transaction costs. More significantly, they are in day-to-day contact with the clients and to the extent there is anything wrong with them, from an electoral point of view, criticism is deflected from the government to the organisation. Where the organisations are faith based (read quasi-religious), they are guided by higher authorities that are beyond question and reproof.

What is not discussed in the literature is the question whether governments have become dilatory, inefficient and ineffective and are engaged in the pursuit of their own agendas that are not related to the public needs, due to political mediation or some other organisational matter. It is a question on the mind of every voter, but somehow it is not sought to be answered either at election time or any other time. Meanwhile, to get over the crisis, tasks are transferred to the corporate sector to be managed by it, while being funded by the public exchequer.

This reluctance to address the important issue is in part responsible for the crisis in governance.

Meanwhile, the functioning of the NGOs has muddled the debate far more than before. They have morphed themselves into replicas of the government machinery. Like the curate's egg, there are some organisations which work well to the satisfaction of the community. They may not be efficient or cost-effective but they are trusted by the clients, and that feature alone has helped them survive against all odds and even flourish. Faith-based organisations bring a good deal of dedication that is lacking in other organisations, a fact that is admitted even by the competing organisations. In general, however, many of the NGOs have been organised to siphon off funds from the Treasury, while enjoying full autonomy for their management. They too have become dilatory.

An organisation based in the Philippines and devoted to the study of NGOs the world over publishes an annual report. These reports reveal that NGOs have also become centres of corruption, much like government. Utilisation certificates are rarely submitted to the government; and when pressure is brought to submit the utilisation certificate, some of the NGOs are wound up and are soon reopened with the same charter of work but under a different name. This transformation takes place with the full knowledge and support of the government officialdom concerned, and then it is business as usual. These are instances where form is obviously far more important than substance. In fact, when officialdom actively connives with the NGOs, they are rarely concerned with the substance. It is form and form alone that is deemed to be adequately compliant with the rules. Experience shows that when a new organisation is set up, new rules are framed to elicit promised results. But once it starts functioning, the objectives are ignored, grantee concessions and privileges are ignored, and a nominal compliance with the rules is shown while the organisation itself has already been converted into a vehicle for the pursuit of private agendas. What is odd is that every bit of this transformation is known to the officialdom but it chooses to cast a Nelson's eye on the goings-on.

India has thousands of NGOs. Most of them, as the reports of the Philippines-based organisation reveal, do not go beyond a post box address. The only thing going for most of these NGOs is the political support they receive. Governments may go through periods of austerity and prosperity, but the government's need for austerity has never crippled the claimed activities of any NGO. In view of this yawning gap between concept and practice, ideal and reality, there is an imperative need to review the working of NGOs and determine whether they provide a sound alternative to government.

6

Delivery of Services

New Stalemate in a Hollow State

Every age brings its own demands, complexities, technologies, theories, and frailties. When the frailties exceed reasonable demands, governance suffers. People then demand more change in the expectation that every change offers more beneficial results, although there are inevitable practical problems necessitating yet another change in mid-course. To gain public confidence, every change is first touted as a panacea until it is found that all that glitters is not gold, indeed not even a metal, but a shining paper offering a putative illusion. Hopes are created, new lobbies are formed, and to propagate the proposed change, a new vocabulary and new slogans are created. Indeed, consultants are hired from all corners and official delegations are sent to the far corners of the globe. These efforts are made to justify the proposed actions that aim at solving a plethora of problems. It is hoped that at a minimum the electorate will be suitably impressed with the ongoing efforts and would extend its support to the party holding power. These features have become all too common, familiar and on occasion banal too.

The major feature of contractorisation is the wall of separation between funding and provision of services. The principal advantage, in the view of the supporters of privatisation, is that the separation facilitates the smooth operation of two seemingly different worlds. In the conventional approaches, a distinction is made between policy formulation and policy implementation in the government. Clausewitz in his classic work made a distinction between grand strategy, strategy and tactics. As propounded by him, grand strategy or the overarching policy goal is determined by the Prime Minister or the President. Within that framework, strategy is formulated by the generals, who are responsible for the prosecution of war—an inevitable stage when all other avenues have failed. Tactics are the approaches followed by the field units under the command of a Major. This analogy can be applied to policy formulation in general.

But very soon the issue arises whether policy formulation and implementation may not be all that different from each other. The assumption that government can follow this distinction between the two phases may not be sustainable. In practice, policy formulation is a complex process in which the administrative class and the political class interact at every stage and it is difficult to demarcate the lines of responsibility between the two or between the legislative and the executive domains. True it is that in a parliamentary democracy the paramount role is that of the legislature, as no policy can come into force except with the approval of the people's representatives. Their role in policy formulation is one of approval and they do not have even the freedom to propose a policy that has expenditure implications, as under the Indian Constitution a "money bill" can be introduced only on the initiative of the executive. The role of the people's representatives in the approval of the appropriations has also gone through a period of adjustment in that the role of legislative discretion has been reduced while expanding the role of the standing and consultative committees. In any event, it is generally conceded that there has been a decline in the role and effectiveness of legislatures. Their role comes into play at the penultimate stage of the policy process when much of the important work has already been done. Within the executive, many agencies have a participatory role in policy formulation. Each sectoral ministry reflects the group interests of those affected by the policies pursued by that ministry. The policies formulated thus reflect those group interests in addition to the macro objectives.

During the last four to five decades, however, the international financial agencies such as the International Monetary Fund and the World Bank, as well as the regional banks like the Asian Development Bank have begun to play a significant role in policy-making, which may not always be visible to the public eye and may not always be transparent (despite the lip-service that they pay to the cause of transparency). Their lending either for specific projects or for overall macroeconomic development and stability is usually accompanied by a long list of conditions and the tranches of money are disbursed to the recipient country concerned after ensuring that the conditions have been adequately fulfilled. The process implies a loss of sovereignty, though no government would be willing to concede that in public. In fact, it is safe to assert that every loan received implies a partial shift of policy-making from the domestic capital city to the international financial centre: the preponderant role that involves identification of problems, measurement of their magnitude, and the formulation of solutions aimed at resolving them as well as financing the operations and their periodic monitoring, is played by the lending financial institution.

There are two other features that need to be recognised in this context. The solutions proffered by the international financial institutions do not reflect either the interests or the policy advocacy of any particular country. Rather, they reflect the collective wisdom of the international community and it is open to the receiving country not to accept them and reject the whole deal. India, for example, rejected the aid offered by the World Bank for the financing of the Narmada River Project. In a few other cases, too, the offers of aid were similarly rejected as the bidding provisions were not acceptable to the Government of India. There is, thus, a lot of to-ing and fro-ing between the governments and the international financial institutions.

The second feature is that this kind of shared policy-making has become a common feature of governance. Policy-making has thus become an open sphere and can never be considered as either watertight or as the exclusive preserve of the government of a country. This reflects the reality of an interdependent world. This process has become even more complex than before in the context of globalisation. A development in one country may have a contagion effect on another country and policy responses may have to be formulated with urgency, for these contagion effects brook no delay. To this complex process must now be added the additional link of contractorisation. When the production and financing of services are delinked from the actual provision of services, the contract itself becomes a limiting factor in policy implementation.

The distinction and the separation of formulation and implementation as two distinct spheres are made in the belief that the role of the political class is confined to the formulation of policies while the implementation part is best left to the administrative class. As an extension of this approach, it is further believed that political interference would be limited to policy formulation and would not be extended to implementation levels. In a way this could be considered as an oversimplification of the process, and to all intents and purposes it ignores the dynamics of policy management as a whole. Everybody in the administrative class wakes up to face a new implementation problem that was not foreseen at the time of formulation. That problem may need a serious adjustment in the policy itself. In India, the implementation reality is that there is very little congruence between the task and the provision of the financial resources. It is common experience that funds are released either by the central government or by the state government long after the need: be it the case of the payment of the wages of a schoolteacher or be it the grant for the purchase of school books, the cycle of activity is different from the cycle of financial releases. Because of this structural lack of congruence the outcome is invariably different and addressing that issue necessitates a change in policy. The policy cycle and the budget cycle, being different, cease to feed each other. As a result, policy adjustment becomes a constant feature and the distinction between formulation and implementation ceases to be tenable. It could plausibly be argued, however, that the distinction may have greater application in the context where the government relies on contractorisation and where it is believed that the contracts contain all the objectives and conditions of payment as well as the estimated outcome; and that to the extent the policies are well laid out, it leaves a clearly delineated space and obligation for the contractor to ensure that implementation is totally in accord with the government plans. As an extension of this belief, it is contended that contractorisation, which is fully transparent and is in accord with the best practices in the world, does not permit political intervention by the ministers or the elected representatives. This argument, as noted earlier, is often advanced by the supporters of contractorisation.

Two considerations, however, have to be kept in view in evaluating this contention. First, there is rarely a case where a policy does not require adjustment. Often, factors such as non-availability of land, ill-timed supply of inputs, and changes in the design of the project because some vital factors were not given the due importance at the time of its formulation, lead inevitably to changes in policy. Every policy works in a dynamic setting and no path can be set in hard concrete. It is also the general experience that possible adjustments are always reckoned as a part of policy formulation and adequate space is provided for their incorporation. Moreover, there are no limits to the ingenuity of the political class. A clever politician has always been a part of the political landscape and intervention is his normal mode of work. The tricks of the trade are learnt quickly and the administrative procedural ropes lend themselves to easy manipulation. The world where there is no political intervention is yet to be evolved.

Secondly, empowerment of the local communities in the process of oversight on contractorisation suggests that political involvement would be greater at the local level. The communities are small and the deliberative channels are even fewer and there is often an informal hegemony of the local elders in determining to whom the contract goes. This fact is not brought out in the annual audit reports as the audit of local finances is an area which is, as noted further on, in desperate need of change. Does the involvement of the local community bring about economies in operations? While in principle it could be said that the association of the stakeholders has the potential of bringing about economies in expenditure, in practice there are many slippages. This is true of even the advanced economies. There are cases in California, for example, where members of the county councils voted themselves high levels of salaries and higher levels of pensions far beyond the fiscal capacity of the county. These experiences suggest that empowerment of the local community is a double-edged weapon that cuts in multiple ways. It also shows that political involvement comes in a variety of ways and every tool utilised in governance could be used for the enrichment of the society as well as to enrich those people who are entrusted with the tasks of governance. The people in government are not endowed with morals different from the society itself.

An important area that needs to be explored is whether contracting out and outsourcing would be far more economical than directly managing the project or programme. Related to this, it needs to be ascertained whether contractorisation confers any particular advantage from an expenditure management point of view on the government. The main reason for choosing the route of contracting out is that the avenue of tendering has the potential advantage of yielding a competitive return in the form of reduced outlays. When a government undertakes a project or a programme for implementation there are, as usual, expenses on human resources, materials, and money transfers (to other agencies). The liabilities on human resources include not merely the pay and allowances for the period of work but also the pension liabilities that accrue. In many calculations, the pension liability is added as an afterthought more for the sake of completion of the estimate than for the purpose of accuracy. These liabilities tend to be substantial for the government. The same job, when performed by a contractor, would have lower establishment expenses or human resources budget, as the employer's liability is restricted to his contribution to the social security-based pension fund, where as the pension is based on a contributory system. In India, however, the contractors work in an informal and unorganised sector and thus may not have to face any pension or liability at all. Thus, more than the competitive edge, it is the fact that the contractor works in an unregulated sphere that provides the prospect of working with a higher margin or a lower bid for the assigned work. In the overall project, however, such economies as are likely to accrue to the government may not be significant, as there are many layers in contracting. With each level of contracting trying to maximise his margin or the rate of profit, the overall expenses on such a project may turn out to be at the same level as would have been the case if the government agency had implemented it directly. The only difference then between the government doing it by itself and through contracting out, would be the quality of work. It could be argued that the government, structured as it is in a pyramidal fashion and prone to inertia and with the diffuse pattern of accountability as well as lack of incentives for the workers, and lacking in customer orientation would be inclined to come out with a far inferior product or service. But then there are exceptions to this rule.

The main argument then in favour of contractorisation is that instead of contributing to a burgeoning growth of the government with attendant implications for continuing tax burdens and personal freedom, it is better to engage in the creation, from a financial point of view, and liquidation of short-term liabilities. These issues, however, are examined and the choice made more from the prism of political ideology than from the point of securing economies in expenditure. Arguably, the latter is often advanced to lend support to a decision that has already been made on ideological considerations primarily. In any event, the issue is not one of contractorisation *per se* but extension of that practice to social and service-oriented fields.

Another major problem relates to the embedded third-party payment system. In general, a payment from the government or even private individuals involves the identification of the person or the institution to whom the payment is made. Any fraud in terms of drawing payments in fictitious names is liable to lead to criminal action and legally imposed punishment. Any time there is no clarity about the payment, there is bound to be a failure of the expenditure management system. The new arrangements in education (which involves millions of students) and medical services (which involve many more millions of clients to whom services are provided) are embedded with too many proclivities to exploit or rig the system in their favour and as a consequence, millions of rupees are spent without adequate documentation and requisite scrutiny. News reports and audit reports suggest that in many educational institutions there are many "ghost" students for whose education the government is engaged in spending massive amounts of money. Similarly, in medical care, there are millions of cases where unnecessary clinical tests are carried out and an equal number of prescriptions are written and paid out. This phenomenon is not, by any means, restricted to India, and is found even in the United States where the annual reports reveal that the extent of fraud is 15 per cent of the total payments made on Medicare and Medicaid programmes. (The potential of abuse under Obamacare, introduced in recent years, is not any less than what it has been in the past.)

The major issue then is to design a system where the incidence of this type is minimised. One cannot totally avoid fraud in transactions involving thousands of service providers and millions of service receivers. Rather, the effort should be to reduce the leakages (while recognising that if one leakage is plugged after assiduous effort, a few others spring up in no time). What is fraud to the government is income (presumably untaxed) to a few others. It should not be forgotten in this context that in India those who are allegedly involved in these transactions also enjoy political support and patronage. In fact, some of the educational and medical institutions are actively organised by political personalities as *benami* owners. Thus, any hopes of major reform should be tempered by a recognition that while immediate beneficial results may be few, the fact that a beginning has been made might itself be praiseworthy. It has the impact of creating hope, and hope is far more sustaining than despair.

The problem of fraud is but one of the many intended or unintended consequences of contractorisation. It may be considered as intended to the extent that the problem can always be anticipated, and the leakages are built into the system not through ignorance but because of a deliberate effort. It may be unintended when all the parties in the agreement arrive at an implementation methodology in good faith but in practice some leakages occur because of human ingenuity and mala fide intent. A lock, when designed, is intended to be theft-proof; but there is always someone who is eager to break it. Governments and corporations have many brilliant people working for them, some of whom tend to be victims of their own greed. The eternal question for expenditure management is to design systems, while being fully aware of the potential that they would be subverted. So far, however, there has been little or no awareness of these systemic slippages and the need to confront them. The efforts are limited to processes, that too on the fringe. The imperative for those engaged in the management of government money is to concentrate on the results.

Quest for a Lower Price or Economies with Improved Care

Governments are by far the biggest buyers of educational services as well as medical services available in the market. In the case of educational institutions, particularly in the medical, engineering and management sciences, the selection of candidates for courses on offer entrance examinations are conducted by autonomous organisations set up exclusively for the purpose by the state governments. The selected candidates are allotted to specific institutions on the basis of what is called as "counselling", a euphemism for verification of the student's credentials. In most cases, particularly for those from Other Backward Classes as well as Scheduled Castes and Tribes, their annual fees and annual upkeep are paid by the governments. In the case of medical services, the insured candidates and others who are eligible for reimbursement of fees and expenses incurred on medications are also among those who are covered under the benefits programmes managed by the state governments and other autonomous agencies.

The question that arises from the expenditure management point of view is whether the government is getting the benefits of a bulk buyer. The evidence available does not even indicate that any efforts are made to alter the management systems of services and other benefits, to reap the advantages of a bulk buyer except in the case of drugs, which in many state governments (the actual procedures vary from one government to another) are first procured by the government, which is also responsible for the maintenance of inventories at public hospitals. (In some cases the supplies of drugs are late and, when needed, the patients obtain the drugs by paying for them from their pockets; the desire for healthy living certainly overwhelms the financial considerations.) In making these procurements, governments often are recipients of discounts for bulk buyers that are extended by all suppliers. In educational institutions, there are no discounts and the state governments have, for all practical purposes, lost their clout (if they had any to start with) as fees are invariably sought to be raised by the corporate sector, which are naturally resisted by governments on the plea of lack of financial resources, and the matter is taken up for adjudication with the judiciary. Thus decision-making, as noted before, has already moved out of the hands of governments, who have now been transformed into supplicants themselves. Thus, in the educational field, the government is at a disadvantage to raise the issue of economies let alone negotiate any discounts.

In the medical field, similarly placed Western governments and insurance companies (this is one case where the interests are common, as both parties are exploring avenues for reducing their own outlays) have been pursuing ways and means to economise on the resources utilised for the purpose. As in India, the universal experience is that costs in hospitals are open-ended and there are no known ceilings on what may be spent. Here there is a distinct discord between the financial controller and the physician. To the latter, the issue is one of providing the best medical care that he/she can provide. Life is paramount and money is not. For the financial controller, it is money that is important; but the relevance of money cannot be evaluated in a vacuum but the prisms through which the issue is analysed are divergent, leading to vastly different conclusions. Moreover, the controls exercised by the respective job-holders tend to be different. The controls of the financial official are oriented to the processes; the doctors' orientation is to the results.

This fundamental divergence poses many insoluble issues to the insurance companies. Governments using insurance companies are broadly concerned with the dilemmas but have not made significant headway in India. The reason for lack of progress is that the governments have not so far focused their attention on the curative aspects and have been primarily concerned with the provision of any type of care and management of payment for benefits. In this context, major insurance companies in the US have been examining the options available to them. For example, in the case of patients needing long-term care (and therefore covered under the Medicare programme, which essentially caters for the needs of elderly people), keeping them in assisted living centres (devoted exclusively to the care of the elderly run on commercial lines) tends to be expensive. So they gave an option for the patients to stay home, if they preferred it, with medical assistants visiting them daily and monitoring the status. This works out cheaper, without any major loss of medical care. Indeed it may work out better for the patient, who continues to be at his own home while receiving medical attention. Similar choices are offered to the terminally ill who often prefer their own homes for the final exit.

In addition, insurance companies in the US are also offering extensive information about themselves through their websites for the benefit of potential clients. This amounts to taking information into the living rooms of the families and enabling them to make their own choices. As they say, an educated customer is the best client (and in cases where resort is made to malpractice claims, the worst clients too). Insurance companies in the US have also initiated a programme called Accountable Care Organisations (ACOs), which evaluates the performance of care-giving organisations and rewards those that keep the costs low. Many of these efforts are spurred by the fact that the costs of medical care often run ahead of the rate of inflation and out-of-pocket expenses met by the client tend to be high, which may lead to substantial additional burdens on them. In India this could very well mean higher pocket expenses for young families who are perforce obliged to take care of the elderly. The absence of a social security system inevitably leads to higher burdens on these families, who are not below the poverty line nor are affluent enough to bear the expenditures. It is an existential dilemma for them, in that they cannot assume a stand-off posture and allow the elderly to fend for themselves or remain unattended. If on the other hand they have to assume the family obligations, they will find their finances severely strained. It is a situation that cries out for relief but the existing assistance plans do not address their problem. It is also a case where the higher expectation generated by social awareness becomes economically unsustainable for millions of people. (The electronic media devote so many hours a week to popular medicine that even for small injuries or aches people rush to a doctor or a hospital. Knowing a doctor itself has acquired a halo of its own and has become a much-valued status symbol.) It is in this context that exploration of cheaper medical care would go a long way in alleviating the financial stress.

The problems experienced tend to be different from one field to another. Each field thus requires a detailed enquiry that is beyond the scope of this discussion. The experiences of the medical field are cited here merely to illustrate that the job of government does not end with the delivery of services. Indeed it is the beginning of another segment of the continuous association between the government as a financing agency and the public as the intended recipient of services. As already noted, an implicit assumption in organising delivery of services is that the services are economical; that their delivery is courteous; and most important, that the services are provided when needed. Only with the fulfilment of these expectations would the public be satisfied. A dissatisfied public is a major problem in testing the resilience of governance as a system. The whole purpose of contractorisation becomes questionable when the costs are high and the service is poor, leading to a frustrated public. It has potential implications for political turmoil and electoral consequences that could be unpleasant for the party in power.

The major issue then is to determine whether government has any option to reduce its own financial commitment. The preceding discussion demonstrates conclusively that government, as a party to a contract drafted by itself, does not have any leverage, financial or otherwise, to improve the financial condition or make the service more effective than before. The only alternative it has is to withdraw from the contract when the actual work is far less satisfactory than estimated. This situation is the result of the handiwork of the government itself; and to that extent, the hollowness which is now the trademark of its operations, is not the making of an adversary but of itself. The reasons for that are not difficult to explore. The rising level of expectations on the one hand, and the high political rhetoric on the other, put the government in a fix in that it had to provide the services that would at least in part assuage the feelings of the public. And this was to be done at no cost or increased outlays. The solution that came in handy was PPPs, which provided a portal to bring in the capital without any short- or long-term impact on government finances. From there, an argument to extend the sphere of contracting to other spheres did not require any additional persuasion. The fact that the State was being converted into a hollow one did not get any immediate recognition. Even when this was recognised, those who were working in the government trusted their own ingenuity and their own capacity to use other instruments available (discussed further on) to improve the situation. There are cases where it is difficult to do so. When there is a failure in the delivery of services, it is immediately ascribed, not to the contractor, but to the government itself. It is that eventuality that government has to guard against. The failure is in the breakdown of services, and not in their expenditure management. The public appears to have enormous patience and a general amnesia to forgive the government for all lapses. But a breakdown in the delivery of services stretches its forbearance, which it finds difficult to forget. And that memory could prevail to the election day.

7

Use and Abuse of Tool Kits

What then are the instruments available to government to ensure compliance with its policy objectives? These are: (i) monitoring of progress; (ii) effective implementation systems *vis-à-vis* the contractual parties or recipient governments or NGOs (non-governmental organisations); (iii) an effective regulatory framework; (iv) effective audit; and (v) effective legislative oversight.

Monitoring of Progress

Progress monitoring is as old as contracting itself. The extent of monitoring and the responsibilities of the partner agency to furnish reports are somewhat sector-specific and vary from one to another. Designing a system too is no longer a complicated exercise: much depends on the function that the reports are expected to serve. Where the projects are deemed to be of vital importance, a more calibrated system with more frequent reporting would be deemed appropriate mainly for the reason that there could be frequent questions in Parliament or even extensive debate, with both requiring a good deal of information with the government.

Two considerations are generally kept in view in designing a reporting system. First, the reports should not be too frequent. This was a caution that was sounded when the systems were manual as it took a good deal of executive time to compile them. This is no longer an issue, given that the systems are computerised at both ends. Since the data are available online, the hierarchical gap between government and the agency has become virtually non-existent. All that remains with the agent is qualitative information, for which the supervising or governmental-level officials are inevitably dependent on the reporting level. The reports should not be so detailed as to rob the embedded autonomy of the agency, nor should they be too brief as to serve no policy purpose.

It is here that the second consideration enters the picture. Any report that is called from the agency should be such as to serve some purpose at the lower level. The report itself should signify, without it stating so, that there is an underlying objective other than simply monitoring what the lower level is doing. If, on the other hand, the report is such that it serves no purpose at the reporting level, that level is unlikely to take any participatory interest in the preparation and onward transmission to the higher authorities. As an extension of this, the quality of information is likely to suffer too. Besides, there is the distinct possibility that data would be manipulated to hide the truth.

In this context, the first step is to determine the objectives of reporting. Although this may appear as self-evident, it is necessary to reiterate them so that there is no fog of confusion among the participants and stakeholders. In designing a reporting system, the respective functions and the limits of responsibilities of the higher levels to whom the reports are sent, and the lower level responsible for the preparation of the reports needs to be recognised first. The level where the reports are received are also the political levels, which have an obligation to keep the stakeholders, *viz.*, the society, informed of the progress. If the progress is not adequate and if it is an important project, then it may be incumbent on the part of the political class to do something about it even if the project is being implemented on an arm's-length basis. Thus, the political objective of being informed is about the most important consideration that should always be kept in view.

The other objectives are more routine, but adjusted to the in-built gap between government and the corporate partner or an NGO or some other organisation which, while being completely or for the most part funded by government, is still given a public space that is far larger than the traditional arm's length. These objectives relate to the approaches to the use of resources. The authority that is providing the resource has an obligation to ensure that the receiving organisation is procuring value for money, that the outlays are being incurred wisely, and that appropriate means are being deployed to secure a modicum of efficiency. It is not adequate to entertain the notion that simply because an activity is being undertaken either on a contractual basis or in partnership with a corporate, the objectives are being achieved prudently. Experience clearly suggests that these financial objectives are too important to be left to the corporation or other institutions receiving money. They need a broader enquiry so that the public may be kept informed about the validity of the political or policy choices made by government.

In the present system, however, reporting is viewed very narrowly, and there is no evidence to suggest that there is either a concern or effort to go beyond the traditional reports despite the growing importance of the joint activities. Money given by government is controlled through the administrative process in that the agency receiving the money submits a utilisation report, on the basis of which the next tranche is released. It is viewed as an accounting transaction and the larger policy purposes are, to all intents and purposes, ignored. It is so even where massive amounts are transferred from the public exchequer to the state governments. The saving grace in the latter transaction is that the spending process is captured in the overall grid of the accounting and auditing system of government.

But the other transactions considered above, are all outside the accounting grid. As more and more services are sought to be provided through the network of linked arrangements such as PPPs (public private partnerships) or NGOs, faith-based organisations or grant-aided institutions, it is necessary that the focus and content of the reporting system is reviewed and improved. Failing this, government ends up looking at an abyss that looks back at it. For a variety of reasons, rightly or wrongly, activities that were traditionally managed by government may be hived off, and as yet not fully developed organisational forms may be devised to carry on the activities. But at the core is government money. Its utilisation is a part of social policy and philosophy and that alone is reason enough for a thorough revamping of the information systems. Not doing so would only mean that in terms of approaches to administration governments continue to be in a colonial time warp.

Effective Implementation Systems

The second instrument available to government to ensure compliance with its policy objectives is to recognise that the fund-receiving agencies or corporate bodies have adequate implementation systems for projects. This task may at first glance appear redundant. In the first place, the project is entrusted to a non-governmental body in the belief (and with supporting evidence) that the recipient has better implementation systems than government. If, on the other hand, its capability is recognised to be less than or equivalent to that of government, there is little point in contracting out. It is essential, however, that in partnerships or in contracting out, a valid contract is drawn up indicating expectations, the tasks to be performed, the risks inherent in the process and their financial coverage, liabilities for fiscal or schedule slippages, and related matters.

Here again, the need for a contract may appear to be self-evident. What needs emphasis, however, is the fact that governments frequently change their own plans and in turn may bring pressure on the partner or contractor to accept those changes. The latter will do this, provided the remuneration package is attractive. It may also happen that the partner faces difficulties, financial or managerial, and demand adjustments in the contract or seek additional compensation. It may even threaten to walk out of the contract if the payments are not remunerative in regard to the changes proposed, and use other means to get approvals from the government. To government, it may appear that it is locked into the contract. A partner walking out can only bring more problems, in terms of loss of prestige or financial losses, and thus there may be no option but to continue with the project regardless of the additional cost involved. In some instances, such as the Enron project at Dhabol (which has been non-operational for several years) government, having provided a comfort letter (euphemism for traditional guarantee and as binding as a guarantee) has been left with no way to salvation. In all these cases, an important element of implementation capacity is the ability to anticipate risks and formulation of ways to address them. Failure to do so is to invite financial complications for which government will be responsible.

Effective Regulatory Framework

Yet another tool available to government in its transactions with the corporate sector is the installation of a regulatory framework. A regulator should be reasonably empowered and endowed with adequate independence to regulate the activities where government is engaged in providing similar services so as to ensure a level playing field for both government and the parties such as in PPP, contracts for major projects, and those corporate bodies who are given the task of managing the State's natural and unique assets, as well as to provide full protection to the interests of the consumer. The regulatory bodies may arrange to collect their own revenues (and thus be financially self-reliant), organise their own bureaucratic structure (either as a commission or as a board), make their own processes and procedures, and issue their regulations from time to time while providing adequate guidance and a time-bound framework for compliance. They should be independent both in appearance and in substance. Any impression that they have been captured by the regulatees is equivalent to a death warrant for them, from which there is no reprieve. The regulatory body should therefore be designed with utmost care so that its objectivity and technical expertise are evident to all, and more so to the bodies regulated by it.

The role of regulatory bodies in contractorisation is an area that is still searching for clarity. Other areas searching for regulatory clarity include financial sector operations in which publicly owned and corporate-owned units work in tandem or in competition. In the era gone by, regulatory bodies announced their processes and procedures through the official gazette and in the press. In the digital age a website would appear to meet this need, though necessarily, the influence would, in the first instance, be limited to denizens of the cyber world. But the spread of information is instantaneous and compliance would be far better than otherwise.

But the world of regulation is not always a happy one, particularly when judged by the outcome of the regulations implemented. The protection afforded to the investor, consumer, a disinterested citizen, and a government whose main concern is the general welfare of the people, are all dependent on the implementation of the regulatory measures. The outcome is itself dependent on the perspective of the regulatees. If the regulations are treated as a necessary evil and therefore compliance is less than ankle deep, then the regulation cannot be considered a success. The risk of perfunctory implementation of regulation is embedded in the operational system. No amount of benign and good natured but arm's-length relationship maintained by the regulator is likely to be of any beneficial impact in view of the fact that the relationship between the regulator and the corporate world is an adversarial one, where trust deficit is somewhat higher than elsewhere.

It is almost like the perspective of the Indian policeman, whose centuries-old outlook is of deep distrust of the "suspect". The first instinctive action, as the inspector in the Hollywood movie "Casablanca" has observed, is to round up the "usual suspects" regardless of the crime proposed to be investigated. In India, the cultural traditions are no different where the patterns of corporate governance are concerned, save a few corporations whose endeavour is to abide by some specified values and which are known to be transparent and are well respected. In this connection, there does not seem to be much difference between private sector/public sector corporate culture in developing and industrial countries. Congressional studies made in the United States reveal that prior to the financial meltdown in 2008, the behaviour and willingness to manipulate operations and data to secure higher bonuses was about the same in government-owned/guaranteed mortgage companies and private sector corporations. Given this background, the regulator has first to fight against the perception regarding what its work involves. If the regulator extends support or tends to accept some management sutras (formulae for success) such as "too big to fail" or is guided by its misguided beliefs, it may be looking into a bottomless pit.

The regulator works in an environment where the heads of corporations have at their disposal a very high level of accumulated political capital, not to mention financial capital and a willingness to use both of them to achieve their business ends. The regulatory agency on the other hand works often in an area of darkness where the subject is evolving and where a lot of midnight oil has to be burnt before its credentials are recognised and accepted. It has to prove itself at every step of the way, where its progress depends, not on the legislative mandate that gave birth to it, but on the purposefulness of the pursuit and clarity of thought that the regulatee can understand and respond to. The first defence of the company or the organisation that is being investigated is to deny the allegations or to say, if they are inevitably conceded, as they must in the light of overwhelming evidence, that its actions were taken in good faith but that it had little control on the consequences. Human nature tends to be the same when allegations are levelled against an individual or a corporation or a government. These factors are firmly embedded in the scene. The only major change that has taken place and that immensely facilitates the work on both sides is the application of digital technology that makes a communication reach the intended party no sooner than when it is ready.

Regulation is, as noted before, as old as humanity itself. The first system of governance included, as Kautilya showed in his still topical book *Arthasastra,* the regulation of weights and measures. Trade, save a few specified areas, was in the hands of a designated group that came to be called a caste later. After the end of the Axial Age, however, the old empires yielded place to newly formed states where economic life came to have a separate form and organisation but was regulated by religious authorities. The traditional government came to focus on other areas. But regulation came to acquire a life of its own, particularly in regard to predatory lending. The widespread practice of lending and borrowing needed regulation, which brought control by the religious authorities[1] into the field. Also, economic life itself became segmented, with one sector engaged in agricultural production and another in consumption of the produce—the rural and the urban sectors. Organisation of trade thus became a field ripe for regulation in that the activities of the merchants were believed to be in need of control in the larger interest of the consuming public. But the role of religious authorities in regulation came to be questioned by Islam, more specifically by Prophet Mohammed, who believed that "prices depend on the will of God" and that government interference in the functioning of markets should be considered sacrilegious (markets were designed by God to regulate themselves[2]). Here was the forerunner of the much-discussed invisible hand. As economic development progressed, and forms of production multiplied in innumerable ways, issues arose that required the urgent attention of governments. Periods of prosperity and depression came to visit countries and peoples more regularly, warranting periodic intervention and day-to-day regulation, and a visible hand to guide the economies.

The fact that regulation has been a formal component of governance and has had many successes to its credit does not by itself validate its existence. In fact, there are many criticisms of regulation. There is even a group of economists who believe that regulation is more of a hindrance and that, in addition to creating a false sense of security, it also leads to greater incidence of moral hazards. Meanwhile, exploiting this situation, there are countries and governments which offer a "lighter touch" of regulation in order to attract international capital. The resulting capital flows tend to have a footloose culture and move to countries and to governments that are favourably disposed to soft-pedal regulation.

There are therefore different ways of looking at regulation in each area. The problems of regulation are often country-specific and

1. See Graeber, David (2011). *Debt*. Brooklyn (New York): Melville House. p.250, for an extended discussion of these aspects.
2. Ibid.: 278.

situation-specific. Thus the word "regulation" should be used with considerable care, as the volume of regulation has grown considerably, reflecting the enormous complexity of the technology deployed and the tools of trade. For example, the bubbles and the consequent losses faced in the financial industry led, during the last decade and a half, and almost in quick succession, to substantial pieces of legislation in the United States alone. These include the Sarbanes-Oxley legislation, and after the 2008 financial crisis, to the Frank-Dodd legislation (The latter contains more than 700 pages of small print written in an exacting legal style. It requires in-depth legal knowledge to comprehend the intent and the content of each article). These legislations and related efforts have spawned a major consulting industry to implement the specific improvements suggested. In addition, numerous new institutions were set up in the United Kingdom and elsewhere to address the problems that arose following the 2008 financial crisis.

Another event, which had a major impact on technology, in particular that relating to offshore drilling, safety of operations, and investing in the response by the authorities, was the Gulf oil disaster, called the "deep water" operation in the United States. The episode involved loss of life, money, and most important of all, the credibility of the company (British Petroleum), not to mention the capability of the regulatory authority. (The problem in the US related to the technology of the operation and its reliability. In India the regulatory problem, relating to the exploration and extraction of natural gas, involved a major issue about the price of gas. Many committees were asked to examine this question. Governments tend to have their own views, considering that the allottees of exploration blocks were endowed with a lot of political and financial clout and a capacity to make the governments accept their terms and conditions.[3])

These instances illustrate the diversity of the fields covered and the range of issues that arise and that may not have been addressed, for a variety of reasons, which again differ from one area to another. (Thus, the factors responsible for the financial disaster of 2008 are different from those that contributed to the oil disaster in 2010, and the ongoing

3. For the disaster in the Mexican Gulf in 2010, see *the Report of the National Commission on the BP Deepwater Horizon Oil Spill and Offshore Drilling*. U.S. Government, Washington D.C., 2015. In regard to the "Slippery Deal of Gas Exploration" in India, see the chapter with this title in Rai, Vinod (2014). *Not Just an Accountant*. New Delhi: Rupa. p.158. *et seq*.

controversy about gas pricing in India). But there are also numerous common factors contributing to the need for a vastly improved regulatory framework. The systems of operations of corporate bodies have become, not out of choice but out of necessity, far more complex than could ever be imagined and failures in such context may also come about, as the U.S. Commission on Columbia Space Shuttle (which exploded soon after take-off) noted, in complex ways. Some of them may lend themselves to anticipation but many of them cannot be anticipated. Despite the enormous development in the science of measurement, regulatory failures may in some cases be anticipated but the severity of the problem tends to be known more in the aftermath than before.

In many cases, the regulatory failure can be placed at the door of the government itself, which often suffers from an immeasurable degree of complacency. The regulated industry may also develop, as was the case with the US financial crisis in 2008, an undesirable degree of hubris that is always misplaced. Often, there are weaknesses in the oversight of the government as well as that of the regulatory agencies, and there are problems in the coordination of the state and central governments. Moreover, there is the inability to read the signals of looming crisis, lack of coherent information, and a pronounced lack of understanding of the risks involved. Often, the proclivity to engage in *jugaad* comes into play and very soon, the problem, instead of being resolved, may become worse. There is also a distinct possibility that the remedy offered may be worse than the problem, as the experience of Air India has repeatedly demonstrated. Added to this is the organisational culture in governments, which includes a large dose of inertia and negligence (a normal feature of most big organisations). When all these factors come together, the price to be paid by the community becomes unsustainable and raises more questions about the directions and content of government policies and associated regulatory institutions. The general public needs to be assured that the regulatory institutions are ahead of the curve (they are paid to be in that condition) and are making every effort to close the gap to serve the community more effectively. In other words, regulatory institutions have an obligation to be better managed than the units they are regulating. Only then do they become credible and the people and the regulated entities repose their faith in regulation.

Inevitably, however, there are many criticisms that tend to be common despite substantial differences in the organisational make-up and cultures of regulatory organisations. At the outset it has to be noted that there are many prominent economists (a few having become prominent by virtue of their highly vocal opposition to regulation *per se*) who consider that government policy measures often end up creating more market distortions than contributing to the smooth working of the market and therefore greater reliance has to be placed on self-regulation than on government regulation. True it is, that government regulation was not *always* successful and that its actions contributed to avoidable crisis. This was also partly attributable to the general belief, as with the events that led to the financial crisis of 2008 in the United States, when an atmosphere was created to the effect that some of the companies involved were too big to fail, although in the event the big size did not prevent them from going under. But the atmosphere had its impact in that even some governments became sceptical about the efficiency of the complex regulatory machinery that had evolved over the years, and urged scaling back.

The significant difference between the Great Depression of the 1930s and the financial crisis of 2008 is the that the former occurred in the absence of a full-fledged panoply of regulatory institutions, while the latter occurred despite the existence of a large regulatory machinery and availability of a high level of financial expertise. But the blame cannot entirely be put at the door of the regulatory machinery. The general lesson from the eight decades of experience (from the 1930s onwards) is that regulation has had its hurdles but that its contribution has on the whole been beneficial.

What occurred in 2008 had several complex but intimately interconnected factors, omissions and commissions that presented a picture of non-compliance on the part of the financial industry both in the US and the European Union. Thus, adequate reserves were not maintained by the commercial banks to cover their risks; provision of home mortgage loans became an end in itself (a politically convenient end too, and thus was blessed with political support in quarters where it mattered most) and risk analysis took a back seat; highly risk-laden derivatives were carried on outside the normal accounting structure (as off-budget vehicles). A benign neglect on the part of the Finance Ministries (in several industrial countries including the UK and the USA these are known as "the Treasury"), paved the way, facilitating every inch of what was a downhill journey. Arguably, the regulatory industry and the eventual rescue packages helped mitigate the impact of the crisis, whose lingering effects continue to be felt to this day. The experience also reveals that in the absence of the assiduous efforts made by the governments, the last-resort regulatory authorities, the effects of the crisis could have been much worse, indeed calamitous.

The generic opposition to regulation does not recognise the nature and structure of regulation but engages at an abstract level that reveals more the ideological prejudices than an objective and well-reasoned approach. Regulation is undertaken by several legislative bodies that include the supranational to sub-national governments; their mandates are specified in several volumes of legislation (some of which is outdated, to say the least[4]) and are administered by several agencies, each governed by a separate structure. There are sector-specific regulatory agencies, and then there are some, such as the environmental regulatory agencies, that deal with horizontal themes. To be sure, not all of them work with the same zeal; indeed, there is a bewildering array of performance levels. In this context, criticism of regulation should be specific rather than being an overwhelmingly political view. The argument that government should not engage in regulation as it causes more distortions, is at heart a political argument and has become a cant reflecting political affiliation.

There are many specific criticisms regarding regulation, however, and much of this literature is based on the experience of the United States, where the regulatory authorities are a legion and have a finger in every human activity. Many critics in the US emphasise the cost of regulation, be it the Obama health care legislation or the Sarbanes-Oxley or Frank-Dodd legislation and associated regulation of the financial sector operations. The complaint about the cost is based more on organisational approaches than on political predilection. Most companies, whose compliance is vital for the fulfilment of the intent of the legislation, may have to internalise the legislative intent in their day-to-day operations. Rather, they hire a consultancy company to oversee the implementation of the proposed measures and this adds to the cost. These costs, in turn, have implications for the price structure. An alternative is to engage in restructuring the operations in a manner that will facilitate the incorporation of the new legislation into the operations. Admittedly, the extent to which this can be done is industry-

---

4. There is apparently a piece of legislation promulgated during the Mughal times to the effect that drinking water should be provided free to anyone seeking it and no charges are collectible from the consumer. This legislation, as yet unrepealed, could, if implemented, put an end to water sales in the capital city.

specific. The implementation of the proposed legislation does, however, offer a choice to each company: whether the legislation should be viewed as additive or whether it should lead to creative destruction in that the old and ineffective operations and systems may be jettisoned once and for all and a new beginning made. New entrants to the industry may not face such a choice at all. Also, in situations where the regulator is already captured by the regulatees, the probability is high that implementation of the new measure will, at best, be notional and the intended benefits may not be derived.

Critics of regulation change their tune from time to time. For example, in the United States, many, including economists, argued that the benefits of regulation were not visible but that the costs were. So, the argument goes: why is so much money spent on machinery where the outcome is uncertain while the process is costly? The validity of this approach was lost in the wake of the financial crisis of 2008. Looking back, many argued that the crisis might have been avoided or would have been lesser in magnitude if the regulations were more effective. A stage has now been reached where the validity of regulation *per se* is no longer a matter of debate. If it is an evil, it is a necessary evil. It is difficult now to imagine a situation without regulation, for that would only mean that sections of the community, investors and consumers would be left without a protective umbrella.

There are also criticisms that are levelled against the structures and the staffing patterns, in short, the organisational aspects of the management of regulatory agencies. To start with, the agency heads are people appointed, and not elected by the people at large or even by the people directly affected by the operations of the regulatory agencies. Their credentials of accountability are vague and are not specified. In government, the Chief Accounting Officer, *viz.*, the Secretary of a Department, is held accountable for all the transactions of the department. His work and accounts are regularly audited by the Audit Department; he is also answerable to the Public Accounts Committee, one of the major investigative arms of the legislature. Besides these checks and balances, there are many others which have a long history and thus a tradition, and a case law, that are even more powerful than codes and regulations. This, however, is not the case with some regulatory agencies.

The Office of the Directorate General of Hydrocarbons in India provides an interesting illustration of the fog surrounding the regulatory agencies. This office was set up in the context of the growing importance of the exploration of petroleum and natural gas in 1993 as an advisory body, and as a regulatory body, as well as to oversee the production-sharing contracts and the Exploration Licensing Policy administered by the Ministry of Petroleum and Natural Gas. But the body has two odd features that are not associated with regulatory agencies. First, it is funded from grants given by the Oil Industry Development Board and not from government budget. Second, being free from the fiscal controls of government, it is also free of legislative accountability framework.[5] This is but one of the many instances where neither consistency nor clear exposition of the rationale has been provided for the final form of regulatory agencies. This contributes to avoidable confusion about the aims of the government in respect of the design and management of the regulatory agencies. While variation in the form and structure of regulation is inevitable in the context of the different industries and services that are being regulated, the underlying premises for the variation should be specified to help clarify matters.

In addition to the lack of democratic underpinning, agencies so organised under bureaucratic aegis become indistinguishable from government ministries and departments at a time when regulatory agencies' legitimacy depends, in part, on the independence they are endowed with to carry on their work. That is the reason why many support the view that regulatory agencies are best established with legislation approved by the legislature than under a resolution or an ordinance or executive instruction issued by the government in its executive power. The lack of democratic form robs the agency of the sheen that it would otherwise have. More important is the fact that when an agency is set up under executive order, there is a distinct possibility that it will mimic many of the ills associated with bureaucratic functioning. Inevitably, this will contribute to inordinate delays and in the end the regulatory agency will be less effective than needed. It may

5. See Rai, Vinod (2014). Not *Just an Accountant*. New Delhi: Rupa. There are many ministries where technical experts in the field concerned are associated with the ministry in various capacities, but their advice is not binding on the government. In fact, there are numerous instances, including the purchase of Boeing aircraft by Air India, where the Group of Ministers took the decision to buy a larger number of aircraft than recommended by the advisory councils, without assigning any reason.

get closer to the minister and the departmental heads in the ministry, i.e. its bosses, but will stray farther and farther from the consumer or the community. This is a danger that should be avoided at all costs. Such consciousness of the possible pitfalls enables the government as well as the regulatory agencies to function better and serve society better. The work of the regulatory agencies should not be seen as an ongoing effort to avoid criticism but as a determined effort at serving society. To that extent, criticism should be seen as a stimulant and as a compelling factor representing the will of the people. Criticism is a part of democratic life and is therefore inevitable not merely when there is a recognised failure in the marketplace but even in normal times. In essence, good regulation requires good management of the regulatory agencies; criticism is but a sharp weapon wielded by society to ensure their smooth functioning and delivery of appropriate results.

There is one area whose final contours have not emerged with clarity and certainty. This relates to the negotiated settlements between the regulatory agencies and the corporations regulated by them. When they find violations in the transactions of the corporations, the regulatory agencies initiate proceedings which often tend to be very prolonged (recall, for example, the Sahara affair discussed earlier) and the outcome is uncertain to both sides. The corporation which is being investigated may wish to reach a settlement with the regulator. The terms of settlement may include the amount of the penalty to be paid and related terms and conditions of payment. These terms are negotiated by the regulator with the corporation and no part of these negotiations is transparent to the wider public. This is akin to the general practice in India of income tax officers determining the tax liability in consultation with the taxpayer. This approach was always considered to be a ripe ground for unlimited corruption. When this practice is extended to the regulating agencies, there is no guarantee that it will be otherwise. When the penalty is determined by the judiciary, there is at least a sense of satisfaction that the penalty was determined by an expert juridical person. There is no such guarantee in closed-door negotiations. So far, however, the practice continues and there is nothing on the horizon to suggest the emergence of a possible solution.

Regulation, as the preceding discussion shows, is a complex field that has been evolving over the years and will continue to evolve in the light of changing conditions and requirements. Admittedly, its problems are not about to be solved by trying to capture every raindrop or by allowing large quantities of water to flow to the sea unimpeded. It is also a physical impossibility to post a constable at every street corner, assuming that the constables are honest and trustworthy. Rather, some degree of compliance is to be expected and rules have to be framed so as to elicit greater conformity and compliance.

Given that there is always criticism about the structure and behaviour of any organisation, it is only appropriate that the regulatory agency takes adequate precautions to avoid many of the handicaps and vulnerabilities that are anticipated and address them at the earliest opportunity. It has to recognise that it is working in the daylight and that the fortunes of many a corporate enterprise depend on the way in which the operations of the regulatory agency are designed. The first step necessarily is to formulate rules and regulations about the operations of the regulatory agency. These rules provide an insight into the techniques and instruments deployed by it to get compliance in the larger interests of the community. Underlying those operations is the basic idea as to how the interests of the community may be served, which always promotes the competitive spirit in the industry. The objectives to be served may be many, such as making sure that the spectrum and digital telephony are within the reach of the common man. The formulation of the rules and regulations may, at first sight, appear to be simple and straightforward. In practice, to stress the obvious, it is anything but that, though the effort of every regulatory agency is to be simple and clear. But, as anyone who comes in contact with official regulations knows only too well, they are rarely simple or clear. Writers of regulations aim to be comprehensive; but to be comprehensive, one has no alternative but to cover *every* possibility that may crop up in a court of law. It is reported, for example, that in the US, the protocol dealing with a patient who has been raped and who has the potential of becoming pregnant and who is brought to the emergency ward runs into 300 pages in small print—a volume of words that is read neither by the treating doctor nor the patient who is already in a severely strained frame of mind when brought to the hospital. If the patient is brought to a hospital managed by a Roman Catholic organisation (and there are many hospitals in many cities across the United States owned and operated by faith-based organisations), this has implications for the treatment given, as anti-abortion medication will have the desired effect only if administered within 72 hours of the incident. But in the triage process, the doctors, not being lawyers, and being under the pressure of the case that needs immediate attention, may not recall the provisions of the protocol that are relevant to the case in hand. This slippage may mean an outlay of millions of dollars in damages if a case of negligence is filed. This illustrates the complexity inherent in the task of compiling regulatory protocols.

This is also true of the corporations, particularly in the financial sector where commercial banks, particularly the big ones, have several intra-financial system chains of exposure. Since these operations have a direct impact on the balance sheet of the bank, it writes the most complex rules governing these chains of exposure. This adds to the already existing formidable complexity, in turn making the task of the regulator even more difficult than it was before. Both ends of the transaction reveal that complexity is not the exclusive domain of only the regulatory agency but also of the corporations regulated by it. In both cases, the anxiety is to please the lawyer and the judiciary who are looking over the shoulders of both parties. It is easy then to say, in an aspirational sense (as used by the Indian Constitution—which is admittedly a very long document—in its first section) that avoidance of complicity should be the primary aim of regulations.

The proposed regulations should first be discussed with the stakeholders and their views taken into account. This gives an opportunity to test the viability of the proposed regulations and the extent to which they are capable of addressing the task.[6] It should be noted though, that the existence of a regulation does not necessarily mean that it will be applied. There is a good deal of wiggle room (as noted further on) for the official of the regulating agency. This process involves the use of a higher judgemental acumen, as every step taken by a regulatory agency is observed by virtually everyone participating in the market.

---

6. It may be recalled in this connection that most regulations governing expenditure management were promulgated during the British period. These, for example, include *General Financial Rules* (2 volumes), *Treasury Rules, Public Works Code* (2 volumes), and *Fundamental or Supplementary* Rules (equivalent to the Esta Code in the United Kingdom). These regulations were periodically revised since independence but essentially, the language and tenor were the same as they were during the British rule. While the continued use of these regulations provides an eloquent testimony to the foresight and drafting capacities of the then ruling elite, it also remains a fact that a greater part of the administrative culture prevalent in the central and state governments is more in the nature of continuities than discontinuities.

The need for a superior judgement arises in two contexts. The first instance is when it becomes known that a company is being investigated by a regulatory agency. The share values of the company concerned then take a beating in the market promptly. People think of the worst possible scenarios that can happen and base their future action on these putative knee-jerk reactions. For all that is known, it may turn out to be an innocuous routine inquiry. The second situation is when a decision has to be taken whether a case and related prosecution has to be launched. Every regulatory agency amasses a good deal of information on the ongoing infractions by many companies, many of which infractions may not merit prosecution, and if taken up with the judiciary may end up in a loss of face. A series of such failures erode the hard-earned credibility of the regulatory agency. But a good deal of trust by the regulatory agency in the corporation could also compromise its judgement, as was indeed the case with Satyam Computers, a case that came to be known entirely from a voluntary disclosure by the chairman of the company in an email addressed to his staff. Even then the regulatory agency did not immediately jump into action, thinking that the whole episode was a hoax. Needless to say, this misplaced trust in the corporation did not earn any kudos to SEBI (Securities and Exchange Board of India, the regulatory agency concerned). Because of this trust and the consequent arm's-length approach to the corporation many an investor ended up with avoidable losses both in India and abroad.

A judgemental call by itself cannot be placed on any rule or statute book. It is here that the leadership of the agency and superior judgement, not to mention negotiating skills, are called into play. There is much that, despite the obvious need of predictability, cannot be anticipated with precision. The responsibility placed on the regulatory agency is admittedly very substantial. The extent to which "public interest" is served depends on its day-to-day actions. More importantly, the argument about the extent of freedom that a market should enjoy depends on the way in which the regulatory agency addresses its own tasks. Its operations need to be fair and objective. The support that a regulatee extends to the regulator depends on the regulator not merely professing these admirable qualities, but putting them into practice. Like the processes laid down for auditors by the International Organisation for Supreme Audit Institutions (INTO SAI), the regulatory agencies also lay down the principles and processes of inquiry so that their operations are clearly understood by the regulatees. The wavelength of the agency should be known to the regulatees so that opportunities for arbitrariness and show of personal vanity (in a hierarchical society as in India, this is an occupational hazard) can be totally avoided.

The Indian Experience

No attempt has been made in the preceding discussion to offer an extensive description of the processes and activities of the vast array of regulatory organisations, nor to provide a comprehensive framework of regulation. Indeed, that is beyond the scope of discussion. The purpose here is relatively limited. It is to provide a basis for reviewing the regulatory experience in India. What has been discussed thus far is adequate for describing the regulatory machinery in India and whether it has developed a capacity to serve the public interest.

Regulation in India should ideally be studied in terms of the jurisdiction of the governing entities. The subjects dealt with by the Centre are different from those allotted for management by the state and local governments. Most initiatives for regulation were taken by the central government, which was also responsible for the central plans which included state plans. It was that responsibility for planning for development that made the central government the pivot of regulatory initiatives. In areas that were the exclusive preserve of the state governments, the initiatives were taken by those governments, although experiences varied from one state to another; the form and content of the supporting administrative structure also varied. In some cases, there were inevitably overlapping jurisdictions but these were sought to be resolved on a case-by-case basis. This does mean, however, that there were no attempts at homogenising with an implicit model of one-size-fits-all. Much depended on the independence of policy-making enjoyed by the state governments although it tended to be a difficult exercise, as the financial power of the central government proved overwhelming. It would not be wrong to say that the domination of the central government was an integral part of the constitutional framework and to a large extent this was also facilitated by the dependency role assumed by the state governments. It was not a role that they cherished and celebrated. Rather, they became fatalistic about events and policies that they could not conceive of opposing and therefore accepted, howsoever grudgingly, the posture of dependence which they frequently employed as a political strategy and as a bargaining point to their advantage.

The story of regulation in India is directly linked to the Industrial Policy announced in 1949. At this stage, the effort was to have a clear demarcation of the industrial areas that were intended to be managed by the central government and the areas that were earmarked for the corporate sector. The lines of regulation evolved from that fundamental schism. The State was designed to own and manage the sectors that were assigned to it and ownership of the commanding heights of the economy became the main feature. The rest was all regulated by the central government in the spheres assigned to it. The regulation had a pronounced bias in that the development of the industry with the inherent feature of licensing and protection of labour came to be adopted. Very soon followed an updating of the Factories Act and the enactment of another piece of legislation known as Development and Regulation of Industry Act and these two became the respective instruments for the protection of labour and for the regulation of industry. These were followed by the Industrial Disputes Act that led to the creation of a whole edifice of adjudication machinery to resolve the disputes between the management and labour. By 1957, the central government had enacted three volumes of labour legislation, all of which gave a prominent place to the newly enshrined right of labour and the obligations of the management. It is hardly necessary to add that these efforts did not really take into account the protection of the investor and the consumer. The visible hand of central government's control extended to all spheres of management and gradually an attempt was made through the Companies Act to specify and guard the rights of the shareholders. The concerns of the government went even into the pay structures of the employees, to the extent that the number of officials who drew emoluments over a specified limit were to be reported to the government annually.

All this was designed to facilitate the establishment of a socialist pattern of society. Landholdings were regularised and tenants were endowed with some rights. Ceilings were imposed on urban land ownership and every sphere of activity was sought to be regulated. Given the enormous landscape of regulation, there were the usual slippages despite serious efforts to establish several layers of regulatory bureaucracy to ensure the fulfilment of the national objectives. The diffuse nature of the extended bureaucracy became in itself a major limitation, while corruption, that now became hydra-headed, crippled the effectiveness of systems of governance. Government efficiency or regulatory efficiency became an oxymoron. There was, as yet, very little opposition to the regulatory industry in view of the fact that those who believed in the socialistic pattern could not set apart the regulatory framework that was also an integral part of that system; the two went together hand in glove. Criticism of the functioning of the system was there, but it gathered no coherence yet and the strangulating effects of the system began to emerge slowly. Many were shy to attack the system for that would give the impression of being not radical enough at a time when the intellectual posture was to be radical or extremely radical.

The saga of regulation has since then moved in various directions and the general effort was one of putting out the individual fires rather than taking an integrated view about the purpose of regulation, the modus operandi of regulation, and the outcome expected as well as the interests that would be served or protected by regulation. The diverse forays in the field can be gleaned from the experiences of: (i) the Atomic Energy Regulatory Commission (AERC), (ii) the regulation of the communications industry, (iii) the sectors of financial intermediation that were not within the scope of the Reserve Bank of India, and (iv) the regulation of PPPs. In a way, these cases reflect the past, the present, and the future of regulation in India. The discussion should also help enable a conscientious reader to reach his/her own putative conclusions about the public interest that is served by the extensive regulatory frameworks extant in India.

(i) Atomic Energy

Atomic energy represented the new frontier that became the dominant pursuit of the government and the nation. The effort was seen as helping the country to emerge from the bullock-cart age to what is decidedly modern. Following the earlier efforts at establishing a Council for Scientific and Industrial Research and a chain of national laboratories, major attempts were also initiated to establish science organisations addressed to meet the fast developing needs of national security. Along with these, a beginning was also made toward the establishment of an Atomic Energy Commission (AEC) with the Prime Minister as its minister.[7] The Department of Atomic Energy (DAE) was

7. For a detailed discussion of the growth of atomic energy in India, see Perkovich, George (1999). *India's Nuclear Bomb: The Impact on Global Proliferation,* Berkeley. CA: University of California.

a small one in Delhi but all its operations were in Bombay, as it was then known. The culmination of the first phase of its efforts was the commencement of "APSARA", a nuclear reactor at Trombay, a suburb of Bombay, in 1965. That event was an announcement to India and the world that the country had arrived at one of its chosen destinations and was part of the international community engaged in harnessing nuclear energy for peaceful purposes. The use of that energy for national security was an aspect that was addressed years later.

Right from the onset of atomic energy on the scene of governmental decision-making, the prestige associated with the attainment of that status played a far more important role than the financial costs involved. It was the factor that dominated the thinking of the science establishment as well as the political establishment. The civil service, for some odd reasons, chose to remain outside these circles or was pushed into the background while all the channels within the government ran only between the Chairman of the AEC (who was also Secretary, DAE) and the minister, who was also the Prime Minister. It was the vision of the Prime Minister about India's future and the role of atomic energy in that which laid the foundation for the efforts that led to the organisation of atomic energy in India. This narrow circle of communication was the one that was responsible for the formulation of policies regarding atomic energy.

The exclusion of the otherwise prestigious club of the civil service (both Indian Civil Service and Indian Administrative Service) merits particular mention in this context. The first Member, Finance, of the AEC was a member of the ICS. He was a student of Physics at Cambridge prior to his induction into the civil service. He was also trained at the Administrative Staff College at Henley, UK. Although very bright and industrious, it is possible that he forgot much of the physics that he learnt in his formative years in India and at Cambridge, while devoting his efforts toward district administration and other activities after he moved to the Central Secretariat. It is debatable whether he played any important role in the finalisation of the financial aspects of the development of atomic energy or went along with the vision of the Chairman of the Commission, who in addition to being a student of Cambridge, had an independent standing (and had direct access to the Prime Minister at all times). Presumably, the civil service did not want to be seen as spoilers in the new game in town.

Meanwhile, the science establishment, whose members considered themselves as a breed apart and heavenly anointed, was in no mood to yield its place to anybody, much less to a regulator. Their technical knowledge was such that it was their presumption that they were the chosen people both to initiate and manage as well as to regulate themselves. Left to themselves, they would have preferred to be without an outside agency as a regulator. But international experience suggested that the DAE should also have a nuclear regulatory commission on the same lines as in the United States. That would enable, it was thought, the establishment to claim to the world, or at least that part of the world interested in India, that there was a regulatory agency.

There were two features that made the Indian regulator different from the NRC in the United States. In the US, the remit of the NRC included all corporations and utilities engaged in the generation of atomic energy, its transmission and distribution, its environmental impact, maintenance of the safety features and related systems, and supervision of the relief measures when needed. In all, the NRC was fully endowed with inspection powers and authority to regulate in the public interest. The public utilities engaged in the production of nuclear energy were mostly owned by autonomous agencies set up by the state governments in the US (one of them went bankrupt a few years ago in the north-western state of Washington) or by private corporations, or by independent agencies such as the Tennessee Valley Authority (TVA). They were all brought under the review of the NRC, which itself was a creation of congressional legislation. In India, generation of atomic energy is the exclusive preserve of the Government of India. As a consequence, the regulatory agency in India, which is a government body, is engaged in the regulation of the government and government-owned agencies.

The second distinguishing feature is that the NRC is an autonomous and fully independent agency. In India, the regulator is attached to the DAE and the regulator himself was a former official of the DAE. Thus, to all intents and purposes, the regulatory agency works like any government department and lacks independence. The feature of making a regulatory body an independent organisation has its origins in the desire to make it a non-political and objective agency and insulate it, to the extent possible, from politicians' interference and influence. Besides, an independent agency does not have to look for legislative favours and therefore can be expected to be fair and objective in its dealings with the units under its regulatory purview. If the agency is seen as working with a political agenda, its credibility would be lost and, with it, its effectiveness. In India, however, nuclear energy is a government monopoly and, as such, arguably, political interference is an integral part of the landscape. One factor that has the potential of reducing political interference is the fact that it is a highly specialised technical field, and the general political class from which ministers are drawn are not likely to be too deeply involved in day-to-day management. The lack of in-depth knowledge of the field could also make the minister heavily dependent on the science establishment. It is possible that this factor alone may have influenced the final determination of the regulatory body as a non-independent part of a regular department.

The tasks of a regulatory body differ from one sector to another. Broadly, a regulatory body is interested in serving the public purpose, which may be stated as providing a service needed by the community at a price (when it is a priced product) that is within its reach and a service that helps it to secure a much-needed higher standard of living. In the case of nuclear energy, the objective of a regulatory body is to ensure that the design of a proposed reactor is properly done, and for the money that is going to be spent on the project, it is the best design that meets the purpose. The need for establishing this beyond any doubt arises even more in the case where the design initially chosen by the AEC is the best in the circumstances, particularly if the design has not been tried anywhere else in the world. A regulatory body is by definition the conscience keeper and people's watchdog to ensure the fulfilment of a specified objective. In the case of the AEC, this objective was "to produce abundant, inexpensive energy to transform India into a modern society"[8] . Within this framework, there is a major convergence of views between the technical and financial points of view. Organisationally, if the former came within the purview of a regulatory body, the latter was at the very heart of expenditure management. Securing cheap energy was the major goal that brought an unexpected unity of purpose between the government, industry, the consumer, and the investor (which is the event in the nation itself). The whole nation reposed

---

8. From the statement of the Head of the Commission. See Ramana, M.V. (2012). *The Power of Promise, Examining Nuclear Energy in India*. Delhi: Penguin/Viking. pp.41. *et seq*. The study offers an incisive look into the management of nuclear energy in India and a series of problems encountered, some of them due to avoidable hubris.

enormous faith in the science community to achieve this much-needed and laudable objective that, when achieved, would have a profound and enduring impact on the life of every citizen.

The achievement of this objective was very dependent on continuing collaborative efforts between the department concerned in the government, which was also the relevant project authority, and the Ministry of Finance and the regulatory agency. Given that the whole area was a new one and also given that the needed technical expertise was available only with the DAE and the regulatory agency concerned, the role of the Finance Ministry was more like a non-expert interlocutor seeking to obtain the best from the other two. Together, the triumvirate had the job of delivering the product within the specified framework of cost and quality. If this appeared to be a stupendous task, the participants, particularly from the DAE, did not appear to be overawed by the magnitude and showed extraordinary enthusiasm bordering on overconfidence. It was almost like launching an expedition to ascend Mount Everest, where the cheerleaders were more than the participants in the exploring team. In retrospect, it may be said that a common feature of all new projects and programmes launched by the Government of India was to display a significant measure of confidence in the project and the benefits that were to be reaped from it by the community. The production of inexpensive atomic energy was no different, in this respect, from all government projects.

The success of the programme so launched is to be seen in terms of the magnitude of the energy provided as well as the cost of production and whether it is any cheaper than thermal or hydropower. From the beginning of the launching of the project, several factors militated against the confidence displayed by the officialdom. As already noted, the type of the reactors initially chosen by the government did not have any precedents, and therefore it was a jump into a realm of the vast unknown. The reactors chosen later were more dependent on the donor than on their conformity with local plans. Donors whose financing helped the establishment of units had different reactor designs (the donors included Canada, France, UK, USA and the then Soviet Union and its present truncated form, the Russian Federation) and differing technologies. Either because of this or for other reasons, "the reactors took longer to build, cost more than projected and have performed worse than had been envisaged when plans were made."[9] The performance of the reactors set up by the Government of India was "spotty at best" and they "were among the poorest performers in the world"[10]. The cost of each project ended up as a multiple of the original cost. For example, the Tarapur Power Project ended up with an outlay that was nearly double of what was originally estimated.[11] Much of this was due to initial underestimation and modifications (they ran into hundreds) in the design of the reactors. Inevitably, the capital cost went up considerably. These features, it must be added, are by no means unique to the DAE. In fact it is a common experience witnessed unfailingly in all seasons. In extenuation, it should be recognised that the task of a regulatory body is not to engage in an analysis of the cost aspects of a project. That is the task of the Ministry of Finance, but it is so immersed in these violations that no experience is big enough to shock it.

So far the discussion has concentrated on the civilian use of nuclear energy. What is not known is the cost of making a nuclear bomb, which also raises the issue of the desirable level of a stockpile of nuclear weapons for India. The answer is more dependent on the strategic posture of the country, and in determining that, cost cannot be a decisive factor. The costs of a national security programme take us into a minefield and are not addressed here.

From a regulatory point of view, there is another aspect which is as important as a nuclear weapon, and that relates to the environmental impact of a nuclear programme. In recent years, this has become a hot potato of an issue. Wherever it was proposed to set up a nuclear energy generating station, be it Tamil Nadu or Maharashtra, there have been ground-level people's movements about their establishment in view of their potential impact on the local environment, in general, and on the patterns of life, in particular. These agitations were given a political colour and it was officially suggested by the Government of India, through its periodic assessment, that the NGOs which were actively engaged in organising the protest movements were financed by

9. Ramana (2012): 41.

10. Ibid.

11. This is somewhat typical of all Plan projects. In almost all cases, costs are underestimated to obtain approvals from the Finance Ministry and the Planning Commission. Ramana observes that "it would have been difficult to garner the large amounts of public funding needed for the nuclear programme" "*if they were to be honest* (emphasis added) in estimating the actual cost of nuclear power, or even to be open about the uncertainties involved in assessing it." Ibid.: 153.

donations from vested interests abroad, and by implication therefore, that the arguments adduced by these grass-roots organisations should be taken with the proverbial pinch of salt. Be that as it may, if it is granted that there cannot be smoke without fire, then there must be something that holds some validity.

What is odd, however, is that the whole experience, which is a continuing saga, throws up some apprehensions about the viability of the regulatory framework set up by the Government of India. Under the procedures in vogue, all the projects proposed to be set up for generating nuclear energy are required by law, like any other power project, to obtain clearances from the Ministry of Environment and Forests. (Ministers in charge of this ministry were moved from time to time because of allegations about their views and capacity to take a non-jaundiced view about the project. There were also inordinate delays in the grant of clearances and pile-up of files, all awaiting appeals or rejections, on the minister's desk. The successor minister reportedly cleared about ninety files on the first day after he took office, which speaks volumes about the style of decision-making in that ministry.) The procedures for clearance, which have been changed from time to time, require, starting from 1994, that an Environmental Impact Assessment (EIA) be made for each project. The findings of the EIA are then examined by an Expert Appraisal Committee and final clearances are issued by the Ministry. The establishment of these procedures suggests that there is a well-articulated machinery to ensure that all requisite questions are addressed by laymen and experts alike and that in the final analysis, the people's representative, *viz*., the Minister takes a decision.

What gives rise to apprehensions is not the existence of the machinery but how it is subverted in practice, among others, by the DAE. The EIA report is prepared on the basis of the views of experts who include the nominees of DAE and the associated science establishment. It is often a small group of elite who are beholden to the establishment in more than one way and it is suggested that the final report is hammered out, in the usual invisible way (What is visible is only the final recommendation), which invariably ends up supporting the view of the establishment. To avoid this pitfall, there is one more layer in the clearance process, which is to hold public hearings. The experience in the USA and in India gives the impression that the companies, which are waiting in the side wings for the final approval, engage in publicity campaigns aimed at influencing the views of the people. As

M.V. Ramana notes, "it is clear that the nuclear establishment treats public consultation as merely a procedural hurdle",[12] which is managed somehow or other.

There is yet another aspect of regulation, which is of vital importance, particularly to those who work in the various nuclear units. Reports prepared by the Atomic Energy Regulatory Board, the Audit Board and other independent studies point out numerous accidents while working, and exposure to nuclear materials, with possible long-term effects. Also, the treatment of waste materials is an issue that has not received adequate attention. In addition to the atomic energy units, there are other institutions which are actively engaged in the use of nuclear materials. Despite their potential adverse impact, the waste materials are treated with cavalier disregard. But these aspects of institutional neglect do not reach the public until some enterprising journalist exposes the failure, as was the case with Delhi University. The promise of corrective action was taken only after the story appeared in the press. For each story that appeared in the press there may be some that have not seen daylight.

Questions are raised whether the failure on the promises made about the provision of abundant (as of now the share of nuclear energy in the total production is less than 4 per cent) and inexpensive energy and the associated neglect of the consumer in whose name and cause so much expenditure was incurred, should be viewed as a major failure of the administrative system or as a failure of the expenditure management system, which consistently cast a Nelson's eye on the bizarre goings on in the nuclear establishment. Or should the blame be laid at the door of the regulator? Would the results have been different if the regulator was endowed with more power and a greater measure of independence? Admittedly, while having an independent regulator could have contributed to a couple of degrees of improvement, it is difficult to be optimistic where the department concerned is regularly engaged in prevarication and persistent lying. The meaning of the term "duty" got twisted in practice and the citizen was placed on the wrong end. Presumably, he alone deserved a Padma Bhushan for his patience and unlimited capacity for endurance.

12. Ibid.: 295.

(ii) Regulation of Telecommunication

Both atomic energy and telecommunications offered avenues for India to forge ahead and harness the advantages of new technology for the benefit of the people, but with a major difference. Atomic energy remained a territory that was, and continues to be, owned and managed by the government and its science establishment. It also was a territory where the traditional civil service was kept on the fringes and where it was never allowed to forge a power base.

Telecommunications on the other hand was a field in which there was a remarkable breakthrough in technology. The emergence of cellular technology offered several avenues which, while yielding substantial revenues to the government, also created a new equaliser to society, where the traditional barriers that it created for itself were ignored and everybody, regardless of his caste and creed, level of education, and professional background had equal access to the new technology for personal use and enhanced personal advantage. It offered an advantage which in its full form was never fully visualised; but once the technology became available, people were quick to see for themselves how that technology could be used in everyday life.

Another major difference between the technology of atomic energy and that of telecommunications was that the former was fully in the hands of the government. Its acquisition, financing, and deployment were all within the realm of policy-making of the government. In the case of telecommunications, the policy-making was fully retained by the government, while the day-to-day management of the telephone service was handed over, for a payment, to private management. That management was allegedly given, on a platter as it were, to the corporate sector, creating a new breed of oligarchs. New mechanisms and levers were created to manage the transition of movement of task management from the government to the corporate sector. There were other discernible differences between the management of the two sectors, with each unravelling a series of efforts to acquire levers of power and use them, allegedly for personal gain, and to acquire major riches while also enabling the companies in the corporate sector to enjoy themselves all the way to the counters of their banks.

The issues for expenditure management in the two cases were different. Atomic energy involved very large outlays from the budget and was always a source of major strain on the budget. The telecommunications sector was a contrast to this. The fiscal issue was not one of determining the annual outlay to be included in the budget but related to the size of the revenues that the government could get and use them for the benefit of the people. The type of regulation involved was also different. In the case of atomic energy, there was a good deal of reluctance to organise a regulatory body but the reluctance was overcome, mostly in a perfunctory way, to establish a Board (a poor sample of regulation) to be in notional conformity with international practices. In the case of telecommunications, there was little reluctance. The benefit was recognised, from the outset, of having a regulatory body that could be entrusted with the task of managing the sector with the new entrants in the game, all from the corporate sector. The approaches of that body were required to be clear and transparent, and predicable, while being fair and objective in all its dealings. Equally important, it had to determine the tariff that could be charged, which was to be within the means of the common man. Telephone was no longer a status symbol but one which was available to all. The regulatory mechanism had the onerous task of ensuring that the benefits of the technology were available to all, that the commercial activities were competitive, and that no unfair advantage was being taken by the corporate sector. The protection of the consumer was the major task that became the important reason for the existence of the regulatory body.

At the same time, the Ministry of Telecommunications wanted to have the best of the two worlds in that it wanted to have full operational control of the regulatory agency, while giving the appearance that it was an autonomous agency. The ministry was also trying to appear to be in conformity with the due process of the transaction of business of a collective entity known as the form of a cabinet government. Thus, it asserted itself from time to time, to prevent the Prime Minister's Office (PMO), Committee of Ministers, Empowered Group of Ministers (EGoM) and other assorted bodies that were periodically appointed to maintain an inclusive process of strategic planning and transactional management. This was done so adroitly that in the context of vigorous efforts to protect its assigned role, it managed to remain outside the sphere of ministerial committees and also managed to have the PMO assume an arm's-length approach to it. Buoyed by the success in fending off the intrusive interferences by the PMO and the Finance Ministry, each in its sphere, the Ministry started using the regulatory process for its purposes that were not always in the publicly known agenda. In turn and in due course, this contributed to an unfortunate outcome, *viz.*, a scam of gargantuan proportions. (There is dispute, which has acquired a major political colour, about the correctness of the estimate of notional loss suffered by the exchequer, calculated by the Audit Department. In this dispute, the subversion of the regulatory agency and the pursuit of the personal agenda of the powers in the game was relegated to the background.) The discussion here, however, is not concerned with the determination of the size of the loss borne by the nation but is about the subversion of the regulatory process. To gain a full perspective of the role of the regulatory agency, a brief discussion of the experience of the US government is provided here. This experience illustrates the changing nature of the problems encountered by government.

Most technological innovations in the field of telecommunications, including in the regulatory field, took place in the United States after the 1970s. By then there was widespread use of the traditional telephone, i.e. land lines. The network was extensive throughout the length and breadth of the big country. The problem faced by the government was not lack of telephone service, except in the remote areas where population was sparse and therefore the demand for the service was not of a "volume" that justified additional investment. The problem was that Bell System, as it was then called, was a private sector monopoly. It provided the telephone services for government and common man alike, and both were at the mercy of the Bell monopoly. Research in the field was also mostly in the hands of Bell System, whose laboratories located in New Jersey attracted the best talent available in the country and outside too.

Where Bell System was concerned, the objective of the government, and in particular the Department of Justice, was to bust the monopoly, busting monopolies having for long been among its pursuits. What followed were highly successful efforts at introducing competition in the field. The focus of the government was on Bell System (and IBM in the emerging computer field). By the mid-1970s, Bell System was broken up. Ma Bell (as it was then popularly called) yielded several baby Bells in that every state began to have a Bell System of its own. More significantly, new companies such as MCI and Sprint entered the field, offering stiff competition to Bell System. The consumer had a choice among the systems, each with its tariff system.

The main objective of the Department of Justice was achieved and the field became highly competitive, with corresponding benefits to the consumer in different ways. It also led to the introduction of peak and off-peak pricing, and the wise consumer took the opportunity to reduce his monthly telephone bills. The companies made huge additional investment to offer their services. They found, not to their surprise, that the usage developed its own patterns. For example, the telephone traffic between Washington D.C. (the seat of the federal government) and New York (the commercial and financial centre), most of which was generated by the federal government, was very high during the office hours and for five days of the week. There was very little traffic during the night hours and the weekend when the offices were closed. The companies had to make large investments to meet the peak demand, which remained mostly unutilised during non-office hours. To attract greater usage of the services, the companies offered lower rates for calls made during the night (after allowing for time differences between the East and West Coasts, as well as Hawaii) and on weekends. Various attractive tariff packages were offered, inducing the consumer to change his habits of telephone usage. Soon after, the companies, in particular Sprint, began to invest in new technologies, such as fibre optics, to attract the consumer. The consumer had a good deal of choice in selecting the carrier. More significantly, the government achieved its objective of breaking the monopoly of Bell System.

The 1970s were also eventful for raising the prospect of a new service: it was raised, not so much for the benefit of the consumer, which followed anyway, but for the improvement of the fiscal position of the government. The impact of the Great Society legislation (which led to the introduction of what are known as entitlements or a series of programmes aimed at providing welfare benefits to the poor) as well as the ongoing war in Vietnam contributed (up to 1975, when the war came to an end) to widening fiscal deficits. The US government had already gone off the dollar-gold link, and the oil price increases by the oil cartel (OPEC came into the picture during this period) and other pressures were having a significant budget impact. The government then, in much the fashion as now, wanted to generate more revenues without, however, resorting to tax increases. In this context, a suggestion was made that the airwaves of the country, whose use was under the control of the federal government, should be auctioned and the proceeds utilised to meet the growing fiscal needs. The airwaves were then under the day-to-day control of the Defence Department, which was far from comfortable in yielding the ground for civilian use. In retrospect it can be said that the idea was ahead of time and had to wait until the dawn of the twenty-first century, when cellular technology became the new toy that everybody came to love. It spanned a new epoch in the telephone industry and now, not a day passes without some company offering a new device that provides all the benefits of technology in smart and portable (pocket size) telephone to the young and old, to the poor and the rich and to all races. In the context of this technological innovation, the consumer has forgotten that Big Brother (the federal government) was eavesdropping, in the name of homeland security, on the telephone conversations. Furthermore, the use of new technology for cyber warfare has also been spreading. The same aspects illustrate the changing nature of regulatory tasks. The issues that are now addressed have little relation to those addressed in the not too distant past. The experience illustrates the benefits of the visible hand, *viz.*, regulation.

As one looks back on the chequered history of the explosive growth of the telecom industry in India, 1994 stands out as a watershed year. In that year, the Government of India decided, in the context of the changing profile of telecom technology, to open the sector to the private sector to participate in the expansion of the industry and to make available the fruits of technology to the people. This was an opportunity for which the private sector was waiting with bated breath, and it lost no time in entering the field, and undertaking massive investments, and of course reaping benefits, as any corporate sector would. Both government and the corporate sector were eager to provide a service; the corporate sector was naturally pleased to have an opportunity to engage in the provision of a service while also making money (profit is a dirty word to some): the social responsibility of the corporate sector does not include provision of a free or subsidised service, although inevitably there would be some degree of cross-subsidisation, as there was even under the postal system. The Hills Principle (named after the New Zealander who suggested this when the postal system was introduced in the world) envisaged that the mail to short distances would cross-subsidise, even if to an unspecified extent, the letter that would be carried to long distances.

The first aspect that needed to be considered was the issue of licences to the corporate sector, determine their entry fee, as well as the tariff to be charged for the use of the airwaves and the respective shares of the Government of India (as the owner of the airwaves) and the corporate sector which was going to be authorised to lease those airwaves and utilise them to provide the needed service. As a part of this whole process, the government was also required to determine the share of the Defence Ministry, which was responsible for national security. The management of these tasks had to be undertaken in a manner that had the appearance of being an expeditious one, while also being a fair one and therefore it was also required to be quasi-judicial. In other words, these were not the tasks to be carried out by a regular ministry but a distinct organisation was needed to be envisaged. While the need for a separate agency was not disputed, what was involved was the creation of an agency with potentially abundant power and also that could eclipse the Department of Telecommunication. Unlike the AEC, the telecom industry did not as yet have a science establishment with the political and administrative clout that the AEC had. Unlike the AEC, which took quite some time to establish an Atomic Energy Regulatory Board, the Telecom Ministry established a Telecom Regulatory Authority of India (TRAI) in 1997, i.e. within three years after the opening of the sector for private sector participation.

The name gives the misleading impression that it was going to be an autonomous agency with a charter of its own, and with its own sources of financing as well. Such an agency, however, was not in the realm of the administrative vision. Rather, what came out was a body that was to *recommend* measures regulating: (i) the timing for the introduction of new service providers; (ii) terms and conditions of the licences; and (iii) efficient management of the allotted spectrum. Following the hoary traditions of the Government of India of creating a vast array of grey areas while seemingly solving the issues involved, in addition to making the body an advisory one, the government further emasculated (or strengthened, from the government's point of view) it, through the staffing pattern envisaged for it. This was done with an approach that bordered on a sleight-of-hand trick, which envisaged the conversion of the existing higher level of bureaucracy of the Department of Telecom into a new designation. Thus, the ministerial setup and head of the department, *viz.*, Secretary, were retained in the so-called regulatory body as well, and were also given full-time members (who would, as earlier, continue to be responsible for functions such as production, technology and finance) and part-time members drawn from coordinating agencies like the Planning Commission, Finance Ministry and others. The full-time members who had operational tasks were given supporting staff in the form of advisors, who also represented the technical jobs that they were carrying on anyway as a part of their daily tasks. In a single swoop, the government wanted to gain the best of all worlds—a regulatory body that was not a regulatory body and a ministry that was also a regulatory body. No part of the existing tasks of the ministry was relinquished, while gaining additional strength in the form of pervasive ministerial (read political) involvement in all phases of the work of the agency for, essentially, it was not different from the ministry at all. All the members continued to operate from where they were working before. The only change, which was entirely nominal, was the change in the designation. For example, the Financial Advisor was now called Member Finance. So the management process continued as before, or *business as usual.*

The potential problem of continuing involvement of the ministers, and the potential for abuse of authority by them or by the supervising political class, came to be recognised from 2004 onwards, when a new coalition came to power at the Centre. The developments hereafter cannot be discussed by abstracting the personalities involved.

At the apex of policy-making was the then Prime Minister Manmohan Singh himself, who in addition to his Oxbridge education, was also, as it happened, the most experienced bureaucrat. He had worked in the ministries of commerce and finance, eventually reaching the position of Chief Economic Adviser, Finance Secretary, was associated with the South-South Conference, and also served for a full term as Governor of the Reserve Bank of India. Later, when it became necessary for the government to move away from administrative controls and licence raj, he was made the Finance Minister and had a major role in introducing reform that contributed to the introduction of market orientation in the management of the economy. The ministers involved—and there were two—were both drawn from the DMK (Dravida Munnetra Kazhagam) party from the south, which was a strong member of the coalition era that emerged after 2004. The leader of the party had full control over the nomination of his party people for the posts of ministers in the central cabinet. It was an unusual departure from the conventional arrangements of cabinet formation, in that the Prime Minister had no say in the appointment of ministers for the Communication Department as it moved to the head of the DMK party.

The Prime Minister was, however, fully aware of the challenges and pitfalls awaiting the grant of licences to the corporate sector and expressed his reservations both in public and in private, as well as in his correspondence to the Ministers of Telecom (which is all in the public domain and got wide exposure courtesy of some enterprising journalists who provided it in the daily press). This is extensively reproduced in the book: *Not Just an Accountant* (Raj, 2014). Although the book was intended as an autobiography, major parts of it are devoted to the treatment of the major scams, including the telecom scam, that erupted during his tenure as head of the audit office, and urging the need for a fair, and equally important, transparent process.

Over the years, transparency and accountability had become the new mantras for improved governance all over the world, largely on account of the advocacy of the international financial institutions. The Government of India did not lag behind any other country in the regular incantation of the new-found pathway for the salvation of the country's economic development. In retrospect, it appears that the Prime Minister had a sneaking apprehension that the nominees of the DMK party then heading the Ministry of Telecom could use the new-found opportunity to pursue their own agenda that could be at variance with what the government as a whole, with the collective wisdom of the cabinet behind it, was trying to achieve.

The choices for the Prime Minister in the circumstances were not many. He could either follow an active interventionist approach by comprehensively monitoring the management of the Telecom Ministry, or follow an arm's-length approach, which meant selective monitoring and even more selective intervention in the day-to-day affairs of the Ministry. In the event, the pragmatic approach chosen was the latter, which meant that the ministers were given adequate flexibility and a long enough leash.

Policy-making in India, particularly at the Centre, is a long and often dilatory churning process in which all concerned are given an opportunity to express their views even if they are very divergent from those expressed by the ministries initiating the proposals for the consideration of the cabinet. The situation is very different from the one existing in many states, where the long shadows of the powerful Chief Ministers are felt at every stage of the process. The central government is much too vast for such shadows to be felt, except during periods when the overwhelming personality of the Prime Minister was, in theory felt, but the object sought to be achieved was often subverted in the course of implementation. Although in principle, all agencies could offer their comments on the proposals going to the cabinet, only those which were impacted by the proposals and thus had a vested interest, and the Finance Ministry and the Planning Commission, singly or, on rare occasions, together, offered more detailed comments (a euphemism for unconcealed criticism). On occasion, when the matters appear to be controversial, cabinet subcommittees are appointed and their views are submitted to the cabinet as a whole for a fresh review of the proposal. The intent is to permit a clash of minds (and hence the churning) but to secure a consensus in the cabinet. That way, the collective wisdom of the cabinet is assured, while the participatory process is explicitly recognised and even supported. But this has also its own drawbacks in that the eventual consensus reached could be at substantial variance with the original proposal, a prospect that is much dreaded but grudgingly accepted.

In the instant case of the functioning of the Telecom Ministry, and given the prevailing aspects of policy-making in the central government, a sort of ring fencing was initiated by the Prime Minister. In addition to the TRAI (which in the event was not different from the Telecom Ministry) and the high-powered Telecom Commission (which also had the usual representatives), he appointed a Group of Ministers (GoM) with its own elaborate terms of reference, followed, later on, by a High-powered Group of Ministers (HGoM). It did not take long for the Telecom Minister to see the direction in which the government was moving. In his turn, he decided to secure his position by not conceding even an inch of his territory.

The verbal defences adduced by the minister give an interesting glimpse into the ways how turf battles are fought in government. In 2006, when these matters were being processed for the appointment of a GoM, a subcommittee of the cabinet with its own terms of reference, the minister wrote to the Prime Minister highlighting the following: (i) the considerable progress made in the telecom sector (and by implication, how it was transforming the nation's pattern of life); (ii) the major issues facing the ministry related to the need for the enlargement of the spectrum and the need for vacation of the spectrum by the Department of Defence; and (iii) the need not "to be diverted by any other issues such as spectrum allocation, state government, etc., which are *solely* (emphasis added) within the purview of this department and which can *well be handled* by it (emphasis added).[13]

The aggressive defence and turf protection offered by the Minister of Telecom had their desired effect. Consequently, revised terms of reference were issued by the Cabinet Secretariat for the GoM, incorporating the lines of enquiry suggested by the ministers. This retreat by the Prime Minister gave a shot in the arm to the minister. Both he and his successor, who was also from the DMK and who was also nominated by the party chief, thereafter continued their aggressive defence, while assuring the Prime Minister all the time that they were observing scrupulous compliance of the cabinet policy, and that they were ensuring that the benefits were reaching the citizen. The Prime Minister was responding to their letters in the form of an acknowledgement, stating, "I have received your letter [date] regarding the recent developments in the telecom sector" or lines to that effect. This approach must have emboldened the minister even further to follow his own agenda. Students of public policy would, however, find the compliant approach of the Prime Minister inexplicable and indefensible.

The consequence of these developments was, however, a series of actions that were not in compliance with the due process specified by the Government of India. The violations by the Department of Telecom, as brought out by the Audit Department in its performance audit report on the issue of licences and allocations of the 2G spectrum by the department in 2012 included the following: (i) gaps in policy implementation; (ii) lack of consultation with the Telecom Commission; (iii) overruling of the views of the Ministry of Finance; (iv) ignoring the advice of the Ministry of Law and Justice; (v) non-observance of the Prime Minister's advice (note the language: it was not "instruction" but "advice"); (vi) arbitrary changes in the cut-off date by the Department; (vii) non-observance of the first-come-first-served policy; (viii) issue of licence to non-eligible applicants; (ix) value of the spectrum allocated to 122 new licensees and 35 other licensees who were allocated the dual-technology facility. The litany was fairly long and it had the effect of an implosion both inside and outside the government.

As noted earlier, the presumptive loss suffered by the government, which the new minister, who was from the Congress Party, declared as

---

13. The minister's letter and the subsequent correspondence are reproduced in full in Rai, Vinod (2014). *Not Just an Accountant*. New Delhi: Rupa. pp.229-48.

"nil", while the audit report gave detailed calculations of the extensive loss, is not an issue that is explored here. Suffice it to say that the matter was later taken up by the Supreme Court, which cancelled all the licences issued by the Department of Telecom, bringing the situation to *status quo ante*. The issue was later taken up by the Central Bureau of Investigation (CBI) and was later followed by the arrest and incarceration in Tihar Jail (Delhi) without bail for one year of the former Minister of Telecom, as well as the arrest and imprisonment of others who were alleged to have had a hand in the rigging of the whole process. The matter is now with the judiciary and it is difficult to say what the final denouement would be. What is clear is the failure of the regulatory process in the management of one of the richest natural assets of the nation. The process was incomplete, arbitrary, unpredictable, and lent itself to full political manipulation by the political class at every stage. It is possible that the political class was aided by the administrative class, though the extent of collusion would emerge in clearer form after the judicial enquiry is completed.

The purpose of reading history is to avoid the mistakes committed in the eras gone by. Viewed thus, it can be safely asserted that had the authorities been more sincere and straightforward in designing a regulatory institution that had legal support, through comprehensive legislation and by equipping it with adequate independence to implement its charter, this kind of abuse would have been pre-empted. Instead, half-hearted measures were taken to introduce a regulatory system that was a regulatory system more in name than in substance. It was bound to fail and it failed sooner than expected. The damage, both collateral and direct, was so substantial that a correct calculation of its extent would never be possible. The damage inflicted on the functioning of the democratic institutions, which are now perceived as serving the vested interests, and are seen as having a good deal of "crooked timber", have eroded the trust of the people in government. Recovery from that level is bound to take a long time; meanwhile, the patience of the people should not be tried further.

From the point of view of financial management, the experience provides new vistas into how the national interest should be managed. The issue is no longer one of managing the allotted budgetary resources, although it continues to be a dominant and vital part of the system of governance, but one of ensuring proper benefit to the people of the country from the utilisation of the airwaves that nature has endowed in it. Abuse of that privilege, as is clear, can have enduring consequences. The system of governance should therefore have the capacity both to anticipate the technological changes that are looming on the horizon, and to formulate a regulatory strategy to address the tasks inherent in such developments.

(iii) Financial Sector

The regulation of its financial sector has a crucial role in a country's life. A government is responsible for ensuring financial stability in the economy. Stability does not mean stagnation. Far from it, it paves the way for economic prosperity that can be shared by all, though inevitably, those shares are bound to be unequal. In a benign way, the regulatory mechanism endeavours to maintain an even keel so that growing inequality does not contribute to social conflict, which can endanger the future of the society. It is therefore essential that the economy is managed in such a way that the potential for social conflict is minimised. Regulation of the financial sector complements the objectives of expenditure management in government. If the financial sector comprises the actions of the community in the market sphere, expenditure management aims at regulating a major part of the financial behaviour of the collective institutions known as government. If they work at cross purposes, which may happen much too frequently than desired due to political exigencies, then the community may have more than its fair share of problems. Ideally, therefore, the two are expected to work in tandem.

The management objectives of the financial sector have a profound effect on the tenor and content of expenditure management. It is also to be recognised that the actions of the regulating agency (agencies) may have, at times, only ripple effects on the economy; but inaction or wrong steps could have devastating effects on the economy. Essentially thus, the task of regulation is to ensure timely action, although like all matters in government, policy-making is a tedious process (the German chancellor Bismarck once noted that policy-making is like making a sausage) and could be more dilatory than needed. The regulatory agency has thus the important task and onerous responsibility for constantly looking over its broad shoulders to see what is happening in the rest of the world and assessing how it is going to impact the nation's economy. It has also to make sure that it is not generating a false sense of security.

These important tasks are managed in India by the Reserve Bank of India. Its role, delicate and crucial, is recognised by one and all, though, inevitably, the opinion is divided about its contribution. A lack of unanimity is part of democratic life and reflects the diversity in society and its economy and plurality of objectives. In its history of nearly eight decades, both before and after its nationalisation, the Reserve Bank has valiantly tried to stave off economic crises and mitigate their effects on the economy. Although, to its credit, it won plaudits from all sides on how it managed to save the country from the engulfing financial crisis of 2008, it cannot rest easy as there are numerous tasks that are regularly knocking at its door. Vigilance is therefore its watchword and its actions reflect that continuing responsibility which society has placed on it.

India is one of the few countries that calls its central bank a Reserve Bank. (The central bank of another BRICS country, South Africa, is called the Reserve Bank of South Africa.) The central bank of a country has a complex web of functions. These include issue of currency, day-to-day management of the economy's liquidity, maintenance of internal and external stability, management of the exchange rate and the foreign reserves (which essentially reflect the gains from foreign trade and belong, as it were, to the participants in the market economy), regulation of the commercial banks, protection of the depositors' interests, and the management of the public debt of the country. (The central government may be taking over the management of its own debt, while, in principle, and since the acceptance of the recommendations of the Thirteenth Finance Commission, the debt of the states has been shifted to the respective states). Several other associated tasks were and are carried out by the Reserve Bank. Many of the current generation may not know that until the early 1960s, the currency used in the Gulf countries including Kuwait, known as Gulf currency, was managed by the Reserve Bank as a part of the colonial legacy.

In managing these tasks, the Reserve Bank has shown remarkable skills and has been a constant ally of the government in managing the economy. The various experiences noted here in the respective decades since independence illustrate both the diversity and the immense complexity of the tasks. Soon after independence, the Reserve Bank had to manage the widespread economic effects of partition and sustain the confidence of the community. Confidence is a fragile psychological trait and may not always be rational or stable. Somehow, this delicate task was carried out with aplomb. Very soon, the rehabilitation of refugees and other related tasks, not to mention the urgent need for launching economic development, led to many strains in the economy. Several innovative departures were made by the Reserve Bank of India to provide new facilities. These, for example, included the provision of a separate credit facility for food procurement, and to maintain the PL 480 food imports and their counterpart funds. (The latter continued until the mid-1970s when, mercifully, thanks to the intervention of the American ambassador, Daniel P. Moynihan, the account was closed and the separate identity of the account ceased to exist.) More importantly, significant forays were made to ensure an extension of the banking system to the rural areas and to provide credit for agricultural operations. This led to the nationalisation of the former Imperial Bank of India and rechristening it as the State Bank of India. The Reserve Bank's own administration was also revamped earlier to include an agricultural credit department that was later siphoned off and given an autonomous status while still working under the guidance of the Reserve Bank, as the National Bank for Agricultural and Rural Development (NABARD). Later in the 1970s and 1980s, the operations of industrial credit were separated into an Industrial Development Bank of India, while housing credit was moved into a newly formed National Housing Bank.

Even as the above described developments were taking place at their own pace, an event that raised issues about the adequacy of the supervisory function of the Reserve Bank over the commercial banks, and its capacity for fire-fighting came to the fore with the liquidity crisis in Palai Central Bank—a bank that oddly enough was considered to be a dynamic one, attracting vast new consumers and winning their confidence. The crisis was denied by the bank authorities and the Reserve Bank seemed to be rather slow, with the predictable result that one fine morning there was a rush on the bank, with the depositors demanding the withdrawal of their deposits and cash. The bank could not meet the demands and became insolvent. (Later, however, it paid nearly 60 per cent of every rupee deposited with it.) The episode revealed that there was no security net, other than vague promises, that offered the much-needed protection to the depositor. Soon, there was a borrowed innovation in the form of a Deposit Insurance Corporation on the lines of a similar institution set up in the United States after the Depression. While the Palai Central Bank could not be saved, the establishment of a security net offered confidence to the depositor and bolstered the stability of the banking system as a whole.

A major development that took place during the 1960s related to the introduction of foreign exchange control system in the Reserve Bank. The shortage of foreign exchange, having exhausted the sterling balances that the metropolitan government wisely left to the Government of India, and with the growing demands, the crisis gained its own speed like the depression in the Bay of Bengal. The Ministry of Finance, which hitherto was both the policy maker as well as the day-to-day manager of the allocations of foreign exchange to all and sundry, divested itself from the latter task, which was shifted to the Reserve Bank. The bank, in its turn, hurriedly organised exchange control branches in its own regional centres, and all the rush which was hitherto aimed at the North Block, now moved to the periphery. In retrospect, it appears that it would have been far more convenient if in turn the Reserve Bank too had distributed its task in this regard to the commercial banks. That step was taken decades later, with the introduction of a new economic regime; and the Finance Ministry as well as the Reserve Bank regained their positions as policy makers and wisely left the detailed operations to the commercial banks—a step long overdue but finally taken.

Meanwhile, in the political field, there was a sudden appearance of radicalism and a new stimulus for growing state ownership in the banking sector. The final event of bank nationalisation came in 1969, leading to a dominant public sector in commercial banking. As is to be expected, the levers of policy control on the nationalised banks came to be exercised by the Finance Ministry, while the Reserve Bank had control of other banks. This split in jurisdiction contributed to a new situation which continues to this day. Some consider it an anomaly affecting the regulatory role of the Reserve Bank.

The banking system in the post-liberal regime hardly resembles the scene that obtained before. There has been a phenomenal growth in the number of banks and in the number of branches offering their services. The customer was the new king on the scene, attracting the attention of the organised and informal sectors of banking. In addition to the commercial banks, which anyway were under the scan of the Reserve Bank, there was also a less regulated growth, at least during the initial years, of NBFCs (non-banking financial companies) that made quick forays into the rural sector, offering attractive terms to the depositors. Very soon, however, questions of two types came to dominate the scene. So far as the organised sector of banking was concerned, the main issue was one of enshrining the facilities and the rights of the depositors.

As a consequence, and following the general approach to endow the citizens with more rights and provision of enhanced accountability to the common man, the banking system too developed a charter for the depositors and each bank also established a system to address the grievances of the public. Banks now boast an ombudsman entrusted with the task of addressing the concerns of the depositors. The situation is less organised and more opaque in the NBFCs. Supervision of these companies was less stringent and, as a result, questionable practices came into being.

Considerable progress was also made in two other areas, contributing to the smooth functioning of the systems of governance. The first related to the payment arrangements of the central and state governments. Prior to the separation of accounts from audit and the establishment of a civil accounts organisation (compilation of defence accounts was a separate organisation functioning under the aegis of the Union Ministry of Finance, while the railway accounts functioned under the Railway Board), payments reflected a long process under which the proposed payments were subjected to a brief pre-audit before the claims were passed on for payment either directly or through the banking system. At the state level, the payments to and by the governments were made through the age-old Treasury system (which, in addition to discharging responsibilities for payments, was also responsible for the maintenance of opium stock). The long-drawn process, which created a separate power corridor, had concerns other than the need and the convenience of the clientele. The transactions conducted by the treasuries were set in the form of raw records to the Office of the Accountants General (the titles have been changed while the functions remained the same—*status quo ante*) which then compiled the monthly accounts. The records sent to them were often incomplete. In turn, this necessitated an elaborate dance ritual of a series of reminders which tended to normalise the situation. But the completion of reports on the money received and spent took a long time and daily management of finances was more a guess than based on facts. This was all changed, for the better, when accounts compilation was separated and now became a part of the tasks of the central Ministry of Finance. As a part of this arrangement, each ministry of the central government was assigned a nationalised bank through which all transactions were made. Since they had the compulsion of managing their liquidity, they made the payments and received payments due to the government in a relatively prompt manner.

The present situation is a refreshing contrast to the one that prevailed prior to the early 1970s. Data on accounts are now available on a daily basis excepting for the Ministry of Supply, which still has several payments due from the state governments, as the initial payments to the supplier are made by the Pay and Accounts Office attached to the Ministry of Supply. The data are by and large detailed enough, save some suspense accounts relating to the advances made to some agencies, and provide an adequate basis for monitoring of fiscal balances.

Moreover, the Reserve Bank has made remarkable strides in the application of computer technology to all its operations. As a consequence, both the governments and the public are now made aware courtesy the print and visual media, of the changing daily trends. The technology has enabled the financial sector to offer improved services to the public, while also providing greater protection to the assets of the public. The Reserve Bank's constant endeavour to improve the service structure has enabled it to consolidate its position as a bastion of strength in a globalised world. More important, its efforts at preventing bubbles in the market and credit management to the community have inspired new levels of confidence in the financial institutions of the Republic. As usual, however, there are many problem areas that need to be overcome; the discussion will be incomplete without their consideration.

The system reveals, from the common man's point of view, three major anomalies that also tend to detract from the valuable progress made in the sector. First, there is a gaping hole in that the *hawala* system, whose magnitude of operations is not known, continues to operate along with the organised commercial banking sector. Large domestic and foreign transactions go through this system, escaping the tax net of the government. More significantly, if anecdotal evidence is to be believed, it is as quick as the commercial banks equipped with high-speed computers, and as trustworthy as the organised sector. Apparently, the transactions reach the intended parties in time and with a degree of courtesy that offers stiff completion to the commercial banking sector. In effect, the *hawala* system, which is as extensive as the commercial banks, has become a parallel system that functions beyond the pale of the regulatory system. It is attracting clients who believe that they are not facing any additional risks by resorting to this system.

Second, as an extension, the money stashed away by Indian citizens in tax havens and other financial centres that offer similar services, represents a major leakage. While it is true that there are other countries, including many industrial countries, with similar features, the daily coverage in the TV channels about the efforts or lack of efforts on the part of the government as well as the hidden presence of political machinations have all created a heightened awareness of the situation.

Third, the functioning of the NBFCs whose operations are at best opaque and at worst a dark operation, and the slow extension of the regulatory tentacles to that sector leave a question mark about the capacity of the Reserve Bank to bring them into daylight. This is not to say that the central bank is not making any effort at all. On the contrary, its diligent work has brought a major operator such as the Sahara Company to judicial review and has created a new revelatory opening into the operations of this system. It is likely that the final judgement of the Supreme Court in the case of Sahara, as and when delivered, will have the desired effect on this aspect of the overall system. The overwhelming question is the attractions, relative to the commercial banks, that the NBFCs offer to the clients. The incentives offered by them and the risks that they pose offer a stimulating research area that needs to be pursued. If it is a case of pseudo-criminal activity that, as in this instance, pays them, it is all the more a reason for initiating detailed studies.

Fourth, the area has also given rise to jurisdictional issues that in turn tend to affect certain types of activities that remain to be brought into the regulatory net. Two activities that need special recognition relate to the chit funds and micro-financing. The former has witnessed a mushrooming growth largely because it is an unregulated activity. It falls within the ambit of the state governments, which have not shown much enthusiasm to regulate it. As a result, there have been many fly-by-night operations that saw a brief spurt of activity and then folded up, much to the discomfiture of the participants. As regards the growth of micro-financing, which again falls within the sphere of state activities, such financing activity was generally welcomed. But lack of regulations led to varying extortionist activities and to high rates of interest charged from the users. Initially touted as a godsend to the financially weaker sections, it soon became an albatross that the people found difficult to service. The bad taste that the practices of these financial institution caused, eventually led to a pioneering legislation by the then state of Andhra Pradesh. Being a state activity, the initiative for enacting similar legislation is left to the other state governments, many of whom have yet to take action.

Yet another feature of regulation which is found at the national level relates to the split responsibilities between the Reserve Bank and the Ministry of Finance, the former being responsible for all commercial banks in the private sector, while the latter is responsible for the public sector banks, which are owned and managed by the central government. The specification of monetary variables and associated requirements of reserves maintenance is the responsibility of the Reserve Bank. Its guidelines in this regard as well as the observance of banking standards are common to both types of banks, but the day-to-day supervision of the public sector banks is with the central government. This split was responsible for the public sector banks pursuing non-commercial policies specified by the central government. In general, however, it is an unholy approach to combine both ownership and regulatory tasks in the same agency. Whether this was a deliberate attempt to create pocket boroughs that are more amenable to the pursuit of politically expedient policies, or the development was a feature that evolved in the flux of time, is a separate issue that is not taken for consideration but is merely raised here as an anomaly that is best eliminated. While it is true that in the United States, there are several regulators and each bank has the option of choosing its own regulator from the veritable salmagundi, it has also thrown up several problems. A regulatory system should, ideally, be a common and uniform one, and the system has not grown too much to fail under its own weight.

Experience shows that while the banking habit has become widespread, the rates of NPAs (non-performing assets) have also been growing. This poses a threat to the banking system in at least two ways. First, it is a threat to the solvency of the bank concerned. Very frequently, however, the effort to collect the overdue amounts is not vigorous, as many of the defaulters are politically powerful. To some extent, this reflects the laxity in the approval of loans in the first instance. People with power and political influence would appear to have ready access to the credit extended by the banking system. In addition, there is the problem of corruption in that the officials concerned tend to soft-pedal the structural weaknesses of the potential borrower, who is anyway rated as a regular customer deserving better treatment from the bank. Moreover, the list of defaulters is rarely in the public domain. In the absence of "naming and shaming" approaches, the borrowers have a greater incentive not to pay. Defaulting has become a practical art and is being practised by many with impunity. Second, the default implies a degree of cross-subsidisation, which adversely affects the regular borrowers who are scrupulous in the observance of the age-old tenet of timely payment and depriving the depositors of the benefits that would accrue to them. Granted that society is pluralistic and therefore the gains of one section accrue at the expense of another section, there is no reason for this to become a regular, institutionalised feature of the banking system. An effective regulatory system would consider this an issue of major importance that needs to be addressed by taking stronger steps. In an open society, this wound, which is a result of lapses on the part of bank managements, should be treated urgently.

Finally, a major area that requires regulatory attention relates to the emergence of quasi-fiscal accounts that have become a part of banking operations by stealth. This relates to the write-off of loans extended to farmers. The spate of suicides by the severely affected agriculturists in several parts of the country, most notably Vidarbha in Maharashtra and Telengana in the erstwhile state of Andhra Pradesh, illustrate the levels of rural indebtedness and the problems that it poses particularly in the lean years when crop failures are more common. The indebtedness is the result of the operations of both commercial banks as well as the local moneylenders. Addressing the problem, the central government announced, a few years ago, an amnesty, and major parts of loans extended by the banking sector were written off. Since then, it has almost become a habit for state governments to declare their intention to write off the loans and to grant freedom to the farmers from indebtedness. This measure does not really distinguish between those who have the capacity to repay and those who have lost that capacity. In the process, the rural divide between these two sections is further widened and, incidentally, the role of rural oligarchs is amply strengthened.

From the technical viewpoint of expenditure management, write-off of loans, whether financed from the central or state budgets, represents a form of quasi-fiscal accounts. In principle, the place of such write-off is in the respective budgets of the central and state governments. Such an inclusion would have provided legitimacy to the whole policy in that it would have been subjected to a policy debate in the legislature, if so desired by it, and an approval of appropriations. In the event, these policies, which aim at creating vote banks and party loyalty, are first announced either in the electronic media or in public meetings. The effort is to create political support, which is then mobilised through protest meetings and other means so that the central government and the Reserve Bank could be persuaded to accept the proposal. The announcement is also timed in such a way that it would be taken up in the five-year financial forecasts submitted by each state government to the constitutional body, the Finance Commission. Once the inclusion takes place, the proposal would have secured acceptance, which then is routinely included in the budgetary expenditures. By this time, it would also have become a non-event, and depending on the situation, would also have received *ex-post facto* legislative acceptance. More recently, the non-event has become an event in that the guardian of the commercial banking system started expressing serious apprehensions about the habit-forming nature of loan write-offs and their consequences for bank balance-sheets. Faced with the opposition of the Reserve Bank, the newly formed state of Andhra Pradesh is setting up an autonomous corporation, a financial public enterprise, to issue bonds for the financing of loan write-offs. Whatever be the final form of the loan waiver, it is appropriate that regulatory measures are put in place to address this major leakage from the public exchequer. Quasi-fiscal accounts imply a negation of one of the cardinal principles of expenditure management. Land grants, or highly subsidised sales (the term sales is a misnomer), which have now become a standardised part of industrial incentives, are recognised as leakages that are legally and technically exceptions to the budget law and should be recognised as such. In their eagerness to gain the electoral support of the people, governments have become, either by intent or by design, a prime violator of the very principle which they are charged with protecting. This is best avoided; and there is no better way of avoiding it than doing it the legitimate way.

The regulatory framework of the Reserve Bank has thus far concentrated more on preserving the structural integrity of the commercial banks and their liquidity status, and has paid, if at all, only lip-service to the issue of efficiency in the banking system. This relative neglect of an important element has its origins in the belief that the maintenance of efficient operational systems is the task of the commercial bank concerned. Because of a lack of emphasis on this aspect, banks have become bloated with large numbers of staff and far too excessive paper work. Both these aspects merit attention from the regulatory agency.

A major question of the regulatory framework of the financial sector is the divisive issue of alleged conflict of interest in the functioning of the regulator, the Reserve Bank of India. Its primary function is the conduct of monetary policy. In conducting that policy it uses the levers or instruments of control on the commercial banks. In addition to this supervision, it also has the task of regulating the work of the commercial banks. As a part of this work, it authorises the establishment of new banks, approves their expansion plans, and broadly acts as the final arbiter on the work of the commercial banks and thus protects the interests of the depositors. Purists of central banking contend, however, that the conduct of monetary policy is a full-time task in itself, without getting involved with the day-to-day supervision of the commercial banks. Pragmatists suggest, however, that this combination of functions has not been without its benefits and that, in any event, it has not affected the work of the Reserve Bank, nor has had any detrimental effect on the commercial banks. The issue deserves yet another look.

(iv) PPPs and NGOs

The nascent stage of PPPs in India and the vast plans that the Government of India has for PPPs in the future have been discussed earlier. In a nutshell, much of the economic development envisaged for the country in the coming decades is dependent on the success in the judicious implementation of PPPs both at the Centre and in the states. A major aspect that needs to be recognised in such implementation relates to the introduction of a regulatory framework to address many of the issues that have already arisen and that are likely to arise in the near future.

In dealing with these matters, a distinction should be drawn between the PPPs on the one hand, and grant-aided institutions on the other. This distinction is essential as much of the following discussion is limited to PPPs. PPPs refer to the participation of the private sector, with its capital and technical expertise, in the projects and programmes envisaged by the government. While there may be some financial transfers from the government to the private sector, they tend to be limited and reflect the contractual commitments entered into by the government. Grant-aided institutions, on the other hand, reflect the initiatives of the private and cooperative sectors as well as the numerous faith-based organisations. While the initial capital and a part of the maintenance expenses may be borne by the sponsoring organisations, it is more than probable that the bulk of their maintenance and capital expenditure may be forthcoming from the government budgets. The role played by these institutions in the educational sector may be gleaned from the fact that about half of the outlays on education in state government budgets is devoted to the provision of grants-in-aid to these organisations.

The relationship between governments and grant-in-aid recipients is an ancient one that predates the colonial era, though the budgetary terminology has been changing over the years. The financial relations between government and them have been codified several years ago and much of this code is operational, though, as is the case with many public operations, there are major leakages too. There is also a supervisory framework embedded in the government administrative systems. For example, in the education field, the supervisory practices that regulate the government-owned and -operated institutions are applicable, for the most part, to the aided institutions too.

PPPs are relatively new. Their operations are varied and so are the conditions attached to their participation. Although the experience is limited to a relatively short period, there is already an impression that the participating corporate units have already exploited the situation for their own extensive benefits that are also seen as disproportionate to their financial participation. More significantly, they are seen as the dominant partners dictating their terms and conditions to the government. It is also perceived that the risk in several of these projects is borne, when all is said and done, by the government itself. It is also observed that in many cases, the government is engaged in gaming against itself and has become the loser, with the government budget bearing the cost of wrong approaches on the part of the government.

For example, in the partnership deal with the corporate sector for the development of a metro system in the city of Hyderabad, there is a provision to the effect that the government would compensate the corporate partner for delays in the acquisition of the needed land and that the compensation would progressively increase with the duration of the delay. In the event, the state government ended up paying crores of rupees even before the project got off from the ground. The fact that a government often tends to be a dilatory organisation is known to the participants and the public alike. Yet the provision is made for these payments in the expectation that it would spur the government into speedier action. Moreover, the absence of such a clause in the agreement could be perceived as a business-as-usual approach. The government, however, ended up paying a higher price for its own optimism and adventurism. What is worse is that the corporation which received these payments went bankrupt for other reasons and was eventually replaced by another corporation. This experience is by no means unique. In addition, there are also complaints about the quality of services, particularly in the field of education, which meanwhile has been transformed from a social good to a highly profitable commercial venture. It is in this context that a need for a well-articulated regulatory framework is felt.

A regulatory framework is needed so that more confidence could be instilled in the public about, not merely the commercial viability of the deal but also restoration of a modicum of social service orientation. More important, from the point of view of expenditure management, it is important that the public is assured about the value for money to the community in these matters. A new centre of authority, responsibility and accountability should be seen as emerging and enriching the fabric of governance in the country. In the evolution of governance, this should be seen as an important, much needed, and urgent step.

True it is that there is some degree of regulation in existence. Most of it is self-regulation. Self-regulation in India, as it is elsewhere too, is an oxymoron. This is evident from the experience of each sector. In medical services, for example, there is the Medical Council of India which has a set of regulations about medical practice and hospitals. The introduction of health insurance services has contributed to a massive explosion in the number of medical establishments. In the former state of Andhra Pradesh alone there were more than three hundred "super specialities" hospitals in Hyderabad and other major urban centres but not even a single one in rural areas. These hospitals have helped the promotion of medical tourism and they now compete with the newly released movies for publicity space in the print and electronic media. Since the provision of medical services is concentrated in urban centres, a new class of touts has grown, who arrange visits, consultations, diagnostic tests and treatment in the hospitals, all for a varying tariff or commission. Even the doctors concede that most of the diagnostic tests may not be needed but are made necessary as they get a "cut" from the diagnostic centres. Medicines are over-prescribed because the doctors are in collusion with pharmacies, which in some cases are owned by the hospitals. The retailers also get a large commission from the distributors and other middlemen.

The corporate hospitals encourage practices that garner higher profits for them. Doctors, or senior consultants as they are called, have to secure growing business for them, as the doctors' own salaries and bonuses are dependent on such practices. The hospitals have become not only profit-centred, an inevitable feature when hospitals are managed on business lines, but the provision of services is afflicted with many other issues. Sanitary standards, to the extent there are any, leave a good deal to be desired. Toilets are cleaned but once a day despite a constant rush of patients and their families. Bed linen is changed infrequently. The proper treatment of hospital bed linen, which has special procedures, is seldom found in practice. Inevitably, hospitals have also become centres of infection. There is no system of grading of hospitals. The situation in government hospitals, which are the only ones that have mortuaries in major centres, is no better. These aspects need regulation and, more important, rigorous enforcement. It is no longer a situation where governments can afford to take a hands-off approach.

In education too, many corporations and organisations have been permitted to offer many professional courses. In many institutions, however, the faculty positions are vacant and less qualified people are appointed. In this context, the major areas of regulation left to the government relate to the admission of students to professional courses, and the organisation of final examinations. Given the large number of educational institutions and the larger number of students, conducting examinations is now comparable to a military operation. While these are regulated well, much to the credit of the autonomous institutions that are entrusted with this task, there are other aspects of the educational system that suffer from lack of clarity of purpose, owing to the jurisdictional overlap between the central and state ministries of education, the University Grants Commission and other administrative machinery. Each level tends to operate not in concert with other levels, but at cross purposes.

One question which is not even raised, let alone answered, is the efficiency of expenditures incurred on these organisations. They work only to spend the allotted amounts and no effort is made to secure economies. The power of government as a major buyer of services (fees for most students are paid by the central and state governments) is neither recognised nor utilised. To some extent, this is an inevitable feature when progress in education is measured in terms of the amounts spent and not on the judicious utilisation of financial resources. The explosion in the education system in terms of creating more opportunities for those seeking education has not been matched by corresponding improvements in the regulation of the institutions. This is equally applicable to all PPPs. They have been offered more lenient terms than were ever envisaged, but these have not been matched by an equal measure of effort to regulate them.

As regards NGOs, the fact that they have become a bone of contention suggests that their development and their role in society have reached a state of maturity. Their operations reflect a mixed bag, some very useful and thus have won a place in the hearts of the people. Some have become controversial in view of the causes taken up by them, and even more by the sources of financing. Some have become "profit centres" in that they are primarily viewed as vehicles for getting funds from various government and philanthropic organisations.

The regulation of this sector is to all intents and purposes weak and lacks a comprehensive design. The components of regulation are: registration of the body seeking financial assistance from government, utilisation certificate of moneys received, occasional inspection, and rarely, a supplemental audit by the Audit Department of the government. The system does not vary with the amounts given or the strategic nature of the objectives pursued by the recipient.

In this context, it would be appropriate to classify NGOs into three groups—(i) those that are more concerned with political causes; (ii) those that receive substantial amounts from the government and where the "own resources" are negligible; and (iii) those that are more dependent on public contributions and are in the nature of quasi-faith-based organisations. In the first type, the motive and the *modus operandi* of the nature of tasks undertaken tend to be primarily political. Consequently, the emphasis should be on monitoring their activities through means other than the conventional financial checks.

It is the second group that is of importance from the point of view of utilisation of resources provided by the government. The very fact that they are primarily dependent on government fiscal support suggests that they have no future as self-supporting organisations. In fact, given their financial dependence, it makes these organisations function like government agencies except that they have been given a large degree of autonomy and are liberated from the financial regime of the government. It is arguable that they have been given that exceptional degree of autonomy for political reasons and the objective may very well be the establishment of domains of patronage. The maintenance of the quasi-personal fiefdoms at public expense is debatable. Also, the submission of utilisation certificate before releasing the remaining tranches of funds is so routine that they have no functional value at all. It is in this context that the establishment of a regulatory institution becomes relevant. The regulatory agency should aim at ensuring that the non-governmental agencies that receive funds from government and that are dependent on government for their sustenance have adequate budget and accounting processes. Such processes lend credibility to the activities of the NGO, and ensuring their orderly functioning should be made the primary task of a regulatory body.

The third type of NGOs, whether they are of a conventional type or operations of a fly-by-night type, do not make a radical difference for the government in the context of the multitude of tasks undertaken by them. In the ultimate analysis, however, the future of the development of NGOs and their functioning is dependent on the establishment of a regulatory agency.

Audit: Current Status and Future Directions

Audit, as pointed out in an earlier section, has a long history which, for the most part, reveals an exemplary record. Although some call it *the* conscience keeper, in reality it is one of the many that can claim that status in a democracy. Its history in India predates the democratic period: it was established within a decade after the baton of administration shifted from the East India Company to the British Crown. Its establishment was not easy, as many of the diehard colonialists doubted the need for an audit agency as its very existence could give rise to issues about the credibility and rectitude of the British administration. But these doubts were overcome and an audit agency was established in 1866. It was, however, not a pure audit agency but an Indian variation of it in that it was a combined audit and accounts agency. Once again, doubts were expressed about this unholy combination, as the agency would be auditing the accounts compiled and consolidated (both for the central government and the then provinces) by itself: it reflected a conflict of interest. But considerations of economy had the better of the argument and, in the event, both functions were combined in a single agency—a feature that continued despite some pilot schemes for separation until the early 1970s, when audit was separated from accounts, though at the level of the state governments it continues to be a combined operation. Whether this has reduced the effectiveness of audit remains, as of now, an academic issue at the level of state governments.

The assiduous efforts made by the Audit Department have made it a countervailing power, an insider critic that is funded and maintained from the taxpayers' money and that plays a crucial part in the democratic functioning of society. It is a testimony to the work of the Audit Department that most scams starting from the jeep scandal in the early 1950s to the coalgate and 2G scam, except the Mundhra deal in 1956, that came out and claimed a good deal of the concerns of the elites in Indian society were the results of the hard diligent staff work done by the sleuths of the Audit Department. Although it gives the appearance of detective work, it is just the normal and tedious work of verification of payment vouchers and the fraud that they involve that bring out the scams. It is all in a day's hard work.

The charter of the Audit Department primarily involves carrying out different types of work. Since the work is carried out by a department that combines audit and accounting work, the department is also consulted, by virtue of a constitutional mandate on forms of classification of the budget (otherwise known as List of Major and Minor Heads of account, which forms the basis for the presentation of the budget and the maintenance of appropriation accounts—a format that was originally designed after the Crown took over the administration of the country: it was changed periodically.)

The audit carried out by the department is essentially of three types: appropriation audit, accountancy audit and proprietary audit. The first two involve a detailed analysis of financial transactions to ensure their conformity with the legal provisions and standards laid down for the purpose. Where a deviation is discovered, a draft audit paragraph is prepared and the reaction of the administrative agency concerned is sought. If the violation is accepted as pointed out by the Audit Department, it has the potential of being included in the final audit report that is submitted to the legislature. Detailed protocols are laid down for these purposes by the International Organisation of Supreme Audit Institutions (INTO SAI), based in Vienna. These types of protocols were in existence even before the INTO SAI was established: only an international ratification took place after the establishment. The audit so carried out is not comprehensive but is based on a random sample or where the department's intuitive approaches lead it to. An exhaustive audit could require a larger department and more expenditure incurred on its maintenance. The selection of what is to be audited lays the foundation for the department's annual work programme. The work programme itself is the result of a judgement call.

Proprietary audit—the third type of audit—is a precursor of what is now called performance audit. It involves an evaluation of the activities of an agency, the financial judgment shown by it, and the probity in its actions. Performance audit is the result of a compact arrived at between the Auditor General (The first part of his title "comptroller" is deliberately eschewed in this discussion, as the constitutional mandate involved in this was never allowed to become a reality. It is an odd feature of the Indian Constitution that some constitutionally mandated titles are to be used even when they are not used) and the Union Ministry of Finance. The charter of the audit does not involve an analysis and evaluation of the policies of the administrative agency. But this technical limitation was and is circumscribed in practice by a curious twist of the argument. The performance audit carried out by the department, which anyway is done on a selective basis, involves in substance an analysis and evaluation of the policies followed, without saying so. This, in a way reflects the Indian preference for *jugaad*. Thus, in practice, a form of policy analysis and related evaluation takes place without admitting that it is in fact being done. In retrospect, however, the nation has to be grateful for the concordat arrived at between the Audit Department and the Government of India. Without that agreement, it is more than probable that many of the scams would not have seen daylight.

While the charter of activities of the Audit Department may appear to be comprehensive, there are some areas which are important from the nation's point of view and need to be taken up by the department. These areas represent the points of departure from the conventional approach. One such area is local finance. Traditionally, local finances are audited by a wing of the provincial, now state, finance departments. There has been, however, an implosion in the financial dimensions of local government activities, particularly after the enactment of the 73rd amendment to the Constitution. Notwithstanding a couple of exceptions, this amendment ushered in three layers of functioning at the sub-national level, *viz.*, state government, district government, and the village *panchayat* or the municipal council. Reflecting the emphasis on decentralised administration, many schemes were formulated to channel funds to the district and village administrations. Some of these financial transfers are directly made by the Centre, and some others are channelled through the state governments. In almost all cases the local financial needs are reviewed by a State Finance Commission and its recommendations are, by convention, accepted by the state government.

As a result of these arrangements, the transfer from other levels of governments—Centre and state—constitutes a substantial part, nearly 80 per cent, of the local resources. The local governments are now "cash rich" and some of them have even started investing the short-term idle balances in government bills. These institutions, in particular the substantial transfers from the central and state governments, are audited by chartered accountants drawn from the large pool available in the country. This audit is less comprehensive than the audit by the conventional Audit Department. Even the protocols and approaches are different. What is important, both for the auditors and for the body of elected officials, is to secure, in the first instance, utilisation certificate so that the next tranche of the conditional transfers may be obtained. Fulfilment of the objectives of the transfers and the programmes for which the funds are given is at best secondary. In fact, the audit by chartered accountants is on legal compliance of the administrative conditions normally associated with the payment process than on the economic objectives of the sponsored programmes. Considerations of economy and efficiency do not even come up for investigation. Furthermore, the administrative machinery at the local level does not have internal audit facilities. To some extent, these aspects are covered, if at all, by the occasional supplementary audit carried out by the Auditor General's Department. The Auditor General is empowered to carry out an audit of transactions following the rupee trail, in that wherever money of the government is spent, he can follow the trail of that spending process and audit those transactions regardless of the place and time where they take place. This audit is, however, not regular and much depends on the process of the annual audit programme of the Audit Department. Thus, in effect, an abyss has been created in an area of immense national importance and that abyss is staring back at the financial leadership of the country, seeking relief. Moreover, the quality and capacity of the accounting personnel at the local level leaves a good deal to be desired, and all statements about the utilisation of funds transferred and objectives achieved have to be taken with, not a grain, but a proverbial "ton of salt."

If local governments reflect one area of operations, the more recent addition of PPPs to the instrumental arsenal of the government raises even more fundamental issues about the audit of the programmes carried out by the partner from the private sector. Local finance has a history of more than two centuries in India, and with all that history and related rich experience, the financial system is archaic and ineffective. If that is the experience of local finance, one would have expected that lessons of that experience would have been learnt and those lessons applied to the new and emerging field of PPPs. In fact, however, the experience shows, not progress, not even stagnation, but regress. Some agreements concluded with the corporate partner do not include any provision for supplemental test audit by the Audit Department. In areas like gas exploration, where audit is taken up by the Audit Department at the request of the government to ensure a modicum of transparency and accountability, the private party introduces so many caveats that the whole process raises fundamental issues about the nature and extent of the audit process as a whole. It is far from clear why this type of arrangements were specified in the partnership agreements, in the first place. A new agency is now proposed to be set up by the central government to promote, and hopefully to regulate, the PPPs which are envisaged to play a key role in India's economic development. The new administrative culture that will emerge as a result of these efforts should include more safeguards to ensure the public interest. (A note is attached at the end on ethics and corporate action.)

Another area where the audit agency and its programme require a boost and warm support relates to a strengthened system of investigative reports. Most of the irregularities, violations, circumventions and conspiracies in the private use of public resources, an aspect that has grown virtually to be a national malady, requires to be addressed more frontally. The litany of not-so-discreet efforts to defraud the government come to the attention of the Audit Department and the public alike long after the event, when the annual audit or performance audit reports are compiled. By that time the officials concerned—both from the administrative and political classes—may be out of power and out of government. Some of them may also have been victims of the actuarial cycle of operations. While the conscience keepers may be keeping the records of the nation, long delays in their compilation reduce their effectiveness. Moreover, the emergence of a scam implies a major institutional failure in that, the internal audit which is within the ambit of the financial adviser attached to the ministry concerned, and the concurrent audit by the Audit Department, have failed to detect it or, if detected, have failed to stem its large-scale outburst. The scope of audit needs to be expanded to include a well-organised system of internal audit and up-to-date process of concurrent audit.

The scope of appropriation audit is rather limited. It is primarily concerned with the task of verifying whether the amounts voted have been spent for the purposes for which they were appropriated and whether the specified legal regulations have been observed in the process. The entire process of spending is now dominated by three phases, *viz.*: (i) appropriation, (ii) re-appropriation, and (iii) misappropriation. *Appropriation* refers to the legislative process of voting the money. This process has become relatively smooth due to the declining interest of the legislators in voting the appropriations. The task of reviewing the proposed outlays for each department is entrusted at the Centre to the Standing Committees, who, after discussing the proposals, submit a report to the Lok Sabha (Lower House). The process has become so routine that more than half of the proposed appropriations are approved in the guillotine hour of debate and voting. In effect, it implies that the budget debate is largely devoted to the "hot issues" of the day and the voting follows the past patterns in the House. It has become so mechanical and lacking in life that the members would not appear to be any more interested in the nitty-gritty of the budget.

Re-appropriation of funds is largely, if not entirely, within the domain of the spending departments. These departments work in a frame of delegated financial powers, and over the years they have been delegated large chunks of power to appropriate funds within a major head of account. The working of the delegated powers shows that there has been abuse of the delegated power. The governments are so brazen about the use of this power that they have subverted the very intent of appropriations. Funds appropriated for the development of Scheduled Castes and Scheduled Tribes were, for example, transferred and spent on the Commonwealth Games, or some other pet projects and hobby horses of the state Chief Ministers. This does not mean, however, that the delegated powers in regard to re-appropriation should be rescinded or drastically reduced (Such an approach would lead to massive centralisation of financial power in the hands of the Finance Ministry and would not be workable) but should be shadowed, where appropriate, through concurrent audit.

Misappropriation, the third phase of spending, consists of embezzlement or siphoning of funds for personal use and related approaches that aim at personal enrichment. The means of engaging in these tricks are a legion and the prevailing view, despite extensive computerisation of payment processes, is that every aspect of the government financial management can be gamed to amass private wealth. What is detected and legally pursued is only a minor part of the total leakage.

The Audit Department's work is largely oriented to the monitoring of these processes and to detect violations and abuses. In the process of counting these trees, it has overlooked the forest of larger issues of fiscal management and budget responsibility. The macroeconomic consequences of the policy approaches have not been subjected to an audit. In fact, a couple of decades ago, the Audit Department took a step forward to review the approaches and mechanics of public debt management. The wisdom of borrowing on the scale on which it is done, and the uses of those borrowed funds, raises larger issues about the wisdom of such borrowing. It has also led to questionable practices. State governments have been engaging in recent years in large borrowing from the public merely because the fiscal responsibility legislation permits them to borrow within an approved ceiling. As the term implies, it is a limit and does not mean that amounts should be borrowed up to the limit even when there is no need to do so. A build-up in idle cash balances is the result of these approaches. These aspects come to light only when the audit shifts its orientation from transactional trees to macro woods. What is involved is the present state of the fiscal health, and the potential state of the nation if the present trends continue unchecked. An objective view of the audit, like the physician's verdict after the annual physical, is an approach that could add a good deal to the constructive contribution of that agency. It is a direction whose pursuit is timely.

Enhanced Legislative Accountability and Participatory Democracy

Legislative control in a parliamentary democracy sets the tone for expenditure management in the country. The legislature has paramount power both in determining the allocations for different services needed by the people and for determining the total magnitude of outlays. The latter refers, indirectly, to the resources that a nation is willing to contribute to its own welfare and economic sustainability. It represents the people's voice. Legislative control, a pattern that is derived from the

Mother of Parliaments, the British House of Commons, was acquired gradually over an extended period. It shifted the power to levy taxes from the Crown to the people, i.e. House of Commons. This power came in slow and painful steps of evolution. From this followed the power to use those resources for the benefit of the people. As part of this struggle between the Crown and the House, the latter also acquired the right to determine the amounts needed for the maintenance of the Crown itself.

India adopted this model of constitution soon after independence and a part of the constitution was devoted to the specification of the legislative functions and duties in framing the annual financial statement for the approval of the House. The constitution reflected the long experience that India had acquired to shape its own financial destiny. The experience was rich, and to use the famous first words of Charles Dickens in his *Tale of Two Cities,* it was the best of times. It is also the misfortune of India that it also experienced the worst of times, particularly during the period 2005-2014, as members came to the House not to proceed with the day's work but to stall it. As the poet T.S. Eliot wrote, "the past has a different pattern". It is instructive to recall the features of that past with a view to ascertaining how far India has progressed in serving its own people and how legislative institutions played their part in the changing contexts.

India's struggle in attaining self-government has been a long one. In the early part of the century, the elected Council was given limited powers to discuss the budget formulated and presented by the colonial power. That discussion was envisaged not merely to provide an exercise to the vocal chords of the honourable members (which they now exercise in a full-throated way) but to illumine the status of finances, the purposes of proposed allocations (A generous part went to the maintenance of the military forces, which at one time drew the ire of the Father of the Nation, who wrote a major editorial titled "The Wrongs of Indian Public Expenditure" in his *Navjeevan:* that issue is a part of the exhibits on display at the Sabarmati Ashram in Ahmedabad) and the checks and balances designed to regulate the outlays.

As an integral part of this effort, two Standing Committees (Members perform their duties while sitting, though) of the House. One was a direct import from the Mother Parliament, *viz*., the Public Accounts Committee, or PAC in short, and the other was an innovation applicable only to India in the form of a Standing Finance Committee or SFC. The two committees had different functions. The PAC was responsible for a review of the annual accounts and the audit reports, both prepared by the Office of the Auditor General. It also looked into excess expenditures, over and above the amounts appropriated by the House, and recommended their regularisation to the House. The function of the SFC was to approve financial proposals leading to expenditures by government. Specific proposals, above a specified level, were submitted to the committee for its approval. In that role, the SFC supplemented the traditional role of the Finance Department, but was given this important role so that the people's representatives could get a taste of governance. Summary records of the proceedings of the SFC were published and were placed in the public domain. The two committees covered the two ends of the annual budget work, i.e. preparatory work leading to the budget, and the conclusion of the budget work.

Essentially, the financial work of the representatives comprised three elements: (i) approval of specific expenditure proposals; (ii) debate in the House on the proposed budget; and (iii) approval of the annual accounts by the PAC first and later by the House. These features were later incorporated into the parliamentary procedure in India after independence, with a major exception in that the SFC was wound up. This step was considered appropriate as the Houses had been given full powers to debate the budget and the approval of the "demands for grants" from the various departments and agencies. The debate was extensive, although no budget was ever rejected, as such rejection is tantamount to a binding expression of lack of confidence in the government. The revival of SFC came up for frequent consideration in the first decades after independence, but the end of SFC proved to be final. It was, in a way, replaced by the Committee on Estimates or Estimates Committee, which, contrary to the implications of its name, was given the task of reviewing the prospects for economies in expenditures in the activities of the departments. Later, the purview was extended to include a review of the current activities of the departments. The three new legs of financial democracy comprised the debate and the two committees, *viz.*, the PAC and the Estimates Committee.

During the 1960s, yet another committee, called Committee on Public Sector Undertakings (Committee on PSUs) was set up to look into the financial operations of the PSUs. In this work, like the PAC, the committee is assisted by the Auditor General, whose reports on commercial audit form the basis of the committee's work. The lacuna felt after the steady expansion of the operations of PSUs was addressed through this committee. The three committees provided membership space for only a few, and the post of the Chairman of PAC was filled up by the opposition parties. Members of the Lok Sabha and Rajya Sabha were meanwhile feeling restive about the lack of opportunities in committee work and related legislative business.

To some extent, this was also a reflection of the tumultuous changes on the political scene when the Prime Minister(s) did not evince much interest in the parliamentary proceedings. The difference between the first Prime Minister and his progeny as well as the next generation of the family who became Prime Minister was that the first Prime Minister was essentially an institution builder and had an enormous respect for the two Houses. His participation in the proceedings was extensive and he sat through the proceedings, even when he was not speaking in the Houses, and frequently intervened to explain his point of view. Those who became Prime Ministers from his family did not share that enthusiasm or respect for Parliament. More significantly, the latter generation did not devote time to make new beginnings that would utilise the local pool of talent from the two Houses. The democratic traditions began to be sidelined.

Meanwhile, however, after the 1980s when Margaret Thatcher came to power, she too began to ignore the concerns and the cravings for public space from the backbenchers in the House of Commons. Eventually, their concerns received the attention of the leadership of the party and they established standing committees and consultative committees in addition to the other financial committees that were already at work. The avowed intent behind the arrangement was to benefit from the wisdom of the members of the House; in practice, however, it was an effort to keep them busy with some semblance of work. It is doubtful whether the ministers paid much heed to the work of the committee or the advice coming from those channels. In fact, one Chancellor of the Exchequer openly expressed the view that he did not find the work of the committee useful. But the fifth wheel also had its political use and was continued.

This example stirred up the imagination of the policy makers in India, though it took a long time to put their thoughts into action. As the legislative history of the Indian Parliament shows, the long shadow of the House of Commons had its impact on the Indian Parliament at several stages. Here too, by 1993, i.e. after the introduction of a liberal economic regime in place of the long and elaborate web of a variety of controls, the government was ready to announce the formation of two committees to review the parliamentary work, both when the Houses were in session or when they were adjourned. The first measure comprised the established Standing Committees to consider the budgetary demands of the various ministries and report on those demands to the full House. To some extent, this measure was intended to provide an expanded opportunity to consider the budget proposals and report on those proposals to the House in the hope that the views of the committee would be taken up for an extended consideration during the budget debate. Membership of the committee, originally limited to 17 when first organised in 1993, was expanded to 24, after a decade of experience, in 2004. In addition, consultative committees for ministries were organised. By the closure of the 15th Lok Sabha, there were 35 committees working with various central ministries and membership of the committees ranged from 10 to 30. It meant that more than 300 members of Parliament were employed with this back-room work. The committees were presided over, when meetings were held, by the minister of the ministry concerned.

Meanwhile, as these efforts for employment generation in the hope of getting some useful inputs into policy-making while permitting the members to acquaint themselves with the legislative and other work of the ministries were moving on, some state governments too were keen to expand their own opportunities and efforts began to revive the second House (Upper House). These efforts were selective and not all states joined the bandwagon. Some states revived the Legislative Council and provided ample opportunities to those who failed in the route of direct election, to crawl back into legislative limelight and pitch their demands for becoming ministers in the cabinet. Thus, there are now abundant opportunities for those eager and enterprising members to join the ranks in serving the nation.

Yet another development was also taking place at the local level in expanding the operational scope of participatory democracy. The stakeholders were now provided with opportunities in the form of User Councils to determine the scope of the services offered to them.

It is debatable whether the transplantation of the British experience to the Indian Parliament has materially contributed to improvement in the nature and content of legislative control and in the pattern of resource utilisation. This in turn involves a substantive inquiry and analysis of the experience. In analysing these improvements, a distinction has to be made between those that have contributed to more effective participatory democracy at the local level and the contribution at the central level. To take up the local experience first, the formation of User Councils has proved to be helpful in resolving traditional contentious areas. One major area was the use of water for agricultural purposes. Although the use of water at the level of states continues to be a hot potato and extremely emotional, as was the case between Karnataka and Tamil Nadu, Kerala and Tamil Nadu, Andhra Pradesh and Maharashtra, Andhra Pradesh and Telengana state, Andhra Pradesh and Karnataka, several measures have been tried to reconcile the conflicting views and to find a way to satisfy the contending parties. Zonal Councils, Autonomous River Management Boards and references to the judiciary have not, admittedly, resolved the issues.

At the village level, the User Councils have in many cases contributed to a lessening of tension, and more important, to a practical way of providing water for irrigation. The usefulness of User Councils in the field of medical service and education continues to be a matter of dispute. The institutionalisation of participatory democracy does not always guarantee a practical solution to problems. Its usefulness lies in bringing the different views together so that a workable solution, at least in the short term, could be evolved. In many cases, however, these approaches may quickly morph into political brawls and extended resort to violence. The traditional physical fights have not been eliminated but have either been exacerbated in some cases or reduced in a few others. These matters are in any event far away from both the central and state legislatures and are to be resolved locally. The formation of the User Council is yet another step, small and tentative, but with greater potential than any other approach in giving a firmer shape to the utilisation of revenues.

At the central level, the issue is whether the Standing Committee has proved to be a useful adjunct to the budget debate and to a more constructive approach for the approval of the annual budget. Prima facie, its contribution is unlikely to be a major one when the bulk of the appropriations, often more than half of the budget, are approved in the last hour of the allotted time and when the voting pattern follows the party pattern. The idea of forming a Standing Committee is based on the understanding that the budget has become too bulky, both metaphorically and physically, to be handled by the whole House.

This problem is not unique to India. In the United States too, a similar problem had arisen and its solution was to subject the budget, which anyway was to all intents and purposes twisted out of shape by the two Houses, to discussion by the caucuses and there was general agreement that the conclusions reached were neither raised nor questioned in the two Houses. In addition, there are as many as twelve Appropriation Committees that are responsible for budgets of various agencies of government. These committees have the power to approve budgets. In India, however, the committees, including the Joint Parliamentary Committees, have followed the predicable approach of the political party patterns. It is not a case where an individual member takes an objective position but is one where the party position is reiterated, often with more emphasis. In these cases, the work of the Standing Committee remains an extension of the budget process except that it shifts the venue from the House to darkened committee rooms and corridors of power. Besides, the occasions where the findings of the committee have become the staple of budget approval are few and far between. In the Indian tradition, a budget proposal can be changed only when the government decides to change its position, either on its own volition or in the light of the changing party pressures.

The effectiveness of the consultative committees is a different matter in that it is an issue between the minister, who presides over the proceedings of the committee, and members of the committee. The minister may choose to be conciliatory or adversarial, depending on how he reads the political situation. If he thinks that the implementation of the committee's recommendations might enhance the prestige of his agency or could even lead to enhanced budgetary allocations in the future, full cooperation would be extended to the committee. One should not ignore the educational value of participation in the committee's work for the new members. But much depends on the inclinations of the members. Their participation could also prove useful in ensuring that the objectives of central assistance provided by the ministries are fulfilled, as members of both Houses are also members of the local, constituency-level committees. It could also be helpful in securing more funds for local programmes. In this sphere, as elsewhere, the consultative committees have the potential of offering a formidable combination of opportunities for expanded deliberations and for greater budgetary allocations in the future.

There is, however, one area which has not yet received the attention due. This relates to PPPs, which on present indications are likely to play a bigger role in the future. But they have been escaping the scrutiny of audit as well as legislative control. When the public sector undertakings were expanding at a rapid clip during the 1960s, Parliament responded with the formation of a Committee on Public Sector Undertakings. It is opportune now to consider whether a similar committee would be appropriate for PPPs as well.

It is essential to recognise that the State has become a Hollow State. Improved ways of ensuring a more effective system of expenditure management require a vastly enhanced monitoring system, a more effective implementation system, an effective regulatory framework, and an effective audit and legislative control system.

8

Praxis of Federalism

Dominance and Dependence

The management of public expenditure throughout the length and breadth of the country involves the combined work of the central government, its Union territories, state governments and local governments. The territorial boundaries of the state governments are determined by central legislation. The functioning of the local governments and the three-tier structure that is envisaged for that level has a substantial degree of homogeneity, though there are exceptions to that approach. The state governments too have more common features, particularly in the sphere of expenditure management, than is generally recognised. The administrative evolution of the state governments differed, in that the territory of the administration of the erstwhile provinces, which were formed originally under the East India Company (the main provinces were three—Bombay, Calcutta and Madras) expanded as also the scope of their administration: new territories were either added onto the three provinces or new provinces were formed. After independence, some parts of the provinces and territories were transferred to the new country that was formed as the spoils of partition. The state governments that were formed in independent India also comprised the 500 and more princely states. Other states such as Goa and Sikkim came into the Union either through annexation or through people's choice.

Given the different administrative traditions in the British provinces, princely states and others, it is only natural that systems of expenditure management differed too among the states. The situation changed, however, after the introduction of a system of planned development, most of which was designed, sponsored, funded, and managed by the central government.[1] The financial functioning of the states is dependent upon the forms and devices through which national resources are divided or devolved to the state and local governments. The process through division and devolution that takes place determines the autonomy enjoyed by the state governments and local governments. This process takes place, throughout the world, through two forms of government that have been recognised for many decades. These two forms are federal form of government and Union form of government. Since the form of the process has a substantial impact on the freedom of the sub-national governments and on the discussion in this section, it is appropriate that it is considered here in a synoptic form.

In the world of today, there are three forms of government, *viz.*, supranational, federal type, and unitary. The first form is unique to the European Union (EU). The Union has a constitution, which specifies the eligibility criteria for becoming members of the Union and procedures of the constitutional organs of the Union such as the European Parliament and other related institutions. The Union has a budget, primarily funded by contributions from member countries, and is the primary vehicle for making transfers to the member countries. The Union has a bank which functions, to all intents the purposes, like the central bank of a country. It issues a common currency and manages the monetary policy of the Union and is responsible for the promotion of economic stability in the Union. Reflecting the recent financial crisis, in part a contagion effect of the financial crisis of 2008 that had its origins in the United States, the Union has assumed additional tasks to oversee the financial management of its member countries that received a fair amount of short-term assistance to tide over the crisis. This group includes Greece, Ireland and Portugal. Their draft budgets are considered by the Union to ensure that proper remedial measures are taken, aimed at resolving the crisis. The Union has rules governing the levels of budget deficit and the levels of outstanding public debt, and any relaxation in these requires its prior approval. The Union has also an office of audit, which is independent, and if its reports are any evidence, too strident in its criticisms. While its reports may not have contributed to substantial improvements in the operational systems of the Union, their findings are subjected to extensive debate.

1. For a recent discussion of the evolution of new states in India, see Tillin, Louise (2013). *Remapping India: New States and their Political Origins*. New Delhi: Oxford University Press.

The Union has not taken over any of the traditional functions and tasks of its member countries, except in the issues of entry into the Union by people of its member countries, customs administration, and the conduct of the monetary policy of the Union. The grants given by the Union to its member countries such as, for example, the development of the southern region of Italy, are governed by a lot of ring fencing and are also subjected to annual audit by the audit agency attached to the Union. In theory, the recipient countries are expected to comply with the conditions attached to the grants; in practice, there are the usual escape mechanisms found all over the world. The functioning of the Union reflects an additional layer of governance. This layer is expected to provide much-needed cooperation and coordination among the member countries. The working of the Union reveals that some members are stronger than others and their power is felt in many ways. The highest level of government, over and above the national ones, is a reality and is an economic solution to an otherwise political problem. The working of the Union also reveals that new coordinating bodies with an oversight can always be established when new problems arise.

The second form of government is at the national level and may be organised either as a federation or as a Union. The scope of working of the former is naturally different from the latter. The former is so designed that the constituent units have their own assigned areas of responsibilities and function independently within those spheres. To support their independence, they are provided with necessary fiscal powers as well as administrative powers. The federation could comprise two or three levels. At the apex is the federal government and at the bottom of the pyramid is the local government. There could be a middle layer in the form of a state or province. Historically, a federation could be an aggregate one or a devolved one. The former refers to a process where a few states could come together and agree to form a federal government. The federal setup of an aggregate type keeps reminding itself that it is there in the first place by virtue of the agreement among the states to form a federation. The devolved type refers to arrangements under which a colonial government brings together some of its territories, generally known as provinces, and forms a new nation, or a new country, and thus, a new national administration. Prominent examples of the aggregative type are the United States and Malaysia. The latter include the former colonies of Great Britain, such as Australia and India. In the aggregative type, each level is assigned responsibilities as well as powers to carry them out. Residual powers that are not specific are vested with the state governments. In the devolved type, the central governments are endowed with greater power and the provinces or states are viewed as subordinate to the central government. Also, residual powers, including the power to create new states or princes, are vested with the central government.

A third form of government is one which has an additional layer between the central and state governments, a form unique to Spain. This level is called zone and each zone comprises some states or provinces. The zones are empowered with a large range of powers, including that of undertaking domestic and foreign debt, and to make grants or engage in financial transfers to the lower levels of government. Zones were devised to quell political opposition and to facilitate greater coordination among the provinces or states. In India too, there are zonal councils, formed in the 1960s, to facilitate greater coordination between the Centre and the states.

A fourth form refers to the state or provincial governments. Like the central governments, the states too are endowed with their own legislature, executive and judicial wings and the powers of each are specified in the constitution. The formal division of powers between the Centre and the states is in the form of three lists—Central, State and Concurrent Lists. Within those spheres, the units have their responsibilities and powers to carry them out. At the bottom of these structures is the local government which has, however, different forms in different countries. Following the 73rd amendment to the constitution, India has three layers of local government—district, *mandal*, and village *panchayats* or city governments. In the United Kingdom, there are only two layers of government—central and local. In the United States, there are basically three levels—federal, state, and county or city governments. The counties are administered by an elected Chief Executive, who is also responsible, among other things, for the maintenance of law and order in the county and therefore has its own police department, not to mention, the jail. The intent behind this complex web of governance is to enable the voice of the people to be felt at all levels and each level has its own elected councils or legislatures that would permit the channelling of people's voices.

The combination of arrangements permits an analysis of the political, administrative and financial aspects of the working of the various levels of governments. Politically, each level reflects an arrangement under which people's representatives are elected, periodically, to transact the business of that level. The administrative level refers to the administrative arrangements in each case. These could be fairly elaborate, as in India, where the constitution specifies the arrangements at the state level (These provisions are too detailed and claim a good deal of space in a volume that is already liberally padded to make it one of the biggest written constitutions and defies the famous dictum of Napoleon that constitutions should be brief and ambiguous) and more so with the state governments in the north-east region.

The financial arrangements are, in principle, expected to reflect the political and administrative arrangements. In essence, each level is endowed with powers to raise financial resources through taxation and through borrowing, though there is a fundamental difference between the former centrally planned communist block of countries and others. In the former, taxes are levied and collected (basically turnover tax and profits from the large sector of state-owned enterprises) by the provincial or state governments, a share of which is transferred to the central or federal government. In the latter type, taxes may be levied, and borrowing undertaken by the state and local governments. In practice, however, there are administrative arrangements that suggest the location of greater power in the central or federal governments. The most important arrangements relate to the financial resources. The division of financial resources has, over the years, become a pivot of federalism in many countries. The political and administrative rhetoric may reveal an emphasis on greater autonomy in the mobilisation and utilisation of financial resources. In practice, most of the resources are located in the federal government, as is clear from the arrangements. In the USA, income tax, which is one of the major sources of public revenue, is collected by the federal government. The state income tax, a supplement of the federal income tax, is collected with the federal income tax. The state governments in the US have full freedom to levy and collect sales taxes, which is their most important source of revenue. At the local level, property tax is the major source of revenue and the governments at this level have full freedom to vary the property taxes and levy other taxes that are within their domain.

Expenditures at each level are determined by the respective legislatures or councils. They also have full powers to borrow from the market or to float special bonds for financing major projects. Each state has its own laws governing the level of deficit that can be incurred by it.

There are more than 23 states with a law that enforces a balanced budget, though the actual content of the revenue and expenditure components differs from one state to another. Many local governments, in particular city governments, also go bankrupt from time to time, such bankruptcies usually being the result of excessive borrowing and uncontrolled expenditure. There are also many cases where the legislators at the local level have awarded themselves generous emoluments and pensions. The only level of government that is permitted to declare bankruptcy and seek the protection of bankruptcy laws is the local level. The bankruptcy laws of this level of government are more patterned after the Chapter 11 bankruptcy proceedings applicable to the corporate sector.

In Canada, the federal income tax is an important source of revenue and is managed by the federal government under a complex agreement with the provinces, where they have ceded the right to it. In Australia, for long an important feature of the federal financial arrangements has been the Commonwealth Grants Commission (which is a precursor to India's constitutionally appointed quinquennial Finance Commission) responsible for devolution of resources to the claimant states. Unlike India, the number of states in Australia is very small, and so is the number of annual claimant states seeking devolution of financial resources.

Broadly, the financial arrangements reflect two features. One relates to the division of resources envisaged in the constitution of the country. This forms the bedrock of federalism. The second is a discretionary arrangement under which federal governments initiate programmes covering a variety of areas that are also funded by them. The difference between the constitutional mandate and the discretionary arrangement is evident from India's own experience in that Article 275 of the Constitution provides for primarily budget support grants (though more recent Finance Commissions could not resist the temptation to make specific and conditional grant-in-aid), while Article 282 was the base for the operations of the Planning Commission until its closure in 2014. The magnitude of discretionary transfers in India—a combination of loans and grants) has tended to far exceed the statutory transfers recommended by the Finance Commissions. During the second decade of the current century this trend has changed, in that the transfers made under Article 282 are less than the statutory transfers made on the recommendations of the Finance Commission.

In the United States, large "discretionary" powers are devised by the federal government only. For example, the federal government makes a grant for each student, who is the child of a federal employee and is getting the benefit of education from the local county government. Naturally, counties which boast a large concentration of federal employees, such as Montgomery and Fairfax that are contiguous to the nation's capital, receive large sums of federal grants. The very size of these educational transfers has enabled these county governments to offer an education that is the envy of many of the counties in the continental United States. In addition, the federal government matches grants for specific purposes such as for the acquisition of equipment for national security purposes. For example, after the Homeland Security Department was established in the wake of the 9/11 destruction of the World Trade Center in New York, the federal government made extensive grants to county governments to shore up the local defences.

In Australia, the federal government finances some programmes and the transfers include both loan and grant elements. In Brazil, the innovative education reach programme is financed by transfers from the federal government. The important feature of such transfers is that they are discretionary and comprise complex financial packages. Their content varies from country to country and depends on contextual factors. In India, for example, during the late 1980s, there was considerable political pressure from many state governments to get central investment in various projects that were sought to be located in the states. The investment brought with it a good deal of economic potential, much more than the assistance provided through the Planning Commission. The pressure was not on what was already decided on, but on what was going to be decided. This kind of pressure, frequently supported by popular protests and organised agitations and part-political movements, also resulted in changes in policies. It was in that context that the Union Ministry of Steel decided to locate steel-making units even away from the source of raw material. In the New York State of the United States, a number of studies including by the Harvard University were made to determine the amounts that the state was getting from the federal government and the amount of tax revenues generated in the state and paid as federal revenues. The contention was that the state was generating substantial sums of revenues, while what they were getting from the federal was minuscule. These episodes, variations of which are found in other federations too, illustrate the contentious nature of resource transfers from the federal government and how every stratagem is deployed to maximise the resource transfers to the respective states. The approach of the states is not directed at enlarging the size of the federal pool of funds, but at enlarging the slice of the cake that is proposed to be apportioned to each of them. The strategies employed to get funds are more in the nature of beggar-thy-neighbour approaches, and each state for itself.

The federal discretionary transfers are not unconditional. As previously noted, these transfers are not for general budget support but for specific purposes that are determined by the federal government and are solely its choice. In order to ensure that the moneys transferred do not become a part of a fungible pool at the receiving end, the ring fencing formulated by the federal government is extensive. The conditionality does not permit any flexibility in the use of funds so given. To ensure continued compliance, elaborate monitoring systems comprising detailed reports and official inspections are devised. As these transfers became extensive and increased in magnitude, the dependence of the states on the Centre also grew. Because of the attractive nature of the assistance, the state governments did not waste any time in seeking it and in becoming eager and willing partners in this relationship of dependency. They took on programmes that they had never envisaged, and they were not about to give them up when the sunset provision of those programmes loomed on the horizon: for the state governments, the continuation of those programmes became imperative in view of the popular support that they attracted.

These illustrations suggest that financial federalism is different from the original canons of federalism, which delineated a world in which the sub-national governments would have complete freedom to operate in any which way they liked, at their initiative and at their volition. The issue of financing the state governments' initiatives was within the realm of their decision-making, subject to approval by their legislatures. In many cases, the legislatures became mute as their political thunder of rhetoric was stolen from them. Instead of being innovators in their realm, they became truly subordinate agencies of the federal governments. Not only were they deprived, not by intent but by default, of the capacity to innovate, but also had no freedom in the use of resources. In the process, a new form of financial federalism, different from the constitutional, political, and administrative federal organisations envisaged by the constitutional experts came into being.

What is now seen as a federation is a group of constituent members in which one member, *viz.*, the federal government, has become the guiding spirit and mentor. It is now a partnership in which there are dominant members and dependent members. It is arguable whether in the process the original intent of federalism was deliberately subverted, or whether the changing events contributed to this change. Both sides of the argument have their proponents and critics. It is not the intent here to engage in a debate about the merits of those changes; the intention is merely to provide a larger backdrop of contemporary developments that would enable us to have a better perspective of the developments in India.

The Indian Experience

Is India a federation or a union of states? The Chairman of the Drafting Committee of India's Constitution, and Minister of Law in independent India, thought that it was a matter of individual perception.[2] As he is reported to have said, with unconcealed ambiguity, if you think it is a federation, it is a federation; And if you think it is a union, it is a union. The Constitution itself took the deliberate stance of eschewing the use of the two terms—federal or federation.[3] Notwithstanding the absence of usage of the term, federalism had a hidden presence in the Constitution inasmuch as the financial provisions, dealing with the central and state powers in fiscal matters, were mostly an extended shadow of the 1935 Act. (It was simply known as the 1935 Act and had no name on the title page—one of those curious anomalies of colonial administration.) The movement leading to the Constitution of India reflected the long-held views of the colonial government and the leadership of the national movement, the Congress Party.

For long, the British administrators of undivided India held the view that India was not a country but a subcontinent, and that its people were not a single nation but a group of nations. The Congress Party, on the

2. The person was Dr B.R. Ambedkar. He was no newcomer to the issue of federalism. His doctoral thesis at Columbia University was on provincial finance. India's second Finance Minister, John Mathai, wrote his thesis at the London School of Economics on local finance in India, which was later published as a book. Thus, there was substantial technical knowledge in the Cabinet on these matters.

3. The apparent confusion did not end there. The chairman of the Third Finance Commission wrote a well-received book titled *Federalism*. Books on the Indian financial system, starting from P.J. Thomas's famous book, were mostly on what they presumed to be a federal system.

other hand, maintained that India was a single nation, notwithstanding multiple religions, numerous languages, and multiple ethnicities, a claim that was disputed strongly by the Muslim League. The credibility of the British administrative point of view was rooted in the existence of more than 500 princely states, each of which had its own legal and financial institutions. This very feature made the series of British delegations that were exploring the path of independence, also envisage the possibility of a confederacy in India comprising the princely states and the territories under the administration of the colonial government. The idea of a confederacy was, however, strongly opposed by the Indian interlocutors. But the idea of a federation had a strong undercurrent from the mid-1920s, when the Congress Party was transforming itself into a national movement, and what it thought was a single voice.

The main worry of the Congress Party was that if India became a federation with the provinces and the princely states having an option not to join the Indian Union, then a form of balkanisation was inevitable. This view continued to hold sway even after independence on the constitution-makers. India, the Constitution announced, was a single country and the newly formed states did not have the right to secede from the Union. Later, in the mid-1960s, the DMK Party, which came to power in Tamil Nadu, officially gave up the demand for a separate and independent Dravidian state. Although there were political movements from time to time both in the northwest and northeast regions seeking the formation of independent states, by and large, the claim of the Constitution of India being a union of states continues to hold. In reality, however, the Constitution of India, to borrow a term used in psychology, had a split personality in that its political and administrative language was different from the financial arrangements, which were, as noted earlier, drawn essentially from the 1935 Act and had features that were essentially federal in content and outlook. This combination may look odd to purists of federalism, but its survival and relatively smooth functioning is to be ascribed to a federal financial arrangement working within a political and administrative arrangement that is essentially unitary in character.

The 1935 Act represented the political views of the period. The demand of the people of colonial India was for self-rule: the demand for full-scale independence came much later. The 1935 Act reflected, thus, the status of a dominion within the vast British Empire. World War II, and the decline of Britain as an imperial and colonial power, did not even appear on the horizon at that stage. The British government was meanwhile engaged in establishing the new forms of government both politically and physically. A massive physical infrastructure began to be laid out in New Delhi. But the colonial powers did not stay beyond a decade to enjoy the new dream capital laid out in all its imperial splendour in what came to be called as New Delhi—a label that was intended to distinguish it from the symbols of monolithic, monarchical power of the Mughals situated not too far from the new capital.

The 1935 Act represented a new era in which politically and administratively attention shifted from the allocation of reserved (to be administered by the colonial overlords) and transferred subjects (to be administered by Indians) to the introduction of provincial autonomy. In administering the Act, financial devolution was a secondary issue and more importance was given to the political aspects. It was the first time that provincial governments were formed with the locally elected representatives of the people. It was an inevitable consequence of the relative neglect of the financial aspects that contributed to the beginning of the dependence of the provinces on the Centre for ad hoc grants, and grants for calamity expenditure. But this was very soon compensated by an independent award of the tax resources that were to be devolved to the provinces. That award, known as Niemeyer Award, arranged the share of the tax revenues to the provinces. This formula held sway even after independence, pending the adoption of the new constitution, and was applied to the post-partition situation.

The Niemeyer formula was revised, without affecting its integrity, by a member of the steel frame, who was then the Governor of the Reserve Bank of India, at the request of the central government. (He later became the third Finance Minister of independent India.) Post-war India, before it became a full-fledged republic, introduced many programmes, as a part of post-war reconstruction, for which grants were given by the central government. These programmes were evolved and managed by the Department of Reconstruction and Development, which in terms of the activities carried out by it was a precursor to the Planning Commission that came into being after independence. Many schemes for grants formulated by this department were carried out later by the Planning Commission with very little discontinuity.

The new constitution ushered in a phase of what came to be called as federal finance. Politically and financially, the constitutional arrangements envisaged the retention of large-scale powers in the

Centre. It had the powers to determine the boundaries and formation of states and to appoint the governors of states. It was also endowed with other extraordinary powers. Financially, for so long as a state government was indebted to the Centre, it had to obtain the approval of the latter for undertaking new borrowing from the market.

Meanwhile, the facility of the Reserve Bank to extend ways and means advances and overdrafts to the needy state governments continued. Broadly, the Reserve Bank was responsible for ensuring liquidity of the state governments as well as the liquidity of the treasuries, which functioned, in the absence of a rural banking network, as the repository of all payments made to and made by the governments—both central and state. There was an elaborate technical infrastructure of accounting inherited from the colonial era that facilitated the maintenance of central and state government accounts. Moneys due to the central government were recorded in suspense accounts and were later cleared through the exchange and settlement accounts maintained by the Accountant General of the Audit and Accounts Department attached to the state government. This department, which functioned under the Comptroller & Auditor General, the new office that came into being after the constitution, combined both the audit and accounts functions and continues to function that way to date.

The separation of accounts and the formation of a Civil Accounts Department was an arrangement that was applicable only to the central government. At the state level, there was, and continues to be, an unusual (but historically it was so arranged in colonial India) feature. The Accountant General (The designation was changed a few decades ago in an effort at being modern: it was a modernity that involved no change whatsoever in the function of the office) was appointed by the Auditor General and was an officer of the Accounts and Audit Department, but his task was to compile the accounts of the state and audit them. His tasks also involved assisting the state Public Accounts Committees of the legislature. The treasury responsible for all payments to and by the governments was a part of the state revenue administration. The initial accounts in the form of collection and maintenance of all basic records of payments were maintained by the treasuries, which later furnished those records to the Accountant General, who then compiled the monthly accounts.

The liquidity position of the treasury system was ensured by the Reserve Bank of India and as a part of this system, currency chests of the Reserve Bank were also kept at the treasuries. (This became a bone a contention in the early 1950s between the Madras government and the central government. Facing a liquidity crunch, the state government threatened to seize the currency chests if immediate assistance was not extended by the central government. The threat remained a threat and was not acted upon.)

The systemic limitations were not given serious consideration. The spur for greater activity and assumption of more responsibilities came from the development side, which became the new dimension of governance. It was as a part of that effort that several programmes were taken up both in anticipation of the First Five Year Plan and as an integral part of it. The programmes were designed by the central government.

On the financial side, some features of the grant system merit recognition. A clear distinction was made between budgetary support grants to eligible states (Article 275 of the Constitution) and other grants. The latter in turn (Article 282) were of two kinds—first, where the work of the central government was undertaken by the state government (such as police work or pre-passport verification, etc.) reimbursement of the expenses incurred was done through the grants.

There was another element which referred to the implementation of programmes that were a part of the assigned list of the tasks of the central government. These programmes were entirely funded by the central government. In administrative parlance, they were designated as centrally sponsored schemes. Second, there were other programmes which fell within the list of work assigned to the state governments. These schemes were known as centrally assisted. Their funding had two components—grant and loan. The financing composition of the schemes varied from one group to another. Although these schemes were, in principle, drawn up as a part of the "development from below" in consultation with the state governments, in practice, they had their origins in the staff work done by the central departments. Both the centrally sponsored and centrally assisted schemes had several conditions attached to them in that they were aimed at achieving the underlying development objectives. In addition there were also grants given to the states to compensate them for the maintenance expenditures incurred on the completed projects and programmes of the development plan.

Most central assistance—of both types, sponsored and assisted—was conceived as a part of the time slice of the development plan. Initially, it formed a part of the Five Year Plan. The recognition that completed projects and schemes ceased to be a part of the Plan at the end of the five-year period, and consideration was to be given for their financing, was an aspect that was thrust upon the central government by the political pressure mobilised by the state governments. The imagination of the newly formed Planning Commission did not extend to this area. Very soon, however, reflecting the new realities, these expenditures came to be called "committed expenditures". Since the Planning Commission did not provide for this, the task fell on the Second Finance Commission, which recommended grants for the purpose. In later years, i.e. from the Third Finance Commission onwards, committed expenditures were included by the state governments in their five-year budgetary forecasts submitted to the Finance Commission and their devolution formula was so devised as to include this element too.

Meanwhile, however, the dependence factor, and the mirror image of it, the dominance factor, came to be a new phenomenon that thrust itself on the national financial landscape. The programmes included in the Plan were mostly devised by the central ministries, which began to reflect a new flow of the development effort. Development began to be viewed as a national effort, primarily designed and directed by the central government. Although a National Development Council was formed providing a forum for the state governments to share their ideas and goals of development, very soon, it became a platform for relating their problems and grievances. At this stage, the political power in the country was largely monolithic in that power at the Centre and in the states was held until 1957 by the Congress Party. Kerala was a brief exception in that it elected to power a non-Congress government that was very soon replaced by the imposition of President's rule. More than the organisational aspect of power, the development effort reflected the overwhelming personality of the Prime Minister, who also doubled, infrequently though, as President of the Congress Party too. In essence, he was the presiding deity, both figuratively and in realty, of the National Development Council.

Meanwhile, the problems of grant-in-aid for centrally sponsored and assisted schemes came to be felt at the receiving end. The schemes were largely in the form of one-size-fits-all and were common to all regardless of their needs. As a Chief Minister wrote to the Prime Minister, he was given funds for anti-filaria campaign, which was not a problem in his state, but did not get funds for the control of malaria, a primary problem in his state. This separation of needs from what was on offer on the financial side generated a different set of problems that were not anticipated by the central planning authorities. Also, the programmes came with extensive conditionality, denying the cognate freedom of action for the constituent units of a federation. The state governments often became mute instruments of the central government. Moreover, the administrative design of the programmes imposed additional strains on the former.

The central government, for its part, took its sponsoring part much too seriously and began to view the state governments as implementing agencies rather than as equal partners. This became evident at every step of the implementation, for example, of the newly launched Community Development programme. It was a programme that envisaged a much-needed multidimensional development in the villages. The common man, as yet, was viewed, not as an urban denizen, but as a landless poverty-afflicted rural peasant who neither had potable water nor a private place to relieve himself. So, in their eagerness and rising ambition, the central officialdom moved in the direction of setting targets, establishing a comprehensive reporting system, and an evaluation organisation to evaluate the impact of the programme in the villages and on the people living there. It soon became apparent that the programme was driven in one way while the financial management processes, conventional and conservative as they were, followed a parallel track. The programme became lopsided in that the central government prescribed more than 300 reports to be furnished by the village level worker, the key official working at the village level interacting with the people and prodding them to action. The programme crumbled under its own weight, in that the number of reports to be furnished to the central government was higher than the number of working days in a year, leaving the officialdom little time for the real developmental work. An inevitable offshoot of the programme was the doctoring of the data claiming progress that only the officials recognised but not the people. In the process, the state governments became mere agencies of the central government, with little or no autonomy.

The financial releases for this and other programmes were painfully slow. In the first phase, the state governments had to defray the expenditure and claim the due quantum of central assistance later. It became a time-consuming task. Meanwhile, the state governments were subjected to severe financial stress and they spent more of their time in getting the money from the central government. It seemed, even in the phase of early development experience, that federalism was experiencing severe stress. The state governments did not, however, press the issue of autonomy in the management of the programme. For one reason, they belonged to the same political party as the one holding power at the Centre. For another, the full contours of the working of the scheme of central assistance were emerging into daylight only gradually. These factors contributed to several features that changed the pattern of central assistance in the following years. For one, the programme of Community Development was quickly given up, a victim, if that is what it was, of its ambition, primarily for the reason that it became unrealistic. The financial working of the central assistance programme was improved in that the reimbursement of the expenses incurred by the state governments was replaced by a system of advances under which tranches of estimated central assistance were released on a pro-rata basis for about ten months of the fiscal year and the remainder released after submitting a pro forma, ritualistic utilisation certificate. Also to relieve the financial stress, another category of assistance, that came to be known as "miscellaneous development loans", was introduced and moneys made available to the states. Moreover, it became obligatory for the state governments to have their Annual Plans approved by the Planning Commission at the Centre.

The introduction of these procedures was followed by interesting deviations and deceptive practices that implied compliance with the revised procedures. The state governments found it far easier to comply with the new regime of virtual subordination and surrender of implied autonomy for so long as their financial needs were met. The approval of the Annual Plans was intended to facilitate the determination of their outlay and to decide on the pattern of their financing. These two were crucially dependent on the amount of additional resource mobilisation (technical terms for the levy of new taxes and fees—shorthand for the annual revamping of revenue administration). As a part of this exercise, the Planning Commission and the state governments were to agree on the quantum of central assistance. In theory, this implied a dirigiste in which every nut and bolt and their place in the structural plan was specified. In practice, however, it turned out to be an innocent folk rite in which economics yielded place to politics. The states did not feel that the procedures of consultation were impinging on their autonomy. Rather, they used the process, including the apparent loss of functional autonomy, to their advantage. Thus, the Annual Plan consultations were leveraged to get higher levels of Plan outlays so that they could get more political mileage, as higher outlays were claimed to be resulting in higher development. Also, they did not want to get bogged down in the nitty-gritty of determining the central assistance which also required a good deal of investment of political capital. So, in an unusual development, they suggested that a part of the central assistance could be viewed as a fixed element, while the remainder was to be negotiated. Until then, each state was vying with others to exploit the situation to get a higher share, but now a part of the central assistance was going to be deleted from annual negotiations.

Thus, in what was known as the Gadgil Formula (named after the then Deputy Chairman of the Planning Commission and an eminent economist in his own right but who regrettably had only a short tenure in office), more than half of the cake of the central assistance was determined on the application of a formula that in turn was based on the backwardness and other indices of development. Very soon thereafter, the Annual Plan discussions degenerated into a one-day farce, a ritual that partook the nature of a one-day miracle, or a much-needed photo-opportunity. Thus, the working of the financial federalism went through any twist in that the lack of autonomy was compensated by improved heft in the determination of Annual Plan outlays. The states also recognised that the best compensation for declining autonomy was to promise more than could be delivered. Gaining more political weightage was more important, or so it seemed. But this apparent happy journey of dominance and dependence was not without its glitches. The first glitch came in the form of central loans to the state governments.

The central assistance programme involved both loans and grants. The loan element, the central government claimed, was primarily for the reason that it came from its own borrowing. Most state governments did not have adequate creditworthiness to borrow on their own from the market. In any event, under the constitutional arrangement, the state governments needed prior approval of the central government for borrowing from the public. The state governments needed to borrow from the market to finance their development finance. It was a soft alternative to the painful task of additional mobilisation of resources through taxation. Also, the burden of the state governments started to grow as they had to scramble for funds to finance the new Plan outlays and the growing administrative expenditure on the non-Plan side. The share of the central loans was a sizeable component of the growing expenditure. The state governments had to make their own matching contribution in order to receive central assistance. The cost escalation of the major projects contributed its own quota of pressures. To meet these growing burdens, the state governments began the practice of overdrafts from the Reserve Bank, which needed to be cleared in a short period in order to be eligible for further overdrafts. The central government had to step in, as a banker without being a bank, and provide additional money in a new form called miscellaneous development loans, a catch-all category that covered transactions other than central Plan assistance. The magnitude of these miscellaneous loans was dependent on the needs of the seeking state government and the terms were onerous and, in any event, were correlated to its repayment capacity. Also, getting these loans involved a lot of investment of political capital on the part of the state governments. If anything, this feature made the state governments even more dependent on the Centre and the irony was that the latter seemed to enjoy its new avatar as the lender of the last resort.

With the flux in time, the amount owed by the state governments began to mount steadily and the scene contributed to a new accounting fiction. The state governments began to liquidate their past debts to the Centre, at least in part, through the new loans they received from it. In short, the Centre was engaged in advancing more loans so that the states could repay the old loans and keep their record relatively clean. The odd feature, however, was that the magnitude of the overall central assistance grew substantially but much of it was returning to the central treasury, leading to a complaint by the state governments that the net transfer of resources was revealing a declining trend. The question ceased to be a political one but emerged as a major financial issue—the states needed relief from their debt pressures, and the Centre needed a way out without writing off the amounts. The alternative presented at the National Development Council by the mid-1960s was that the Centre should take over the major multipurpose projects whose financing needs were contributing to the states' growing indebtedness in the first place. The idea was, however, dropped, as it involved, what came to be called later, a moral hazard. The takeover, if administered, was not going to put the states on the path of financial rectitude. If anything, they were going to be more dependent on the Centre for financial assistance. The framers of the Indian Constitution did not certainly envision this mushrooming growth of complex financial issues, all stemming from the need for prior approval of the central government for the states undertaking borrowing from the market.

The situation, with all the accounting fiction that it involved, continued into the late 1990s. The issue of persistently mounting state debts was not addressed, as no senior official of the central Finance Ministry wanted to consider write-off during his/her watch. Meanwhile, on the international scene, efforts began to be made (thanks to the enthusiasm of a most unlikely avenue, *viz.*, a rock singer from Ireland) to take up "debt forgiveness" to be extended to poor African countries. In due course, the international financial institutions began to recognise the inevitability of debt write-off. They undertook it under a new programme, of course with new conditionalities, extending to a set of poor but highly indebted countries. Necessitated in part by this development and by political developments in parts of the country where secessionist movements began to gather momentum, the Centre was forced to write off portions of its loans to the states. What was but unthinkable a few years earlier, now became a reality, also demonstrating in the process that the central government had adequate discretionary power to go beyond the box and envisage much-needed radical solutions.

This did not, however, lessen the dependence of the state governments on the Centre, as new spending pressures were gathering speed. For example, the implementation of the Pay Commissions' new scales of pay called for large public outlays. At the request of the state governments, the Centre was willing to provide more money if they were willing to undertake structural adjustments in their management. These and other interventions illustrated the inherent flexibility in the system, if it could be used judiciously. The final nail in the coffin was provided by a recommendation of the Twelfth Finance Commission. It distinguished between the outstanding debt owed by the states to the Centre and the new borrowing that they could undertake from the market based on their own creditworthiness, thus removing the major hurdle between the states and the markets.

There were several contextual changes which paved the way for this change that converted dependence into freedom. For a starter, the passage of the Fiscal Responsibility and Budget Management (FRBM) legislation both by the Centre and the states suggested that the national governments and the sub-national governments could chart out a medium-term fiscal strategy on a rolling basis, and a commitment to adhere to that strategy. It was a new form of policy accountability that went beyond the conventional legislative accountability of debate and the work of the two financial committees. Second, the freedom to borrow from the markets but within the limits specified in the FRBM legislation gave a new impetus to the state governments to look inward and set their houses in order. Third, the substantial remittances from the denizens of some of the states working abroad in the Gulf and other regions provided additional stimulus to their economy outside the conventional development plans. And finally, the opening of the economy to direct foreign investment, and to loans and other forms of assistance from international and regional financial institutions, opened a new area of dialogue and brought sunlight to many areas that were hitherto opaque. In theory, the central government still had many levers to oversee the use of the new avenues by the state governments, but it tended to deploy them more selectively than before. Also, there was another change, which has not been given the recognition due. This is the fact that the assistance from the Planning Commission at the Centre came to be overshadowed by the statutory transfers envisaged by successive Finance Commissions. The budgetary support grant recommended by the Finance Commissions provided the much-needed cushion for the state governments.

These positive factors need, however, to be tempered by recognition of the conventional conditional assistance provided through the Planning Commission. The development programmes taken up as parts of the five-year plans and related central assistance were conditional and specific. In its anxiety to oversee the implementation of development, the Planning Commission formulated conditions that were too elaborate, with such a strong ring fencing, that they allowed little flexibility at the receiving end. That said, it should also be recognised that compliance had its own leakages.

The experience of the last six decades shows clearly that in the name of fiscal oversight, the central government strengthened its own financial power substantially. As a consequence, the state governments lost their limited freedom and became dependent on the Centre, becoming regular supplicants for federal funds for purposes that transcended the developmental needs. The roles of the sub-national governments in the national plans were assigned by the central government, though formally approved by the National Development Council in which the state governments were also members. To that extent there was an appearance of partnership and joint responsibility, but in reality the latter were mostly engaged in role playing. Decision-making was concentrated in the central government, even to the extent that local issues were frequently brought up, that would normally have been dealt with at the sub-national level. Administrative decision-making thus reflected the highly centralised financial arrangements. It appeared frequently that the higher power acquired or embedded in the situation was something that the central departments relished, in the knowledge that the expansion of the central ministries was entirely the result of the dominant role that they assigned to themselves. In theory, the central programmes provided ample room for the views of, and occasional lobbying by, the state governments but the latter had no illusions about their own role. The dependence had other effects too.

Part of the dependency attitude of the state governments had its origins in the approaches of the central government, which never conceded its own preferences. Its preference was to secure economic development first. To this end it was always willing to press its own political advantage and financial muscle. These two in combination gave the Centre an overwhelming power base from which it could dictate, and it dictated to the point that the autonomy of the states was never an issue. The state governments, for their part, were also anxious to secure as much of central assistance as possible and at any cost. It saved them from mobilising revenue resources at their own level, given that the levy of new taxes or upward revision of the existing taxes would not make them politically popular. If central assistance reduced their own freedom to act and flexibility to adjust, and converted them into routine compliance with what the Centre wanted, it was, in their view, a small price to pay. Instead of undertaking the risky course of raising taxes, they began to invest their political capital to secure more funds from the Centre. It was dependence, they must have reasoned, that was remunerative, and politically advantageous in the short term. In the long term, as the economist J.M. Keynes noted, with his tongue firmly in his cheek, we are all dead.

But it needs to be emphasised that the whole process contributed to a total subordination that robbed the state governments of their initiative and the capacity to deal with the local needs and issues from their perspective: the only valid currency was the point of view of the Centre, which was overly conscious of its advantages in the game. As these approaches continued with only a rare, *pro forma* demur from the state government, and history or experience or the acceptance of the precedent, all of which have a powerful role in government, contributed to the process of central assistance becoming too complex, and the triumph of process over purpose became a common occurrence. The process also suffered from the growing complexity of the assistance schemes. By the end of the century, there were 261 programmes that were under the supervision of the Planning Commission. This too contributed to avoidable anomalies, considerable overlap and distortions. In their anxiety to spread their wings and influence, the central departments did not recognise that all of them were thinking alike and taking too similar initiatives. The overlap among the schemes came to be noted only after prolonged and frequent criticism from the state governments.

Ideally, in that situation, the Centre would be expected to seize the initiative and revamp the whole system. Such a revamping could have involved a rationalisation of the schemes of assistance, changing the loan/grant ratios of programmes, converting specific, conditional grants into general grants for broad groups of schemes, and introducing a degree, however small, of decentralisation. Toward the end of the previous century, there was a movement in the direction of decentralisation (in addition to transparency and accountability) and the implementation of the principle of subsidiarity. This principle had its origins in the ecumenical instruction issued by the Vatican. The principle stated that it was a sin for a higher authority to do what a lower authority was expected to do. The then chairman of the European Commission, a French socialist but by faith a Roman Catholic, endorsed this warmly in the management of the supranational authority of Europe. This also became the new mantra of the administrations in various countries. India, which always excelled in canvassing for borrowed innovations, lost no time in supporting the new philosophy.

What followed was the appointment of committees, which were naturally headed by the Cabinet Secretary at the Centre (There were only Chief Secretaries in the states but not a Cabinet Secretary until one was appointed by a newly elected lady Chief Minister in Uttar Pradesh) to deliberate on the matter. They did that task with the usual diligence (or, as some point out, inertia) and undertook a regrouping of the schemes into more meaningful clusters that in principle gave more flexibility in the use of funds. The reduction in the number of schemes was, however, nominal. Also, the two major issues that arose in this context were left unaddressed. The conversion of specific and conditional grants into broad-based groups of general grants was not taken up for consideration. There was also no reconciliation of the vocal emphasis on decentralisation with the creeping centralisation and its concomitant effects. The appropriateness of the discussion of "sin" (arising from the regular violations of the subsidiarity principle) was not taken up, presumably because the "sin" already accumulated by the central departments was so heavy that even a few pilgrimages to Benaras, Haridwar, Amritsar, Mecca, or the Holy Land could not have extinguished it. In the event, the effort at rationalisation was more in the nature of an eyewash. Overall, the impression generated was that no serious effort was being made to analyse the impact of the existing patterns of assistance and the stultifying effect that these had on the capacities of the state governments. Regardless of political affiliations, the general view of the state governments was that the design of economic development was such that the states had become, partly out of their volition but mostly because of the biased systems, subordinate to the Centre, making redundant their own legislatures and constitutional arrangements for governance. The alternative often suggested was that an effort should be made to make the states own the idea of development and treat all programmes as their own. The idea, an appealing one on paper, had no real merit and thus did not lead to any less frustration on the part of the state. Every programme is the end result of a lot of policy churning and it is difficult to pinpoint its fatherhood. In any event, it is not the idea but it is the associated financial arrangement that demeans the state governments and robs them of legitimacy in their cognate sphere of action.

This, however, is not the case with the other main actor specified in the Constitution. The Finance Commission is a body which comes but once in five years. Its membership is believed to sponsor a quasi-judicial approach to financial matters. To ensure this, traditionally one of the members of the commission was drawn from the judiciary. In the case of the Fourth Finance Commission, 1961-1965, the chairman was a retired Chief Justice of Madras state. His interest in the subject was such that he deemed it appropriate to add a supplementary report to the commission's report with a view to explaining the legality and thus the legitimacy of the arrangements specified in the Constitution. The first few commissions also had a member drawn from the political class to bring to bear the common man's point of view on their proceedings. In fact, at least three commissions were headed by members of the political class—one was a former Chief Minister and later a minister in the central cabinet, while the two others were purely creatures of the central cabinet. The commissions used to go around the states rather than the states reaching the nation's capital, though the procedure was partially changed depending on the convenience of the chairman of the commission. The state governments expend enormous effort to ensure intellectual coherence to their argument. The arguments are heard, given due weightage, and the result of the deliberations are submitted to the President of India. So far, there has been no major dispute on the commissions' findings. In one case, however, the findings of the majority of the commission, including its chairman, were rejected, and the note of dissent prepared by its member-secretary was accepted. That instance alone was enough to demonstrate that on occasion, the Centre accepts only that point of view which is palatable to it.

The grants-in-aid devised by the Finance Commission are specifically tailored to the fiscal needs of each state. Even when it makes specific grants, i.e., conditional as is the case with the Planning Commission's assistance programme, the quantum is adjusted to meet the fiscal needs of each state. The commission is obliged, by virtue of the provisions in the Constitution, to develop its philosophy of the scheme of grants-in-aid recommended by it. In the case of the first few commissions, there were very few conditional grants. It is only from about the Eighth Commission that some grants, fairly negligible, became conditional. In at least one case, for example, the computerisation of the state treasury system, the need for such grant, which was more in the realm of the Planning Commission, was not obvious. Gradually, however, the commissions expanded the scope of their grants. From being the arbiter to determine the budgetary support grant for deserving states, they moved into quasi-developmental grants, and finally, as in the case of the Thirteenth Finance Commission, an agent for ensuring fiscal stability was established through the introduction of an incentive grant system if the levels of deficit were not exceeded. The conditions and their implementation in this regard were guided more by a system of honour, for there is no looking over the shoulders of state governments to verify whether the grants were utilised for the stated purposes. There was also no problem of its "committed expenditures", as the outlays incurred over the grant-aided services were included as a part of regular outlays in the forecasts submitted to the Finance Commissions and were thus eligible for the financing envisaged by them.

To some extent, this was also true of the Plan programmes that reached their "sunset" at the end of the five-year plan period. The state governments were saved from the submission of utilisation certifications, which in any event provided only a fig leaf of evidence of the amount spent. What was most significant is the fact that the gravitas shifted from the Planning Commission to the Finance Commission in that a major portion of the financial sources reaching the states was from the recommendations of the Finance Commission. While this did not materially change the financial dependence of the states on national resources (the states continue to get more than 65 per cent of their resources from these arrangements), the fact that they were general grants and thus gave more flexibility and responsibility to the state governments altered both the perception and reality of dependence. As an extension, the dominance of the central government became less and the long shadows cast earlier became less distinct.

It is becoming clear that the effects of dependency have come to be recognised rather implicitly and some changes have been taking place by stealth. No government will admit in public that its processes were spawning a culture of dependency and that it also revealed "a desire for dominance": such admission would further erode the little credibility it has. That said, a curious feature of this dependency should also be noted. If the state governments have been complaining about the dependence (It is possible that like Sisyphus, they enjoyed that experience), they do not seem to have recognised that their treatment of local governments is no different from the approach of patronage and uncertainty of financial releases that characterises the relationship between them and the Centre.

In reality, the dependence of the local governments is far more acute than the relationship between the state and the Centre. In the central-state nexus, the number of participants is limited. In the case of local governments, the number is much higher and the technical infrastructure of consultations is much less formal (apart from the State

Finance Commissions, whose appointment became mandatory after the 73rd amendment to the constitution) and less transparent. The issues, being local, are deemed to be the issues of a few. The representatives of the local government have come to be dependent on what the state finance departments have come to believe is their munificence. The releases are at the discretion of the state government and are not predictable. The local governments' work tends to suffer because of this unpredictability. To some extent, this has been relieved by direct transfers from the Centre to the local governments. In the case of a few programmes, the entire annual outlay was transmitted in a single tranche. Moreover, the submission of the utilisation certificate by the local governments, an eligibility criterion before the release of funds, is more of a formality as all that it involved is clearance from the chartered accountant entrusted with the audit of those funds.

The problem of dependence came to be realised by some state governments and they began to alter the patterns of assistance. The government of Kerala, for one, shifted from the specific conditional grants to general assistance and left the powers of utilisation to the initiative of the local governments. This implied a belated recognition that the local needs vary from one locality to another, and the best way of contributing to their development is to allow them to address their own requirements. Gone in the process are the so-called oversight of the state finance departments. The release of authority to spend has enhanced the participation of the stakeholders and the process of accountability. It has also demonstrated that local initiatives, which are now encouraged, can lead to a successful introduction of a decentralised form of government.

From the expenditure management point, the point of departure made by the Kerala government has ushered in a new pattern of administration. Over the years, the links between the central, state and local governments, in the realm of finances, have become so many that a considerable overlap has come about among the various levels and the distinguishing lines have blurred. Now, while the source of funds continues to be most centralised (more than 80 per cent of the local resources come from the central and state governments), the utilisation part of the task has been left to the initiative and imagination of the local leadership. It has been noted in an earlier section that the difference between allocation and resource utilisation and consequent warped outcomes was the result of a skewed pattern of management.

Liberating the local governments from this dependence framework is only one step. More steps are needed if the national complementarity among the central, state and local governments is to be supplemented by an expenditure management system that is truly decentralised.

9

Crises and Renewal

Evaluation of a deep-rooted system of management is a delicate exercise and also an essential one. The current system of governmental management in India traces its antecedents to the tentative steps taken by the East India Company in the years of its infancy. Later it went through a series of unforeseen strains and stresses and the government as an organisation was buffeted by several crosswinds. Administrators often wake up wondering what the new dawn has in store for them. All these have a discernible impact on the way in which government organisations work. Although each organisation has its own objectives and work programmes to attend to, some of them have more, profound, and an enduring impact on the lives of people. What organisations in government do is as important, paradoxically, as what they do not do. They are the biggest organisations in the country, employing more than twenty million workers, ranging from sweepers (the only professional category mentioned in the Official Handbook of the government; the other groups are mentioned in terms of their pay categories, such as A, B, C, D) to the highest level of policy-making.

While government organisations are, in theory, expected to be objective, fair and anonymous, in practice, in course of time all the three features have changed their colours, reflecting the changing political environment. Government organisations are no longer deemed to be objective, as many of their personnel are deemed to have compromised themselves with their hidden collusion with vested interests. The presence and activities of these lobbies are, though not transparent, no longer hidden. Some of them have extraordinary clout and their money bags testify to their growing influence and power. Some of them, as recent revelations suggest, have even an influence in the formation of the cabinet and in the allocation of ministerial portfolios.

The fairness of government organisations is also raising more eyebrows than in the past. Administrative decisions are contributing to the establishment of oligarchies and numerous fiefdoms. In the process, the very political foundations that reflect the inalienable links and bonds between the people and their institutions are changing. Reliance on administrative decisions, rather than market discipline, has altered the way in which government organisations work.

The organisations have also ceased to be anonymous. When governments were working in an environment when the Fourth Estate was dominated by the print media, the public hardly knew who the Principal Secretary of the first Prime Minister was. (His photograph or name rarely appeared in print.) Now with the virtual displacement of the print media by the electronic media, there has been a sea-change in the situation. It is the publicity that the administrative class craves or gets without its urging that is the dominant feature of the day. Even in those areas where decisions are yet to be reached, the media are abuzz with speculation, or "reliably learnt" guesses, or substitution of public judgement for the private decisions. The public is often at a loss to distinguish the grain from the chaff.

These factors have contributed, inevitably, to changes in the way in which government organisations work. They are under the constant glare of the media, and to appease the hungry news hounds, policies are made on the spur of the moment. What passes for government policies then are, in reality, knee-jerk reactions. The hard part, as a consequence of the displacement of known traditions by as yet nascent departures, is that government organisations are under varying degrees of strain and stress.

The growing pace of globalisation has also had its own impact on the functioning of government agencies. They are called upon to make quick decisions, be it a tax on a multinational company which is using its financial clout by employing highly paid attorneys, or the payment of a subsidy to a major industrial house, or the determination of the price of a commonly used commodity like onions or natural gas (Both have a tendency to incite public riots in urban centres and tectonic shifts in political alignments) or the acceptance of the recommendations of the latest Pay Commission that affect the millions of people who ostensibly serve the public (and there were cases when decisions were taken in the most flippant manner, with the Finance Minister abstaining from participation in the proceedings) and on numerous other matters. The viability of the policies they make adds strength to the organisations; and ineptitude, on the other hand, not merely weakens them but leads to periodic crises that severely erode their credibility. Once credibility is lost, the effectiveness of government organisations is also lost. The crisis is followed by sustained efforts to bring them back to life. Survival for organisations is as vital as it is to the human race and the animal kingdom.

The system of public expenditure management is not an exception to the organisational cycle. As of now it appears, if government announcements are any indication, to be creeping through an existential crisis. It is no longer disputed that the system is in the throes of a crisis. The causes of the decline and ineffectiveness are to be found in both external and internal developments, and in organisational factors, and traditions, as well as administrative cultures. Organisations such as the Finance Ministry/Department have been there for centuries, and have spawned their values and distinctive features that have influenced the patterns of expenditure management. The values too changed as expenditure management moved from counting paise and compiling their accounts, to a recognised major role in achieving economic stability. That long journey has also contributed to a new path where the public, being at the receiving end of the effects and outcomes of expenditure management, has also been engaged in forming its own perceptions. A combination of organisational and traditional factors and changing public perceptions has contributed to an expansion of the criteria for evaluation. It is no longer a matter simply of a narrow judgement of the organisation. More constructively, it involves the assessment of the role of expenditure management in serving society and in being a part of society's life.

From society's point of view, all governance systems deserve to be adjudged in terms of three criteria, all of which are larger than life but have a substantial impact on how a society, developing or developed, looks at its own needs. The first consideration is whether the systems of government, including the system of expenditure management, have reduced social conflicts and promoted social harmony. The various layers of society have varying needs, and they look to the public bodies to address them. These needs are broadly group needs; and the needs of one group may be met, given the shortage of resources, only by denying the needs of another group. This effort at managing the embedded conflict in society is generally undertaken through the participation of elected representatives in the functioning of the legislatures. Elected representatives vote for their needs. The eventual allocation of resources is done through voting and the majority gets its votes to determine the extent to which their needs are met. This process leading to the allocation of resources is, both at its heart and in the style in which it functions, essentially political in character. It has been so for centuries, even when the forms of government were non-democratic. The role of expenditure management in this context is twofold. The first is to supplement the political process through a comprehensive analysis of the implications of various needs and their funding arrangements and thus clarify, for the political decision-maker, the likely benefits that will flow from the proposals to society—in short, explain how society stands to be benefited. The second function of expenditure management, as illustrated in the preceding sections, is to ensure that the allocated resources are utilised for the stated purposes. The actions of the expenditure management system determine the extent to which society benefits from the preceding two phases. Implicit in this process is the constant endeavour to resolve the conflicts in society and bring about a modicum of order.

Second, it could be argued that the first criterion may make many tall demands on the expenditure management system. It could also be argued, on the other hand, that the societal conflicts can now be fully resolved in a heterogeneous, multi-cultural society like that of India, with more than four hundred political parties seeking to represent it. The second criterion thus reduces the broad questions to more manageable proportions in that it seeks to answer them within a specified dimension of time and space. In participating in the elections once in five years, the voter raises and seeks to answer the question—once his personal predilections and preferences for caste, liquor and money as inducements to change his voting preferences are decided upon—whether he is better off or worse off than before. His preference for change depends on how he evaluates the benefits, no doubt from a self-centric standpoint, from public outlays.

Admittedly, there is a substantial herd mentality in voting on public issues. But it has also to be recognised that the voters reveal a good deal through their electoral choices. Those choices offer a sufficient basis to attempt an anecdotal assessment of the effectiveness of the expenditure management system. They also indicate whether the system is in a crisis; and if it is, then ways have to be found to resolve the crisis. On the other hand, available evidence suggests that people could also be indifferent to the expenditure management system and may be apathetic to further involvement. It should be parenthetically noted that this was indeed the case when a finance minister (V.P. Singh, who subsequently became the Prime Minister for a brief period) sought the views of the people as to how the expenditure process of the government might be improved. The underlying attempt was to make the system more responsive to the demands or views of the people. The invitation for suggestions proved infructuous, as the response was nothing but a long silence.

Any number of reasons could be adduced for this studied silence. But it also needs to be recognised that the reform of the expenditure management process has, by default, always been a bureaucratic rather than a political process. Problems were recognised by the bureaucrats and solutions were also proposed by them. Since their attitudes to reform were influenced, to a substantial degree, by the extent to which the proposed reform would not disturb the existing situation to their disadvantage, they ended up introducing reforms that did not envisage any wholesale change in their status or functioning. In turn, their actions were approved by the political class, who are perceived as not having any technical views of their own. These aspects illustrate the limitations inherent in any evaluation exercise; but they do not fundamentally negate the utility of an evaluation as such.

The third criterion for adjudging governance systems, from society's point of view, is to evaluate them in terms of an ends-and-means framework. The objective of an independent India has always been to seek to establish a just society with just means. While the objective was always clear, there was less clarity on what the just means are. The terms could be interpreted both in political and administrative terms. Politically, the implicit faith was that a just society would be achieved through the assurance that each individual would be guaranteed the fundamental freedoms and that in that framework, governments would aim at providing the basic needs for improving the standards of living of society while ensuring that there was an economical, efficient and effective use of its resources.

These considerations are raised here, not so much to carry out a systematic evaluation of the expenditure management system, but to provide a philosophical base to determine whether the system is in a crisis. Since no attempt is made to cover society as a whole, all that is proposed to be done is to examine the issue from the perception of the common citizen, the quintessential representative of society.

The question may be raised whether perceptions alone provide an adequate justification for assessing the effectiveness and broad role of the administrative machinery. Perceptions, it may be argued, may depend on fleeting moments and may reflect the individual's predilection rather than the reality; that the experience may be personal, narrow and biased; and that there is often a Roshomon effect in the individual's perceptions, and the final story that emerges may be warped to some degree. In the individual's intellectual make-up, however, perceptions are a first step, followed by feelings, followed next by action. This continuum is a part of the make-up of an individual. William James[1] wrote in the nineteenth century that the bodily states follow perception, and feelings, the first perception being "purely cognitive in form, pale, colorless, destitute of emotional wealth". Impulses are primary and their effective manifestations are secondary. The argument that man is rational is applicable, under this approach, to a later stage. In this secondary stage, man may apply reason and take action. Perceptions tend, however, to dominate thinking.

It may be added in this context that the compilation of the annual corruption index by Transparency International is based on opinion or perception surveys. A single incident is enough to colour judgement and the action that follows from it. Thus, notwithstanding all its limitations as an analytical tool, perception is still relevant as it tends to dominate the determination of the action eventually taken. The perception may not be purely personal but may reflect group thinking when an individual is a part of a group that is going through an experience. The formation of a perception may also not be a one-sided affair in that it depends on the actions of the important "other" in the experience. *Vis-à-vis* the State, an individual's perception is dependent on what the State does and does not. If it does nothing or is merely drifting, looking for a policy, still the phenomenon forms a basis for a perception.

There is no perception on governance, if there is no State. That may be one reason why the Adivasis, or the original inhabitants who are dubbed by the Indian constitution as scheduled tribes (a description that is far from complimentary and yet is an integral part of daily discourse and the law of the country), may not have a perception on the State,

1. James, William (1890). *The Principles of Psychology, New York:* Henry Holt & Co. p.449

for they are, in principle, remote from the actions of the State. An Adivasi has, however, a perception, when the reality strikes him in the form of State action to displace him from his abode, to make place for submersion that will be caused by the construction of a dam to serve the cause of development for the benefit of the larger society.

The perception of the past and current generations may be substantially influenced by myths[2]. Thus, the concept of Ram Rajya dominated the perceptions and thinking of the Father of the Nation at the time of India's independence. It continues to form a political goal for a few political parties in the country. It is, however, not a very practical idea for the simple reason that Rama never explained his approach to governance.[3] It is adequate for this discussion to recognise that myths have decisive influence on the perceptions of people.

No attempt is made here to chart a chronological development of the Indian state. Rather, the intent is limited to note the changing patterns of the perceptions of the people on the State, and the state of its governance. It therefore starts with the colonial administration whose laws and administrative approaches continue to dominate governance in India. The system has, however, gone through major changes in that numerous other tasks generally associated with a welfare state have been added to the tasks of government (See Table 9.1).

The systems of governance that were in force during the colonial period were systems of convenience that were intended to serve the needs of the colonial power. The colonial power was very successful in translating and applying the "danda" principle of governance enunciated in the classics of Indian statecraft, *viz.*, Manu's laws and Kautilya's

2. For a cogent discussion of the myth of the State, see the classic by Cassirer, Ernst (1946). *The Myth of the State.* New Haven and London: Yale University Press. Cassirer's work, however, is largely a discussion of Western philosophers and their thought.

3. In Valmiki's *Ramayana,* there are only three occasions when Rama explains his and people's duty, other than the starting point of the obligation to follow one's father's wishes (a resounding endorsement of the principle of patriarchy). The first is when Bharata, his brother and the pro-tem ruler of the state, visits him in the forest where Rama is staying with Sita and Lakshmana. Without even raising the usual pro forma well-being questions, Rama asks Bharata, not so much as a question but as a process of validation of his presumptions, what he has been doing. The second occasion is when, after the death of Vali, Sugriva the new king asks Rama how he should rule. Rama's answer is simple and direct. "Rule them as a mother would look after her children." The third is when he meets Sita, for the first time after her liberation, and proposes that she should go through the tests to set at rest the possible wrong perceptions of the people. It was a process of internalising the people's voice in his rule.

Table 9.1

India: Administrative Evolution—From Colonial Regime to Date

↑	Citizen-oriented administration: Empower
↑	Beginning of a hollow state: Emphasis on contracting out and PPPs with corporate sector; issues of market experimentation
↑	• Emergence of a new face of governance
	• Committed bureaucracy
	• Fundamental duties of citizens
	• Authoritarianism; stricter laws and curtailed civil liberties
↑	Soft state: Management issues
↑	Emphasis on state's role and efforts to address major administrative issues—issues in Indian versions of socialism
↑	• Development-oriented regime with emphasis on state ownership
	• State involvement in science and technology
↑	Constitutional regime
↑	Post-independence quasi-colonial regime
↑	Colonial regime

Arthashastra. It was the fear of punishment that made the people law abiding. There were actions such as famine relief programmes, irrigation works, establishment of a transport network, and the foundation of an educational system. They had the intended benefit for the people, while serving the interests of the colonial power. The people were under no illusion about the intent of the colonial power (or the vestigial laws that are in force even now). Within this broad framework, people pursued their own economic and financial interests. Thus, over a period, they gained entry into the administrative system, first as "babus" or writers (the Secretariat in Kolkata is still known as Writers Building) and later as members of the armed forces, though entry into commissioned ranks came decades later. Opportunities came to be opened gradually. The investment in transportation network, in particular in the establishment of Indian Railways, witnessed large-scale internal migration of labour within British India. Very soon, this was followed by movement of indentured labour to other British colonies such as Burma (then), Ceylon (then), Fiji, Caribbean islands and others. In all this the main feature of governance was that all the initiatives were taken by the government.

Although there were political movements, particularly after the 1920s, aimed at securing self-rule, they did not have much impact on the way in which people channelled their desires, needs, anxieties and insecurities. The onset of the Second World War brought about major changes in the economy. Shift of materials for war needs contributed to shortages in the economy and there was rationing of foodstuffs in the urban centres. There were also massive failures. The Bengal famine, in which millions died, was a consequence of those failures. The war gave an impetus to the economy: but there was also the emergence of a "black market", which everybody knew existed, but could do nothing about.

These events were followed by partition and independence. The attention of the new government was focused on addressing the consequences of partition, in particular the displacement of people and the dislocation in economic activities. The administrative challenges that the infant government faced were many. These could not be called crises, as barring a few, they were not of a sustained character or prolonged. They are best considered as administrative challenges in the context of changing policies and economic structures. These challenges continue to be faced to date. It is only natural that governments, for so long as they exist, will continue to face challenges . With a view to providing an essential background to a discussion of the changes in the pattern of administration and the ways in which the presumed needs of the people, basic and others, were met by the governments in India over the decades these are stated synoptically in Table 9.2.

Table 9.2

Administrative Reform: Challenges and Response

Period	*Challenges*	*Response*
1947-1965	• Refugees	• Rehabilitation and resettlement
	• Political consolidation	• Integration of states
	• Civil services	• Reorganisation
	• Corruption	• Enactment of legislation
		• Limits and monitoring of acquisition of assets by civil servants
	• Economic development	• Establishment of Planning Commission
		• Beginning of a new process
	• State involvement in science and technology	• Establishment of a National Chain of Laboratories
		• Changing the defence profile in technology
	• Development of rural India	• Community Development Programme
	• Management of state enterprises	• Establishment of an Industrial Management Pool
		• Centralised monitoring of enterprises
	• Improved internal management in departments and agencies	• Establishment of Organisation and Management Units
		• Delegation of enhanced financial powers to departments
		• Introduction of measures aimed at improving efficiency in Plan projects
1965-1975	• Corruption	• Appointment of Administrative Reforms Commission
		• Appointment of ombudsman machinery (Lok Pal and Lokayuktas)
		• Appointment of Vigilance Commissions and Anti-Corruption Bureaus
	• Improved democratic governance	• Establishment of Panchayati Raj Institutions

	• Improved governance	• Introduction of performance budgeting as a supplementary measure • Streamlining personnel management through the introduction of a revised performance reporting and monitoring system • Rationalisation of the management of state-owned enterprises • Improved coordination between central and state governments
1975-1990	• Citizen empowerment	• Inculcating responsibility and social discipline in the people–constitutional amendment carried out • New patterns of local government introduced • Creation of new states to avoid allegations of internal colonialism • Post-Emergency measures to restore normalcy
1990-2013	• Citizen empowerment	• Right to Information legislation enacted
	• Management of a liberal economy	• Old system of controls replaced • India's own new management philosophy • Appointment of Second Administrative Reforms Commission
	• Internal reorganisation	• Introduction of e-governance • Establishment of websites for all agencies • Introduction of outcome budgeting • Revised performance review system in government and budget-neutral incentive system • Strategic human resource management
	• Hollow State	• Selective privatisation • Public-private partnerships • Contractorisation of selective tasks • Strengthening of regulatory framework
	• Improved policy management	• Fiscal Responsibility and Budget Management legislation

A few features of the developments may be noted. First, all the changes reflected the initiatives of governments. People had very little to do with the changes, though, to be historically accurate, there was a People's Plan for economic development prepared during the period immediately preceding independence. But the people, or the common man, had very little to do with it. In fact what comes out of the historical experience is that the people, despite being at the receiving end of all government actions, gave very little thought to the means, other than political, that needed to be devised to address their own needs. The means, it was felt, were to be devised by the administrators who were managing the government. In effect, it meant that the government was engaged in treating itself for all the maladies created by it and identified by it in the first place. Neither the people nor their elected representatives contributed anything of significance either to the debate or to the formulation of remedial measures.

The political parties, particularly the Congress Party, had an informal two-item agenda to serve the people. One was the establishment of a Ram Rajya, a kind of a myth or utopia, about whose content nobody was clear, except for the end product, which was to make the people happier. As an inspiring notion it continues to have sway on sections of the people and their memories, as well as demands, which are stirred up at the time of elections. Second, the aim was to make the civil services more civil and service-oriented. Here again there were very few specifics about how those twin objectives were to be achieved. The task was left to the domestic experts, and the visiting experts, who provided a series of reports. Despite the growing awareness[4] and greater availability of literature, the formulation of specifics continued to be elusive.

It is small wonder then that the government opted for continuity of the inherited traditions, structures and administrative cultures. It was a time when there were no "witch doctors", otherwise known as technical experts. As a result, the aloof, distant and generally imperious attitude continued though the "subjects" now became the people and members

4. The lack of general awareness of the intricacies of public administration may in part be ascribed to the fact that public administration was not a separate subject taught in Indian universities. To the extent that it was taught at all, it was as a part of Political Science, and more specifically, the Constitution, Parliament, and the Cabinet Government. Financial Administration, as it was then called, did not receive much attention. The literature was limited, and some of it was contributed by serving or retired officials of the government.

of a community. It was at the same time deemed essential to elicit the views of the people for running the administration of the country. The first President of the Indian Republic, who was also the President of the Constituent Assembly, drew pointed attention, in both capacities, to this need. He said in 1949, "Whatever the constitution may or may not provide, *the welfare of the country will depend on the way in which the country is administered.* That will depend upon the men who administer it" (emphasis added). Another occasion to drive home this point came when the Prime Minister wrote to him expressing a sense of satisfaction with the way in which his government was functioning. In reply, the President wrote (on 18 December 1959), "It is not enough that you are satisfied that all is well. *A popular government's duty is to give satisfaction to the people also*" (emphasis added).[5]

There were several dimensions to installing a system of improved governance to secure the satisfaction of society. It was, however, becoming increasingly evident, as Machiavelli pointed out in his *The Prince,* that the ruler who aspires to provide public security and good government must be prepared to compromise on his own values so that "taking everything into account, he will find that some of the things that appear to be virtues will, if he practises them, ruin him, and some of the things that appear to be wicked, will bring him security and prosperity". This aspect was becoming evident in another sphere as well.

This contributed to the third feature, i.e. growth of corruption. Corruption is not by any means new. It was there a long time ago primarily because of the large gap between what leaders professed to do and what they did in practice. Thucydides noted several centuries ago that "such things have occurred and will always occur so long as the nature of mankind remains the same. The leaders in cities made the fairest professions. On one side with the cry of political equality of the people, on the other of a moderate aristocracy, but they sought prizes for themselves in those public interests which they preferred to cherish." Centuries later, a young Prime Minister, who came to that position in the wake of the assassination of his mother and the previous Prime Minister, and attained the highest majority in Parliament, noted, in an address to the Congress Party that "millions of ordinary Congress workers are handicapped for on their backs ride the brokers of power

5. The correspondence is available in the Nehru Memorial Museum and Library, New Delhi, in the volumes of correspondence of the first Prime Minister of India.

and influence who dispense patronage to convert a mass movement into a feudal oligarchy. Corruption is not only tolerated but even regarded as a hallmark of leadership." As a description of the growing national malaise, it was a precise and prescient statement.

Corruption had a hallowed history in British India. During the eighteenth century, Warren Hastings, the Governor General, was impeached in the British Parliament for corruption but was exonerated when he pleaded that he should be judged on the financial performance of the East India Company, which under his leadership reached very high levels. The lack of a punishment in his case contributed to a situation where the lower officials exploited the situation, particularly in the Madras Presidency, where in their dealings with the nawabs, they made personal benefit their primary goal. The phenomenon was never absent but was a constant feature. Efforts were made to address the situation to include the broadest possible definition of corruption as Section 161 of the Indian Penal Code. Available evidence also indicates that the new laws did not prove an adequate deterrent to the growth of corruption in the country. Table 9.3 provides a quick glance into the efforts made in India, commencing with the colonial times and until recently, to curb corruption.

The first known major case in independent India involving corruption was the deal to buy jeeps (hence it came to be known as the jeep scandal) for the Army from British suppliers, in which there were allegations of payment of kickbacks. The episode brought to light the possibilities inherent in the procurement process for corruption. Such corrupt practices were extensively prevalent during the Second World War. The growth of corruption and the efforts to contain it have been the two main constants of Indian administrations. That these efforts were far from successful is evident from the facts presented in Table 9.4.

What is also evident is that the expenditure management system failed to cope with the growth in expenditures. Effectiveness apart, these scams illustrated the growing abuse of the management processes of public money. While it is difficult to say what the future has in store, it is clear that the enactment of new legislation and the establishment of new machinery have not contributed, from the citizen's point of view, to a discernible improvement in the situation. The scale of efforts initiated to detect fraud in public transactions has not yielded, at least so far, commensurate results. This also raises issues about the adequacy of existing legislation, and the capacity of the expenditure management machinery to deal with corruption in all its manifestations.

Table 9.3

Landmarks in Addressing Corruption

1770s	Impeachment of Warren Hastings
1840	Inclusion of the broadest legal definition of corruption in the Indian Penal Code (Section 161)
1947	The Prevention of Corruption Act 1947
1960s	• Establishment of government commissions to enquire into allegations of corruption by the Chief Ministers • Appointment of the Administrative Reforms Commission and a beginning toward the establishment of Indian versions of ombudsman machinery
1980s	The Prevention of Corruption Act 1988 • Powers to enquire into acquisition of disproportionate assets • Extended powers to police to carry out raids • Appointment of Special Judges • Specification of a punishment schedule Others: establishment of anti-corruption bureaus • CBI to look into corruption cases Judiciary: • Avenues to file Public Interest Litigation in courts • Vigilance Commissions • Economic Offences courts
21st century	Citizen empowerment: • Right to Information Act 2005

Table 9.4

Scams in the Country

Year	*Number*	*Amount involved (in ₹ crore)*
2005	52	19,426
2006	58	16,367
2007	34	11,249

Source: Kumar, Arun (2013). *Indian Economy since Independence*. New Delhi: Vision Books.

Fourth, the growing availability of alternatives to government monopolies has created new employment opportunities and ushered in numerous changes in the formation of consumer and clientele groups in the economy. The opening of the economy to greater corporate participation and the introduction of cellular technologies have opened up new vistas. People are no longer dependent on what the government is engaged in doing, though paradoxically, nearly one-third of the population continues to be dependent on government handouts in terms of new programmes aimed at creating income and food security. But the standard of services provided by government has been continuing its downward journey. People are removing their children from government schools, preferring private schools, are opting for corporate water supply in place of government-supplied water, and installing protective devices to save their few electrical appliances from the vagaries of supply. The affluent are getting more affluent and the growth of oligarchies has become a daily feature. On the other side, the public squalor too has been increasing at a rapid clip. The urban consumer is being cuckolded with subsidised rice, wheat and other essentials. The compulsions of electoral politics are such that two vote banks are being created. The misery of the rural farmer has gone up as he has to fight for a minimum support price for his product while his costs have been going up despite the subsidised supply of fertiliser and free supply of electricity. The problems of daily life, which are now being brought into the limelight, courtesy of the electronic media, are further exacerbating the discontent among the middle class. The new-found paradox is the growth of opportunities and the simultaneous growth of discontent. Demands for improved governance have become a common feature.

Equally, the inability to raise the standards of governance illustrates the growing ineptitude of governments at all levels. Finance continues to be a serious limitation and the governments at the sub-national level give the impression of being immobile without the cash releases from the central government, which have now morphed into an ATM in the country. Finally, there has been a massive change in the functioning of the State itself.

After independence, the Indian State became a huge administrative machinery that tried to manage the economy and society through what was called a socialistic pattern. This big task was rendered difficult by the acute shortage of financial resources, a shortage that was sought to be relieved by annual visits to the capitals of the donor countries with the proverbial begging bowl. The regime of state-directed and managed economy gave rise to a licence raj and a policy of import substitution that exacerbated the shortages felt in the market. Those who had access to power benefited from this regime and those who did not, lagged behind and so did the common man.

Corruption, political and economic, became more ubiquitous, while those engaged in corruption were sufficiently insulated from retribution. Taking action against an alleged corrupt minister needed the prior approval of the President or the Governor of the state. Action against a civil servant drawn from the All India Services needed prior permission of the Union Ministry of Home Affairs. The implementation of the national ombudsman recommended by the Administrative Reforms Commission could not make much headway even after years of "deep thinking", while all concerned expressed their anguish at the slow pace of reform.

Meanwhile, even as the State was drifting into a state of near failure, came the traumatic military debacle of 1962, from which the national psyche took a long time to recover. The sociologists in their turn came up with the view that India was a soft state, incapable or unwilling to promote social discipline among its citizens: the country was not moving ahead because the citizen was not doing his bit in meeting his obligations to society. Measures were required to make him more responsive and responsible. And so the government amended the constitution to make the citizens recognise and perform their duties. This amendment, which is still a feature of the constitution, and a unique one in that no other constitution has a similar feature, is still read and rarely practised. The younger generation, the backbone of the middle class, is hardly aware of this. It is a feature that illustrates the futility of undertaking social engineering through legal fiat.

Hitherto, the State had gone through three phases—an administrative state; an administrative and a corrupt state; and a soft state. The fourth phase, which started with the introduction of liberalised economy in the last decade of the last century, transformed the State into a hollow state. It is not that this new form lacked positive or laudable objectives. Its broad objective was to come to an arrangement that permitted the release of the energies of all participants, *viz.*, government, service providers, service producers, and service consumers, and to achieve a reduction in public expenditure (It was implicitly assumed that the services would be economical and efficient since the providers functioned in an environment of competitive markets). To some extent, the aim of reducing public expenditure, and thus the burden on the taxpayer, became an election slogan in 2014—Minimum Government with Maximum Service. As usual, the specifics as to how this happy state of affairs would be reached were lacking. Much of it was left to the fertile imagination of the voter.

The hollow state also meant an admission of failure of past policies and related administrative reforms. The new approach was to cease doing what was done in the past and to entrust the job to the corporate sector through public-private partnerships. As discussed before, PPPs have their advantages, particularly in compensating for the decline in capital expenditures. They provide avenues to the government to augment the public outlays, notably on national security. The success of PPPs, however, is crucially dependent on the regulatory framework and on the expenditure management system. In both these respects, no attempt has been made to strengthen the systems. All that the public perceives is the excessive expenditure of governments, at all levels, on the corporate sector, and the growing financial prosperity of the latter. It is a case of corporate affluence and public squalor all over again.

Has this change materially led to an improvement in addressing the issues that dominated the sphere of public policy-making over more than six decades? The perception is that not much has changed. Table 9.5 summarises the themes of administrative reform during the past years. The themes continue to be operational for the simple reason that while the issues were attacked, success continues to be elusive. Corruption continues to be the dominant, if intractable, problem. There has been a significant growth, at all levels of governance, save the local level which continues to be an unfathomable abyss as before, in the corruption fighting machinery. New laws are being made and new efforts are being tried to bring the "black money", whether kept in India or in other countries, into the tax net.

Table 9.5

India's Themes of Administrative Reform

Description	*Period*	*Corruption*	*Service to the public*	*Performance and efficiency*	*Citizen empowerment and duties*	*Internal management improvement*	*Contracting out and PPPs*
Administrative state	1947-1965	✓	✓	-	-	✓	-
Soft state	1975-1990	✓	-	✓	✓	✓	-
Hollow state	1990-	-	-	✓	✓	✓	✓

Notes: (i) – indicates that no major initiatives have been taken.

(ii) Some of the themes illustrated here have been pursued over extended periods and should not be considered as being limited to some periods only. ✓ denotes the period during which major initiatives were taken.

It is the lack of results that worries the citizen. He finds it difficult to appreciate the goings-on in the government—where it is headed, the purpose of its actions, and the likely outcome of the policies pursued. For him, government remains mysterious as ever. Notwithstanding all the talk about accountability, that is the one thing that is lacking. The channels of accountability were established soon after independence but it is their effectiveness that is increasingly debated. Meanwhile, the executive power has increased substantially, while the legislative power has declined.

The hollowness of the state is becoming abundantly clear to the people. So far as they are concerned, the talk of reform is mostly talk and little action. Suggestions for improvement made by commissions are studied from all angles and then are allowed to be swept aside by the stress of developments in other spheres. Surprisingly, the state has become hollow, not for lack of power in the executive branch of government but despite the growth in its discretionary power. Reform is seen as an exercise carried out by the civil servants, for the civil servants, and with the civil servants. The internal processes of government are opaque. And given the record of the government, its periodic announcements about its determination are received with derision and extreme scepticism.

Meanwhile, the voter's discontent continues to fester. While it is perennially simmering, it implodes whenever there is a spark that ignites it. That spark came in 2012 when Anna Hazare came on the scene and when a new political party was established that also gained power in the Union Territory of Delhi. The movement and the political party concentrated, however, on one issue—the setting up of a national ombudsman (Lok Pal) that could be the new czar to fight corruption. This was to the exclusion of all other issues that afflict governments in India and time has proved that such a misplaced effort is far from a panacea and is in fact a major problem in itself. Thus the public is back to where it was—hoping for solutions that will come one day. Meanwhile, the systems of governance, in particular the much-neglected expenditure management system, are in crisis. They need to be understood, recognised for what they are, and addressed.

The scepticism of the public is fuelled by the conventional belief that governments have been marching on the path of folly. As Barbara Tuchman points out in her historical survey,[6] "rejection of reason is the prime characteristic of folly" and "non-rational human frailties—ambition, anxiety, status-seeking, face-saving, illusions, self-delusions, fixed prejudices"[7] have all had their impact on governance to the point that the "impotence of reason" has become dominant in governance. This impotence of reason is not by any means new, nor is it unique to India. Long ago, Plato pointed out that when desire disagrees with reason, there is a disease of the soul. The second President of India, an eminent philosopher in his own right, called it a crisis of character, a feature that continues to afflict the country. These factors have contributed to a State moving from an administrative state, to a corrupt state, to a soft state and to its present incarnation, a hollow state. Walter Bagehot pointed out in his classic work, *The English Constitution*, that the British constitution had continued "in connected outward sameness" but had gone through "hidden inner change" and was "like an old man who still wears ... clothes in the fashion of his youth: what you see of him is the same, what you do not see is wholly altered". It is that altered state

6. See Tuchman, Barbara W. (1984). *The March of Folly.* New York: Ballantine Books; more specifically, the epilogue.

7. Ibid.: 380.

that has become the problem. Historians like Tuchman provide ample evidence as to how governments reach the altered state with many features still hidden. Her analysis of history over centuries reveals a long list of problems, which are mostly universal in nature, and some specific in time and space. Some of the problems identified by her also illumine the Indian experience.

First is the lust for power. Associated with it is what Jefferson, a founding father of American democracy, pointed out: "Whenever a man has cast a longing eye on office, a rottenness begins in his conduct"—a tendency that was further elaborated by Adam Smith in his *The Wealth of Nations* to the effect that it ended up introducing "all the rapine and injustice" and "avarice and ambition".[8] As a part of that lust for power, which is a continuing trait of the political class, they hanker for privileges and perquisites. Even today, Members of Parliament in New Delhi seek these perquisites. A good illustration is their demand that when they travel by Air India, they should be received at the gate and conducted through VIP rooms and other exclusive corridors all the way into the aircraft, and they should be given higher baggage allowance. Regardless of political affiliations, they consider these demands as "normal", with one member going to the extent of saying that they were "essential" for them. They want bigger accommodation and want changes in the form of additions and alterations in their quarters even though the existing laws enacted by these elected members bar them or the Central Public Works Department from making any changes in Lutyens' Delhi (named after the architect, who with Herbert Baker designed the whole complex of office and residential buildings that came to be called as New Delhi). The desire of India's elected representatives of the people for comforts is such that when a lady Chief Minister of Delhi demitted office after her party was defeated at the polls, it was found that her official residence (which incidentally was far from her office) had no less than thirty-six air-conditioners. Such comforts shock the poor voters, who wonder what all the talk about service to the poor was about.

Once the political class reaches the portals of power, they want to have more personal power. The centralisation of power is inevitable, with the consequence of favouritism and patronage. The power should be such that it alone attracts cronies and sycophants. Exercise of power, which is constitutional and legal, becomes personal and a form of

8. Cited in Ibid.: 382.

personal fiefdom (eventually becoming a dictatorship in a democracy) emerges and consolidates to the point that it becomes a hallmark of a Prime Minister's tenure.

The desire for more power goes together with a "mental standstill", comprising ideas that do not go beyond the convictions that the political class developed before getting into positions of power. While their views do not broaden, their hold on power becomes such that they brook no opposition. The ideas acquire rigidity and service to the people would be rendered only in the framework of those rigid views. To some extent, these arbitrary approaches and extreme personal rule tend to be smoothed at the edges when the countries become members of a globalised world and when financial connections become dominant. At such times, the personal convictions may be replaced by the management philosophies of the corporate world. Their nostrums such as open capital flows or "too big to fail" mantras are offered and practised as shortcuts to distinction or to economic salvation. The people have only a choice between personal and arbitrary rule, on the one hand, and forced practice of ideas that have not been subjected to tests of empirical validity. The profits of that experience go to a select few while the losses, which are evident but rarely admitted, are invariably socialised as additional burdens on the people.

With the ruling class refusing to re-examine its policy prescriptions, the persistence with the socialistic patterns continues. The country is declared a socialist republic, even if there is not even an ounce of that approach in practice. To the political class, and to those who run the government and hold the reins of power, "to recognise error, to cut losses, to alter course, is the most repugnant option".[9] In the world of today, however, governments are forced to recognise the effects of their folly when they are on the brink of economic disaster, and assistance from the creditors would be available only when the course is altered.

It has been recognised all along that the quest for excess power would very soon lead to the abuse of power. It was expected that the rule of law, and an objective civil service based on merit would, to some extent, mitigate the ill effects of excessive personal power. Experience does not, however, support these beliefs. The rule of law is often subverted to favour the privileged class and becomes an instrument of oppression. Even the objectivity of the civil service may not play a

9. Tuchman *op. cit* no. 5: 383.

significant role when career prospects depend, not on merit, but on loyalty to the provisional master. The political class deploys all the stratagems in the world to solidify its power base in every way it can. For example, a minister of finance in the central government packed the ranks of joint secretaries in his ministry with officers from his state, and preferably with members of his community, so that they remained loyal only to him. Thus, whatever techniques can be used to pursue a personal agenda, it may be affirmed, would be followed without fail. Also, whatever parts of the law are inconvenient, there are more than a hundred ways by which compliance can be avoided.

These and many other faults have their applications and counterparts in the world of today. Some of the impressions regarding any country have been formed on the basis of the observed historical trends. There are, in addition, two other forms of public discourse aimed at illuminating the performance of countries and their governments all over the world. These discourses enable the citizens of every country know not only how their government is performing in the country but also where it stands relative to other countries.

The first form of public discourse is that of human development reports. From the beginning of the current century, these reports have come to be prepared both at the international and national levels. At the international level, international organisations and countries have been issuing annual reports on various aspects of human development. Similar reports are also being issued in India and many state governments have also been very active in issuing such reports, if only to buttress their development record. In addition, non-governmental organisations and international financial institutions have been issuing indices about transparency, corruption, ease of doing business, patterns of behaviour, and other aspects. Although there are several methodological limitations to these studies in that some of them are based on perceptions and therefore lack empirical underpinning, they have come to be accepted both by the common people and by policy makers as useful indices. While they do have technical limitations, a compensatory feature is their consistency. They have become popular, as their findings are publicised both in the electronic and in the print media to add a degree of verisimilitude to popular impressions. A result is that countries whose ranking is way down are engaged in making renewed efforts to improve their place in the international comity.

The other form of public discourse relates to the introduction of a whole new vocabulary to describe the existential status of various countries. This vocabulary includes terms such as failed state, fragile state, disorderly state, shadow state, mediative state, unstable state, and states descending into chaos. The list is not exhaustive and is growing by the day, depending on the creative imagination of the analyst. The use of these labels, while illustrating the plight of the countries, could also contribute to the hastening of the formation of donor countries to offer aid to the affected countries.

Coincidentally, as the literature on these aspects grows, there has also been burgeoning growth in the consultancy services, all offering their expertise, at a remunerative price. It is a booming business, lending credence to the old saying that the distress of somebody could be the basis of a good business for somebody else. (Readers in a senior age group may recall a scene in a Charlie Chaplin movie, where he offers his binoculars—for a fee, of course—to watch somebody who is threatening to jump off the top of a building.) That apart, the growing discussion has helped focus on the problems of governance in some of these countries. In particular, a recent book by Ghani Ashraf and Clare Lockhart, with a not-too-modest title—*Fixing Failed States*—discusses this phenomenon.[10] The authors characterise a failed state as one where the rule of law, legitimate use of force by the state, administrative control, sound management of public finances, investment in human capital, creation of citizenship rights through social policy, provision of infrastructure services, formation of a market, management of public assets, and effective public borrowing have failed. Some of these (and only some) themes are reminiscent of the themes pursued by the Government of India. The substance of problems experienced in each of these segments is summarised in Table 9.6, which also indicates, albeit briefly, the relative conditions in India. The basic point that these studies reveal is the "sovereignty dividend" and the "sovereignty gap" that a country has and illustrate the catch-up that they have to undertake. The list is fairly comprehensive, and much more than what the Department

10. Ashraf , Ghani and Clare Lockhart (2008). *Fixing Failed States*. New York: Oxford University Press. Ghani Ashraf is a former staff member of the World Bank. He successively became Finance Minister of Afghanistan, and is now the country's President. He was the Finance Minister at a stage when Afghanistan was dependent, to a very substantial degree, on foreign aid.

Table 9.5

State Functions and Issues

Functions	*Issues*
1. Rule of Law	• Legislative overload • Law relating to regulation murky and frequently lacking comprehensiveness • Arbitrary application. Redress through the judicial system takes a long time and is so expensive that it is beyond the means of the common man • The law may be biased in favour of oligarchs • Frequent revisions in law • Evasion of law pervasive • Lack of enforcement capability • Compliance involves too much paperwork • Illusion of safety • Extensive prevalence of organised opposition to proposed/ enacted law • Poor record maintenance and powerful vested interests with political backing often deprive the citizens of their property rights • Existence of a parallel system of governance with its own legitimacy • Separate rules for the armed forces and civil services in designated areas • Favours the elite groups
2. Legitimate use of force by the State	• The armed forces play a major role in maintaining internal security: they have a privileged role • Use of force by police is arbitrary and the methods of crowd control are primitive at best. Individual rights do not count for much as the police force rarely takes them into account. No accountability for the killing of people or for the destruction of property • Use of force is influenced by ethnic considerations • The reach of the law-and-order forces is limited. In rural areas, there are local hegemons whose authority remains untouched • Armed conflict is far too common: as a consequence, the credibility of the legitimate power to exercise force is vastly eroded

...contd...

...contd...

3. Administrative control	• Overlapping jurisdictions • Excessive centralisation • Emerging patterns of patronage and corruption • No firm schedules for delivery of services • System not geared to the efficient delivery of services • Focus on fulfilling centrally determined targets for completion • Regulatory framework for outsourced work remains to be developed in most cases • Mismatch between administrative and financial regulations • No congruence between tasks, responsibilities, finances • Unpredictable application of rules • Accountability is very diffused • Inefficiency is not penalised as it is hard to prove waste • Government employees are well protected as the web of rules protects them rather than the complaining citizen • Corruption is widespread
4. Sound management of public finances	• Budget outturn is often different from estimates, revealing substantial fiscal slippages • Tax collection is generally lax • Both tax expenditures and subsidies are frequently determined without substantive analysis of their financial implications or impact • Expenditures are generally perceived to be wasteful, with extensive leakages • Physical progress in projects and programmes has little relationship with monetary flows • Budget implementation phase reveals a lack of balance between central controls and internal controls in the spending agencies • Pursuit of efficiency is not the most common objective of government agencies • The anchor of expenditure management is never obvious either to the citizens or to government employees • Payment arrears, including in payroll payment based systems, is fairly common • Internal audit and pre-audit before payment are not always well organised • Audit is often delayed and the officials responsible for the problem areas identified in the audit reports would have retired by the time action is contemplated

...contd...

...contd...

	• Legislative review of the audit reports and the comments thereon by the legislative committees reveal a partisan approach, reducing the effectiveness of legislative control • There are many activities which are not within the budget or the financial management system of the government either by design or default • Most governments lack an inventory of their assets or liabilities • Audit of local government activities is too selective to be of much use • In many areas benefits conferred by government programmes remain to be utilised • Cost control is non-existent; indeed, cost awareness itself remains an issue • The central concerns of society in the management of its finances remain to be addressed
5. Investment in human capital	• Several of the key elements of education and health sectors are now carried out by the corporate sector through PPP arrangements. In the process, the state has been hollowed and most officials in the ministries have become coordinators and reviewers. The regulatory frameworks dealing with the corporate bodies engaged remain to be formulated • Those institutions which continue to be operated by government have come to be poorly maintained and their capacity to render services is vastly eroded • Vast grey areas in the production and delivery of services have emerged • From an administrative point of view, accountability remains to be ensured • There are areas where there has been rapid growth in the expectations of the citizens and they tend to believe that they are not sufficiently empowered to oversee the work of the corporate bodies. The right to information, which is a feature found in about 80 countries, is often delusional

...contd...

...contd...

6. Creation of citizen-ship rights through social policy	• Social and economic policies are generally believed to be the best equalisers. Although they take a long time to be effective, the fact that those policies are there strengthens the resolve of the affected citizens. But these policies have also created protected classes more interested in entitlements that tend to create more divisions, and consequently fractious relationships, in society. Pacification of those tensions has become the job of the judiciary. What has become contentious is the determination of the eligibility for inclusion in the entitled class • What is delivered as a part of these entitlements also reveals several problem areas. Scholarships are not paid in time as are the grants for the purchase of books. Those who are not treated well consider themselves to be children of lesser gods. (Gods in Hindu society have a hierarchical order of their own and defy any attempt at conceptualisation) • In regard to health, the issues go far beyond the fiscal ones such as the appropriate level of health expenditures (which, admittedly, is very low in India) and their linkages to the recognised health indicators. Lack of progress in attaining higher levels of public health is a reflection of the failure of health policies at all levels • Social policies have a major role in the shaping of public perceptions about the effectiveness of government. The demands often include provision of free services as well as effective delivery of services. This process involves the operation through forward and backward linkages; they also involve frequent comparisons with private sector operations (often as paid agencies of the government) which work in competition with government agencies that are fully owned and operated by them and yet are perceived to be inefficient. The general complaint is that the government agencies do not even try to be efficient. Fulfilment of government-formulated targets does not mean that the agencies are efficient. The public has no role in the determination of targets at all. • There are also areas where a form of rationing through political interference is often found to be at work, creating in the process yet another group of privileged consumers/users. There is usually a scramble for political patronage and this form of rationing works, not in tandem with government, but as a separate stream

...contd...

...contd...

7. Provision of infra-structure services	• Public agencies are expected to provide clean air, potable water, well-organised sewerage systems, and a transport system with enhanced connectivity through air, sea and road. In all these areas, what has been achieved is considerably behind the recognised need. The gap between ideas and the reality is substantial and the credibility of government stands considerably eroded now. In an attempt to shore up their image, governments tend to promise even more (much of it deliverable in the distant future, as for example, is the case with the provision of atomic energy) and continued lack of progress adds to their discomfiture even more • Pollution has become a major issue during the last few decades. The understanding of the public of the ecological disasters that government policies have either contributed to or caused has increased steadily as sections of the community are direct victims of industrial and other forms of pollution. Lack of balance in the use of chemical fertilisers and natural, organic materials has contributed to declining soil quality while contributing to polluted water supplies in rural areas. The citizens' visits to health centres reveal a bleak picture and indications are that major health crises are looming on the horizon. A major challenge to governance is to launch an effective programme of action in this area • Drinking water availability remains a major problem that touches the daily lives of millions of people. Five-year plans are routinely announced but they do not have any impact in transforming the community. Major cities offer no better facilities. Water supply is at best intermittent. Seasonal variations are high and long lines of people waiting at the pumps is too common a sight as is the acceptance of the inability of the government to provide water. Life has become a series of adjustments to the shortages created by government agencies. From the common man's point of view, there is no respite in sight. Indeed it is uncommon to find anyone with optimism and governance limps on, with or without reform. The country is meanwhile dubbed as a NATO country (No Action, Talk Only). The issues are so common that the threshold levels of acceptance of governance failures is part of the people's psyche • Sewerage systems are few and far between; where they operate, their capacities are in need of immediate upgrading. In several cases, sewage streams run very close to the supply lines of drinking water and seepage from the former to the latter is a common occurrence. Facilities in the rural areas hardly exist for treatment of human waste. No effort is made to create them in the new housing colonies that are not a part of an urban municipality, and in any event require large investments that are beyond the financial capacities of a *panchayat*. In the process, a new excluded class of citizens has emerged

...contd...

...contd...

	• Much has been done to improve transport connectivity through air, road and sea lanes. There is, however, a good deal that remains to be done. The regulatory framework remains to be effective. Maintenance remains a major area in need of development. The pervasive corruption has seen to a massive decline in construction standards in that lining of canal and river beds would appear to vanish after the first monsoon, as do the roads.
8. Formation of a market	• A major function of the government is to facilitate the operations of a free market in which the rights of the consumer and the liabilities of the investors are protected. In principle, the level of regulation should not be so intrusive as to dampen the creativity of the producer, nor so light that the investors exploit the light-touch regulation and the consequent losses are nationalised • The regulatory framework of each industry is, by definition, different from the framework applicable to another industry. The underlying considerations have, however, identical purposes, viz., the interests of society. In India, much remains to be done in refining the role of the regulatory framework. An additional feature of the Indian system is that many industries continue to be owned and operated by either the central government or state governments. (Unlike China, local governments in India do not own or operate any public utilities or other enterprises.) The regulatory institutions engaged in the regulation of government-owned enterprises are not endowed with the requisite degree of autonomy. This is evident in regard to atomic energy, banking industry in so far as government-owned banks are concerned, communications, civil aviation, electricity industry, broadcasting and others. Clarity is still needed about the way in which the regulatory institutions work. Greater reliance continues to be placed on administrative controls than on market mechanisms. Predictability is not a virtue of the operations of these institutions. Public hearings are seldom held and very few attempts are made, unless forced by public pressure, to consult the consuming public
9. Management of public assets	• In the absence of accrual accounting, there is no inventory of public assets (primarily land, forests, buildings, plant and equipment, etc.) or their valuation. Moreover, grant of land does not require legislative approval. As a consequence, all public assets have become centres of patronage. This is true for cantonment lands managed by the Ministry of Defence as well • Very little is known about the way in which the discretionary power vested in the executive domain is utilised. Notions of accountability have yet to enter into this realm • The utilisation of the assets is a major question that remains to be posed and answered. Public sector undertakings (PSUs) also have large assets and are retained by them long after they cease functioning.

...contd...

...contd...

	• The ecological impact of the use of government assets is raised only when there is a new project proposed to be undertaken (as the enterprise is required to submit a report on the ecological impact) but not as a general issue in itself. • Emissions from PSUs have a major impact on the quality of air and water.
10. Effective public borrowing	• Until the submission of the 12th Finance Commission report, public borrowing both by the centre and the states was largely coordinated by the Reserve Bank. That job has since been decentralised. It still remains a task where state governments tend to rely on the commercial bank with which they conduct their operations. There has been a growing awareness of the fiscal impact of the borrowing operations as a result of the Fiscal Responsibility and Budget Management legislation. A good deal remains to be done • Payment arrears: many state and local governments have long delays in payments, including wage payments • There are large amounts owed to electricity companies, distribution companies and to commercial banks. The size of this informal or unrecognised debt fluctuates during the fiscal year and over the years • The credit rating of the country as a whole is, in part, dependent on the outstanding debt and the pattern of its utilisation. In turn, it affects governance too. A government that does not pay its bills in time cannot be expected to win the trust of the people

Note: The enumeration of the functions is based on the inventory developed by Ghani, Ashraf and Clare Lockhart (2008). *Fixing Failed States*, New York: Oxford University Press. The authors suggest that when these functions are well performed, they produce a sovereignty dividend and that failure to do so creates a "sovereignty gap". The list is more illustrative than comprehensive. Three notable omissions are, defence management, working of the representative institutions, and the functioning of the judiciary. Governance is significantly affected by the operations in these sectors. Defence is also an opaque area about which little is known and what is known may not be too complimentary to that agency. Representative institutions have largely been in decline and they have surrendered their oversight functions to the executive domain itself. The judiciary is not without its own quota of anomalies and problems. Litigation continues to be a long-drawn-out process and its costs are formidable. It also is tainted by corruption. Besides, it is not accountable to the representative institutions.

of Administrative Reforms of the Cabinet Secretariat has been issuing over the years.

The conclusions that emerge from the preceding discussion are that in the perception of the people and those of the analysts, there are far too many issues that remain to be addressed. Whether the present situation is such that it can be called a crisis is a matter that requires further discussion. A major factor that influences the formation of perceptions is the administrative culture of the government. This culture is indicative of the underlying human face of the administrative system, the face that it collectively presents to those whom it is serving. Here again the culture is viewed from the perceptions of the people and not that of the administration, who anyway spend a good deal of time justifying their actions or the lack thereof. Coincidentally, the participants in the processes of governance also tend to blame the systems for all their failings, though it should be recognised that they tend to be more vocal as they are about to retire from government service.

A major question raised in the literature is how institutions think, and following from that, whether institutions differ in what they think. One view is that "they are part of the universe" and that "they survive the stage of being fragile conventions: they are founded in nature, and therefore in reason."[11] They move beyond abstraction and, over the years, they develop a case law, a kind of informal convention that is far more powerful than a law enacted by the legislature. These conventions influence their outlook and frequently their judgement too and their behaviour becomes predictable. These are generally considered as being part of a shorthand expression, "finance mentality". As a management expert has noted, "Where one stands depends on where one sits." Finance mentality is viewed as being conservative and its approach is derisively called as ostrich-like or stick-in-the-mud. The people with the finance mentality are guided by, according to the general perception, by precedent, and are risk averse. Their notions of economy are arcane and their action consists in paring down all demands for budgetary allocations to what is considered as acceptable minimum. Their attitude is further described as "wood pecking", "cheeseparing" and perennially

---

11. For a comprehensive discussion, see Douglas, Mary (1984). *How Institutions Think*. Syracuse, N.Y.: Syracuse University Press. p.52. Also see Khare, R.S. (1985). *Culture and Democracy*. Lanham, MD: University Press of America, on how cultural patterns affect democratic functioning, particularly in a patriarchal society.

niggardly. These perceptions are not vapid notions borne out of cussedness but are solidly based in fact and experience that date back to the colonial experience.

The cultures of expenditure management cannot be viewed in isolation from the general cultural pattern of government administration. As a part of the colonial administration, the administrators learnt to be distant and adopt a so-called magisterial outlook. To them, compliance with the rule and the process was sacrosanct, regardless of the context. But it must also be noted that if there were many adherents to this approach, there were also a number of officials who rose above it and brought to bear a liberal outlook toward those governed by the colonial administration. The magisterial outlook of the general run of administration springs from the power and prestige conferred on it by the people, with the result that the assertion of power, to the exclusion of service to the people, has become the dominant theme of bureaucracy even in non-colonial times.

Ivan Turgenev satirised this phenomenon in his novel *Ghost Souls* (he was also the author of *Inspector General*) about czarist Russia. Even as recently as 1980, Deng Xiaoping, who led the reform in China and was responsible for mentoring it as an economic giant, pointed out that "bureaucracy remains a major and widespread problem in the life of our state". He added that the harmful manifestations of bureaucracy included the following: "standing high above the masses; abusing power, divorcing oneself from reality and the masses; spending a lot of time and effort to put up an impressive front; indulging in empty talk; sticking to a rigid way of thinking; being hidebound by convention; overstaffing administrative organs; being dilatory, inefficient and irresponsible; failing to keep one's word; circulating documents endlessly without solving problems; shifting responsibilities to others; assuming the airs of a mandarin; reprimanding other people at every turn; vindictively attacking others; suppressing democracy; deceiving superiors; being despotic and arbitrary; practising favouritism, offering bribes; participating in corrupt practices in violation of the law." And winding up the long litany, he added, with unusual candour and a sense of urgency, that "the above have reached intolerable dimensions both in our domestic affairs and in contacts with other countries" (*A Report Submitted to the People's Congress, 1980*). After perusing this list, the reader might wonder whether Deng was describing China or India. The difference is that the Indian leadership might entertain similar views but they have not been known to be as vocal or specific as the Chinese leader.

The effects of this culture are to be found in the daily work of the finance ministry (as well as other nearly one hundred departments, not to mention the numerous second layer of semi-autonomous bodies that comprise the central government and other layers of the sub-national government) at the centre and in the states. Those who are at the receiving end of the work include the numerous government agencies and the public. Within the government, it is frequently said that the finance ministry as the chief executive of expenditure management (without being an exemplar) cannot claim a friend in the vast and transient world of central bureaucracy. It is viewed as comprising all-purpose critics (without pointing the way for a more constructive agenda) with unpredictable reactions. Budget demands are pared down to the bone, and the release of funds is rarely on time and bears little relationship to the budgetary allocations, with the consequence that the spending agencies develop the compulsive disorder of spending more money in the last two weeks of the fiscal year to avoid lapsing of budgetary grants.

Cash releases are often behind schedule. The grants intended for primary and secondary schools for purchase of books reach them by the end of September as they are about to close for vacation at the end of the first term. The grants to local governments and municipalities are usually delayed and the employees are paid their wages with a lag of three months. The implementation of the recommendations of the Pay Commissions, which come once in ten years, involves the payment of arrears of wages and pensions too. The final decisions on the payments are usually delayed and the government employees are paid, not in cash, but in the form of bonds payable at a future date. In the process, the government employees end up as involuntary lenders to the government.

State governments and central public sector undertakings usually maintain liaison offices in Delhi. One of the major tasks undertaken by them is to chase the bills due for payment. Payments due to contractors are rarely made on time. This affects a whole chain of sub-contractors who provide their services through the primary contractors. All the delays in payments are internalised by the vendors in their cost structures. Inevitably, the cost of projects moves up in the northerly direction. These irritations coexist with a computerised system of payments. A computer makes a payment only when it is programmed to do that, be it a payroll or a payment to the vendors. That requires human action, which, however, moves reluctantly, and that too only when the palms of the authorising officials are extensively greased. These problems are experienced mostly at the counter level and do not go up to the higher echelons. As a consequence, these issues are not taken up with them. Even if they are taken up, there is little effect, as the final action has to come from the bureaucrat who is at the end of the chain of authority. That official tends to work at his own convenience. It also means that the elaborate edifice of the government and its credibility is dependent on the official who is at the street level of bureaucracy. He is impervious to the efforts of government to introduce reforms. But reforms are introduced, as they must, from the top, often at the urging of the international financial institutions. When all the layers are peeled, it reaches this core on whose slender shoulders the reputation of the government depends. The human face of the core is very different from other levels and reformers of government in general, and more specifically the expenditure management system, have rarely reached this level. Meanwhile the problems continue, and the public as well as all other vendors develop high levels of patience, as impatience leads them only to hospitals but not to banks with the newly minted currency or the issue of a long-awaited cheque.

The mental standstill involved in the process remains to be addressed. Meanwhile, the management system continues to limp and be dysfunctional, a feature that has become pathological to the organisations engaged in this sordid business. The officialdom lives in a world that is, it appears to many, completely isolated from the society in which it is supposed to be living. Because of this structural disconnect, the perceptions toward governments tend to follow the same direction as before and no part of it has been helpful in rebuilding confidence in governmental machinery. Apart from perceptions, which anyway are close to the reality, there are structural features which have made the system dysfunctional, and thus ineffective. These features merit detailed consideration for they reveal the core of the system.

One of the main objectives of the system is to lead to the establishment of financial discipline in all government agencies. But this objective stands self-defeated by virtue of some of the principal tenets of the system itself.

Organisational Realities

An odd feature of expenditure management is that everything that needs to be regulated is specified in the rules, but in practice, compliance with the rules is not obligatory. The exceptions tend to be common, and these may be contrary to the very purpose that is sought to be achieved. The following examples illustrate the point.

It is expected that the budgetary appropriations enacted by Parliament are not exceeded. Excess outlays constitute a violation of the legislative prerogatives in that no expenditure may be incurred except with the approval of Parliament. In practice, however, expenditures are incurred and these are pointed out in a comprehensive manner in the audit report. Appropriation audit consists in pointing out the excess, as well as under-expenditures as both indicate, even if in a selective way, that the canons and wishes underpinning parliamentary control are not being fulfilled. The excess expenditures are regulated on an *ex-post facto* basis by Parliament, long after the completion of the fiscal year, on the basis of a routine recommendation by the Public Accounts Committee. What is odd is that in many cases the excess expenditures occur under the public debt accounting head, a head that is controlled by the Ministry of Finance and that is also based on accrual method of accounting. Since these outlays are met from *charged* expenditures, they do not require legislative approval at all. But that this happens at all should be a matter for deep introspection, but nothing of such re-examination of the issue takes place at all. In the end, it is business as usual.

Another instance relates to the approval of supplementary estimates. Both under the prescribed rules and conventions from the colonial period, supplementary estimates are processed for legislative approval on three occasions per fiscal year. The legislative calendars are so devised as to provide time for the approval of supplementary estimates. In theory, an annual budget is expected to be so framed that the supplementary estimates are few and far between. In practice, they are a regular feature of the annual budget cycle. This has been happening for three reasons.

Estimates for projects are approved in three stages. At the first stage, a token grant is processed for parliamentary approval as full details of the project are being worked out. Once the details are available, they are processed through the supplementary estimates. Supplementary estimates are also processed toward the end of the fiscal year when the excess expenditures incurred in the yesteryear are also regularised. Supplementary estimates are also deemed to be necessary as the budget estimates for public debt are generally understated. These supplementary estimates have become so routine that they have the effect of diminishing the utility, not to mention the sanctity, of the annual budget. In terms of fiscal policy, the annual budget is deemed to be the primary instrument of policy both by the executive wing of the government and all the corporate houses, which plan their activities on the basis of the annual budget of the government. But by making the supplementary estimates a routine affair, the government is sending wrong signals to the vast array of government agencies.

From the point of view of the spending agency, the occasion for a supplementary budget is yet another chance to continue the budget dialogue through the fiscal year. It offers an opportunity for a moral hazard in that the limits of budget estimates have only a formal purpose and can always be incurred with impunity, while the annual budget tends to be viewed, in the context of thrice-a-year supplementary estimates, as a year-long exercise. An inevitable consequence of this perverse incentive (in that the perceived limitation of resource ceiling can always be overcome) is the loss of financial discipline in the government itself. But in support of this practice, it can always be argued that the procedure is legal in that it is provided for in the rules. The purpose of these rules then was to reduce the rigidity in the system (for excessive rigidity contributes its own quota of distortions) and add a touch of flexibility. It was never expected that it would become the normal practice rather than an exception. The moral of the story also is this: that in government the unexpected ends up as the rule.

Another point of practice relates to the payments to contractors and other vendors. As has been repeatedly pointed out in the preceding discussion, there is often considerable delay in these payments. One reason for this is that the numerous functionaries in the ministries wait for their kickbacks before processing the claims. These delays and kickbacks are already factored in by the vendor in his bid, and the government ends up paying for all its delays and for the venality of its employees. Government, which is expected to be cost conscious and make every effort to reduce the costs, ends up adding to the costs. It is not the government that suffers, because in the final analysis, it is the poor, voiceless public that ends up paying for this. The lack of attention to these aspects makes the people wonder about the adequacy of the governmental systems. But then, the wonders never cease; they end up being routine.

Structurally, a system is designed, in general, to achieve a stated objective. The Indian expenditure management system basically was designed by the colonial government more than one and a half centuries ago to provide a decent rendition of accounts indicating the amounts received and spent. The intent was also to monitor whether there were any major leakages in the system in terms of embezzlement. Furthermore, to prevent unauthorised transactions all the controls were concentrated in the finance department in that no money could be spent without its approval. It meant that the finance department would not initiate any actions on its own but would only react to the proposals of other departments.

In adopting this framework to post-independence India, the authority for approving outlays was split into two stages—one, legislative approval; second, approval by the finance department. In technical parlance, the second stage was known as "prior approval" which was needed to be accorded by the finance ministry/department. As governments grew in size and complexity, it became impractical to get approval from the finance ministry for all items that were already approved by the legislature which, under the constitution, was the only designated authority to approve expenditures. So, the items for which "prior approval" was needed, was limited to selected items. In either event, the process changed the finance ministry to an agency that only reacted to proposals, but did not initiate proposals on its own except in so far as regards selected proposals that were announced in the budget speech. Essentially thus, the finance department never became a proactive agency anticipating situations and seeking solutions. A proactive agency would have an opportunity to "steer" the government and the economy to outline a spending scenario that would enable the spending agencies to prepare advance action plans.

A necessary consequence of this "reactive" approach has been the conversion of an annual budget exercise into a regular exercise, with no defined periodicity, throughout the fiscal year. Over the years, this situation was sought to be corrected in two ways. The preparation of a development plan implied that a good deal of preparatory work would take place well before the beginning of the formal budget season. This, however, limited the exercise to plan programmes only. Nevertheless, the plan did provide tentative estimates for the next five years. These were more in the nature of projections and lacked detail in terms of the outlays of each agency.

Financial control was, however, in the details but the devil in the details was not identified as the exercise was a projection only. Second, the opportunity of analysing the detailed trends was presented in the context of the Fiscal Responsibility and Budget Management legislation that mandated the preparation of medium-term rolling plans. Here again, it was an exercise that was carried out in highly aggregative terms and not in terms of detailed programmes. As a consequence, two paths, independent of each other and mutually exclusive, came to be followed. One related to the aggregate picture and the other related to the annual budget. The fact that the former was an exercise prepared mostly by economists, while the latter was carried out by the financial advisers and controllers, contributed to the firm separation of the two approaches. Thus, with all the introduction of budgetary innovations that involved macroeconomic planning over the medium term, the business of preparing expenditure plans continued as usual. A result of this is the absence of a forward look or the provision of a proactive guidance to the spending department. These were opportunities that could have been seized by the finance ministry to become a proactive, steering agency. It opted for rowing than for steering. Expenditure management came to be trivialised in the process, with attention to the minor details, while the major underlying trends and related policy themes came to be ignored.

This structural bottleneck was partly abetted by a traditional choice in the finance ministry. The Economic Division was responsible for the budget speech and the preparation of the several documents that went along with it. The preparation of the detailed "demands for grants", a complicated but routine task, was a part of the domain of the Budget Division and the Department of Expenditure. The two, however, spoke different languages. The Economic Division spoke in the language of the economists, a feature that it also shared with the (erstwhile) Planning Commission. The second group spoke the language of an accounting controller.[12] This separation contributed to the growth of two cultures, one forward looking but with no responsibilities for the management of

12. It may be noted that the Department of Expenditure in the Union finance ministry was never headed by an economist but was always headed by an officer from the All India Services, or from the Accounts Services. The first Secretary of the Department of Expenditure headed the budget division of the Ministry of External Affairs before taking up the new assignment.

the budgetary trends, and the other that was responsible for the details but not with an analysis of the trends and what they implied for the management of the economy.

The two cultures were so separate that a comprehensive policy base combining the two was possible only at the top, that is at the level of the Finance Minister. This crucial task was never examined in its own terms, partly for the reasons that the ministers were too busy in frying their own fish and fighting their political battles. The first two ministers after independence were drawn from the corporate sector and had, in any event, only a brief tenure. The third minister, himself a member of the Indian Civil Service and a former Secretary of Finance in one of the British Provinces (Central Provinces and Berar) presented five budgets and brought a degree of consolidation to the process but could not go beyond that. He was followed by a politician who had to leave, after a brief tenure, amidst allegations of corruption. He was followed by a former provincial civil service officer, who brought solidity to his position but could not go beyond. He too presented more than five budgets. Thereafter came a series of ministers, including a professional lawyer, a retired major in the armed services, and another who was a member of the All India Services. In between, the two Prime Ministers presented two budgets in their capacity as provisional finance ministers. The highest number of budgets were presented by a lawyer/politician, while another former Chief Economic Adviser also had a long stint as finance minister. The view held all these years was that the position of a finance minister was so technical that it required somebody other than the regular political class representative. Neither the professional politicians nor the professional administrators nor the economists showed enough of leadership to merge the two cultures. They, therefore, continue, and the role of steering the expenditure management system remains to be fulfilled.

The management system of the country, the composite of the central, state, and local administrations, has the immense responsibility of maintaining the natural assets of the country and enriching them. This task is not centralised in any particular agency at any level. Rather, it is fragmented among the many agencies. For example, the defence forces have large areas of urban lands. At one time, they were located away from the densely populated urban areas. The defence lands were utilised to house their soldiers and other fighting ranks, but also involved the maintenance of stables and ammunition depots. In some ways, they posed inherent risks both to the military personnel as well as the civilian population. Now, as the urban areas grew and more population moved to the urban areas, what was once deemed to be remote came to be smack in the centre of the city. (It is projected that in the near future almost half of the Indian population would be living in urban spaces. The pressures for urban development would be greater as the "smart cities" idea catches up further pace). Apart from the security risks, the urban lands of the defence ministry form a component of the richest assets of the nation. More or less, the same holds true for the mines, including those not yet surveyed, and the sandy areas that also would hold metals needed for nuclear energy and related security uses. The maintenance of the rivers and the forests is also a major task.

Some of these tasks were anticipated in the First Five-Year Plan, when the idea of preparing a national resource budget (including the natural resources and human resources) was mooted but very little was done in the area. As a result, ad hoc decisions, neglect, and deterioration of the assets, not to mention the transfer of natural assets to private sector management have tended to dominate the governance landscape. Some agencies like the defence cantonment services do not have a precise idea of their land assets in the country. The ministry of civil aviation has suddenly woken up to the fact that it owns more lands located along with the airstrips it has known. The situation with the railways is no different. The use of lands has created more problems due to lack of or poor planning. Pollution is the order of the day than an exception.

Arguably, the position could have been different if there were an accrual accounting system in place indicating the natural assets and their growing value. In the absence thereof, lands are granted to corporations and other autonomous institutions as a part of the industrial incentives packages in place in the state governments. Although some of them are given away (and not sold) at throwaway rates on long-term or perennial leases, and therefore continue to belong, if only tenuously, to the government, they have become earning rich assets to the corporate sector. These arrangements do not require legislative approval. The anomalous situation is that while every paisa spent by the government needs prior legislative approval, land grants form a part of the executive's discretionary powers. While the finance department or ministry may be consulted in granting these assets, they have not become an organised part of the expenditure management system.

The most important issue is whether the administrative agencies of governments have moved from the accounting of the trivial and the minutiae, to a system of orderly management that would provide an effective combination of the financial and physical resources and provide a focus on the best way of achieving results. The answer, regrettably, is in the negative. This happens to be the case despite the introduction of performance budgeting and outcome budgeting in most departments. Both, it may be noted, are supplementary to the existing system and have not replaced it. Outcome budget is, in reality, an extended Plan exercise. Both documents provide large amounts of data on the activities but are not deemed as beacons guiding or regulating the internal management of the agencies. The agencies lack the internal accountancy infrastructure to control the costs of programmes and projects for the simple reason that no cost data are compiled. Thus, the costs of programmes remain unknown as the cash-based expenditure systems do not permit the computation of costs. The existing systems are elaborate rituals performed in a perfunctory manner by the policy makers and the executives.

It is not that the virtues or the usefulness of performance budgeting are not known to the decision-makers in the government. Rather, they were reluctant to introduce the new systems. (Parenthetically, it may be noted that when the introduction of performance budgeting was recommended by the Estimates Committee of the Lok Sabha in 1960-61, it was virtually rejected by the mandarins of the finance ministry. The idea was revived by the First Administrative Reforms Commission in 1966.) The new system did away with the exercise of piecemeal controls. But that is where the sinews of power lay and no administrator was willing to give up his fiefdom. So the old system limps on with a few bits of improvement here and there, like the Ambassador car which continues to be on the roads.

The accounting system shows signs of awareness of the advances made in the field in other countries, particularly in the introduction of computer technology, but also reveals that the system is archaic in many other ways. The structures remain deep-rooted in the traditional practices and very few efforts are made to measure the costs of programmes. Asset accounting remains an unexplored territory and there are no accounting standards evolved for the government. The accounting personnel are aware of the generally accepted accounting principles and they are also aware of the lack of functional utility of the systems they operate. The end of all existing systems is to prepare the annual appropriation accounts and not to explore an analysis of the underlying trends and weaknesses. This reveals a lack of understanding of what accountability means.

The allocation of resources as a part of the annual budgetary process shows that there is no anchor now on which the expenditure management process rests. Traditionally, the anchor was the control of staff complements as it was believed that was the area in which rapid expenditure increases take place, and once admitted into the budget, they gain an inertial weight of their own and become difficult to be reduced or dislodged. Staff reorganisation units have come and gone as the plan programmes came with their own yardsticks and staff norms and once approved, they came to be seen as inscribed in granite. When as an economy measure, creation of new posts was denied, political expediency had the better of the administrative judgement and contractual employment became the new normal. Expenditure control then moved from staff control to the total programme outlays but that approach proved impractical as anything deemed a part of the plan stood on a higher pedestal with its own allure. Investment control moved from the finance ministry to the Planning Commission and from there to a high-level committee under the belief that a policy approved by the collective wisdom of the many senior civil servants was better than the rulings by a single agency. But the approvals by the committee take a long time and are approved without adjustment for the potential level of inflation. Provision for additional money becomes yet another tortuous exercise. Meanwhile the expenditure management system has become highly fragmented, so much so the absence of a unified approach is revealed on every occasion. It is difficult to say whether these ad hoc changes were part of a design or had their origins in a convergence of accidental factors.

The budget has ceased to be an instrument of economic policy in that it lacks an anti-inflationary expenditure strategy. All find it easier to advocate the need for economies and they lack clarity about where and how these have to be achieved. Meanwhile, every action becomes a token one (symbolic actions are far more important than substantive actions) and a few posts are kept vacant, a few visits to foreign countries are selectively promoted, and the purchase of new office equipment is deferred to the following year. In the process, decisions of today are postponed for the next year and the problems end up becoming more complex and intractable. There is little recognition of the tenet that expenditures have to be treated unequally if an anti-inflationary strategy has to be successful. Rather, ad hoc percentage costs are imposed, as such an approach is easier to negotiate politically through the wild complex of political corridors and lobbies. Instructions are issued to the state and local governments, where they are routinely received, read even more routinely, and thereafter carefully filed.

This is not to say that there are no exceptions, or that the policies are inflexible. Those with high political connections or those who can thump the tables much louder than others continue to get their way. The central government views these developments as a part of the routine and gives the impression that it has no intention to become an exemplar. If the budget is needed to fight an emerging recession in the economy, a slew of projects are approved in what are known as a category of quick-yielding projects, with the usual emphasis on quick implementation but little supporting action to support that strategy. The strategy does not raise and therefore answer the question as to how the ratcheted levels of outlays are to be financed at the end of the recession. Also, the objective of quick action is subjected to a thousand pinpricks in that cash releases often lag behind the progress in the field. The inescapable conclusion is that the system is obsolete, that there is no driving force (and there is no impetus for such a force either), that there is no detailed strategy and that the strategy, when formulated, is not supported by a detailed plan of action. Meanwhile, the expected economic correction yields place to an unplanned drift.

The finance ministry has not explored how a pattern for securing technical efficiency could be introduced into the system. Neither the spending agencies nor the controlling agencies have spent time to devise and deploy levers of efficiency. But that has not prevented them from a regular incantation of the mantra of "economy, efficiency and effectiveness" in the ministry's budget speeches and other public pronouncements. The desire for attaining financial salvation is unattainable. In the absence of specification of ways and means through which that salvation is to be attained, the repeated expression of that desire remains an empty rhetoric. Lack of action on these fronts has effectively crippled the main organ of the administrative body of the government, *viz.*, the finance ministry.

Normally, any systematic failure is expected to be compensated by political leadership through other means. The experience in this regard, it is fair to say, is disappointing. There is no political party which has paid attention to this in its manifesto or in the common minimum Plan agreed with among the coalition partners. The Congress Party has at least delivered two economy reports (in the 1950s and in the early 1990s) that eventually became the basis for governmental actions. The other parties have devoted their energies at an emotional level on emphasising the need for reducing subsidies and on attacking corruption. Specific measures were never suggested to provide an alternative forum.

What is more, the budget debate in the Lok Sabha is generally vapid, with token expressions of local grievances, and the annual legislation is approved in the guillotine hour. Even the legislation for raising the salaries of the Members of Parliament is passed amid general approbation without much of substantive discussion. In their quest for securing more benefits and privileges, the concern of the legislators for the common man has been ignored. Neither the members of legislatures nor the government would appear to keep in mind that public expenditure management is primarily a people's issue. While the members of legislatures may not be knowledgeable about the intricacies of management or the ways of the working of governments, their efforts should pave the way for greater recognition of the problems. This has contributed to a situation where no effort is made to identify the capacity of the government and the willingness to correct the situation; and much of the valuable legislative schedule is in fact utilised for stymieing the programmes of the government and thwarting the efforts to introduce any innovation. The combined indifference of the legislatures and the government has tended to push the main issues aside. For the first time, however, the new government that came to power in June 2014 has announced an expenditure management commission. Its tasks remain to be specified. But it represents an attempt to prevent a fatal organ failure and to engage in transfusion or transplantation efforts.

Renewal

The preceding discussion illustrates the immensity and persistence of the problem. When a problem persists and manifests itself in many forms, it should be recognised as a crisis. The fire brigade has already been called in—in the form of an expenditure commission. Its plate is full. The effort is limited to raising some important issues and no attempt is made to claim the high ground.

The first issue relates to the role that should be played by the central agencies in the management of expenditures. What kind of power should they exercise? What kind of stress tests should be devised to sustain the day-to-day tasks of expenditure management? And finally, what are the areas that need to be looked into?

The main problem of expenditure management has been the excessive, hegemonic, and colonial type of power exercised by the central agencies in general and more so by the finance ministry and other central agencies. Thus far these agencies have wielded a three-legged system of control: (a) the power vested in the finance ministry both by convention and by the legislative instrument of transaction of business rules that are applicable to the central government; (b) provision of central clearances and related approvals as well as the management of the annual budget cycle; and (c) provision of cash support for the payments to be made by the spending agencies and the maintenance of the broad accounting functions which continue to be managed by the accounting services that are working under the control of the central finance ministry (the exceptions are defence, railways and posts and telegraphs, which manage their own accounting services). These three functions formed the core of the system of hegemony exercised by the finance ministry. At one stage, when the government was relatively small and compact and the functions as well as the structure of objectives of policies were fairly simple, this system might, arguably, have worked well, though it developed its own hiccups. As the size of government began to grow at a faster rate, it became evident that the administrative culture it spawned became more of a liability, and in any case ceased to be an asset. It contributed to a culture that has a heavy and substantial dependence of central departments, state governments, and on occasion, the local governments on the central governments. Such dependence, apart from sapping the initiative of other agencies, also contributed to a situation where financial discipline was there only in name.

It is obvious that this dysfunctional culture cannot be permitted to continue, as continuation would only mean prolonged agony and distress to the community. It is essential that in place of this dependency culture, a foundation is laid for the growth of a new culture that would permit the growth of unfettered creativity in managing one's own affairs. The agencies must become responsible and it is only when that responsibility becomes functional and not formal that the utilisation of financial resources would have the focus and energy that it deserves. The seed needs to be planted as soon as possible if it has to germinate properly and grow into an orderly tree, with its own pruned branches so that it does not end up like a banyan tree where nothing grows under its shade: such an experiment could only mean that the remedy may be worse than the malady.

With this caution noted early on, it is appropriate at this stage to briefly note the types of power and their implications for the management of the government and the national economy. The concept of power has thus far been mostly analysed in terms of the role of superpowers and the type of international relations that it would foster.[13] The ideas contained in these strategies for managing international relations have only inspirational value for the management of finances and are so considered here. Basically, power is seen in terms of a prism that has two sides or two types of power—hard and soft, the former referring to military and economic power and the latter referring to cultural power. Military power achieves its objective through a regime change and by imposing a new regime that secures the results that the military power desires. Soft or cultural power works through quiet persuasion, more by example, of ideas and ideals. It is like the introduction of the socialistic pattern in India. Although a discredited system (India remains, as proclaimed in its constitution, a socialist state) it was based on the ideas of the Fabian socialists (Sidney and Beatrice Webb in particular) and the post-revolution government and society in the Soviet Union that came into being after 1917. The main virtue of soft power is that it encourages freedom of thinking and action but it is the "power that comes from the setting the agenda and determining the framework of a debate."[14] The terms of reference are sought to be so framed that they provide ample freedom and creative leadership to the participants or the spending agencies in the context of our discussion. Freedom, as the ancient Greek thinkers and others have pointed out, creates a good deal of anxiety but could also encourage the adoption of a more prudent behaviour, and a capability to adapt to the changing situation, not to mention a growing awareness of the fact that the world is always changing and of the essence of governmental management in

---

13. See Nye, Joseph S. *(2002). The Paradox of American Power: Why the World's Only Superpower Can't Go It Alone.* New York: Oxford University Press; and Mead, Walter Russell, *Power, Terror, Peace and War: America's Grand Strategy in a World at Risk.* New York: Vintage Books.

14. Nye's remark quoted in Mead, 2004.: 25.

keeping with the changing economy. In the financial literature, this type of power is analysed in terms of steering versus rowing.

At the first stage, it is necessary for government to make a choice about the nature of the power that it wishes to exercise and also make a choice between two binary sets: (a) proactive or reactive, and (b) macro or micro management. It is clear from experience that a reactive stage of control in which the finance ministry makes policies only on the basis of proposals reaching it is not constructive, as by this time the spending agencies would have already made up their minds about the content of their programme for the next year. The only item on which they are waiting for a response is the level of resources that would be available and their energies would be devoted thereafter to devising strategies that would bring their goals to fruition. A proactive stance on the other hand involves a preliminary exercise in the likely quantum of resources that could be made available to each agency. For a knowledgeable finance ministry, and for a central agency that wishes to exercise central control of the soft type, the way to management is to determine the ceilings for each ministry so that its creative efforts could be geared to the determination of priorities that could be pursued within the ceiling .

This choice has to be followed by another complementary one: whether the finance ministry wants to engage in macro or micro management. Experience is conclusive in this regard. In the current world, ministries have grown to be too big to make micro management by them feasible (although many finance ministries continue to nurse the delusion that they are capable of such micro management). The efforts of the finance ministry should ideally be geared to the maintenance of an arm's-length relationship with the spending agencies. Too much of intrusive, detailed control would make the spending agencies forget their own role in the functioning of a system of financial discipline. Far too little control could on the other hand have the effect of making the spending agencies far more creative, particularly in ways and methods that are far from welcome.

In devising the control framework, the finance ministry has also to be mindful about the extent of detail that it wishes to present to the legislatures in the demands for grants. Members of Parliament tend to demand more detail even when they are not engaged in approving appropriation bills except in the guillotine hour. But the legislature being the paramount power needs to be given the detail that it seeks. It has also to be realised that the legislatures do not have the time now to absorb the excessive details that they are being provided in the existing system. It is averred in some quarters that excessive detail has the effect of diverting attention from the important policy questions in a context where the members are stuck in the pool of detailed information . Essentially, too much detail masks the choice of control. The nature of financial management is that its life is one of a series of discontinuities; the issues that the ministries handle keep changing every year or even during the year. This necessitates a frequent change in the anchor of expenditure management and in shifting from one anchor to another: anticipation is half the game. This approach proceeds on the assumption that spending agencies need plenty of freedom and open space in which they manage their programmes. In doing so, the voice of the finance ministry should be that of an expert who is able to achieve more through the timely provision of advice without leaning too heavily on the spending agencies.

The task of the finance ministry extends beyond the rendering of policy advice to ensuring that the administrative ministries have adequate financial management systems and that they have the willingness to deploy them for attaining the collective goals of government. The importance and content of the systems vary from one ministry to another. The defence ministry, for example, is engaged in spending the money on itself, on its human resources, machinery and materials. The task of the ministry of rural development tends to be different in that a substantial part of its budget is in the form of grants-in-aid to state and local governments. The task of the ministry, crudely but realistically put, is to be an ATM for the sub-national governments in the sphere of rural development. Both ministries form important links in the chain of the central government, which, however, is only as strong as the weakest link.

It is therefore necessary to form a series of "stress tests" that ensure that the proper financial management systems operate in these ministries. Stress tests aim at identifying the vulnerable areas of the ministries and analysing the adequacy of the systemic responses to the changing needs. These could involve the management of human resources (the defence ministry continues to suffer from severe manpower shortages, affecting in turn the tooth-to-tail ratios) or management of contracts, be they for construction or the acquisition of crucial equipment that essentially determines the level of defence preparedness or the public-private partnerships engaged in the provision of services on behalf of the government but entirely funded by the government, or pending legal cases where the outcome is uncertain, which makes it difficult to formulate contingent policy responses. By their very nature, the stress tests cannot be uniform; the uniformity is limited to the range of choices in policy actions available to government. Stress tests have the potential of making the expenditure system more responsive in anticipating and in dealing with the dynamic situations. The tests should be broad enough to enable the central agencies to deal with the vulnerabilities inherent in the situation. They have the potential of ensuring a much-needed shift from the philosophy of one-size-fits-all.

The final step in the renewal of the system is to undertake systemic reforms. Many of the issues that are currently faced have been enumerated at various places in the preceding discussion. Without being repetitive, some of them may be synoptically noted. The structure of the system needs to be reorganised to be more inclusive: also compatible systems should be developed at the sub-national levels, more so at the local level and among the non-governmental organisations that are virtually functioning as extended arms of the government. The resource allocation systems need to be revamped with a clearer understanding of the profile of each agency. Toward this end, detailed forward planning at programme level should be undertaken on a rolling basis. The annual guidance should be based on the economic outlook and should include an identification of the programmes that need to be pruned or altogether eliminated. The outcome budgets should reflect the changing priorities as well as the economies that are sought to be achieved.

As a supporting technical measure, the system should include the development of costs of programmes and projects, distinct from annual outlays. The budget should become a firm beacon rather than being changed too frequently during the year. A systematic effort should be made to reduce the moral hazard inherent in the existing policies of dealing with the spending agencies and with the sub-national governments. The financial risks and systemic hurdles should be analysed in terms of their impact on the course of budget implementation. The process of resource utilisation should be congruent with the budgetary intent and a consistent process of funds release should be an essential ingredient of a revamped process. More important, constant vigilance should go beyond monitoring the trends in financial utilisation to the social effects of such utilisation; the budget, as an extension of government's policies, should become, in addition to being a financial instrument, a means of achieving a just society. That goal should be evident at every step of the process.

It is only then that the expenditure management system becomes a valued instrument in the arsenal of the government to serve the interests of society. Anything less is tantamount to maintaining a ritual, ignoring the vital purpose for which it was designed in the first place. A renewal of effort to make the system a vibrant and responsive one is not a matter of choice. It is a necessity mandated by the times.

Appendix

Ethics and Corporate Action

Like any other activity, corporate activity and associated management gives rise to many ethical questions. Like all decisions in economics, corporate decisions also relate to the allocation of resources. It is a matter of choice between labour and technology, e.g., employment of advanced technology could require, as a complementary effort, additional investment and hiring of labour. Alternatively, more technology could be considered as labour saving and far more productive than may have been the case. In developing countries, where more emphasis is laid on greater employment of human resources, governments may provide incentives to the corporate sector to maintain, as a minimum effort, the existing level of staff. The alternative would be retrenchment, where the labour would be shifted to receive unemployment benefits or additional efforts may be made to "retool" the workforce to learn new skills for which there is demand in the market. These multiple facets illustrate the choices that are made both by the corporate sector and by the government. Although the corporate sector does not have specific social responsibilities (its primary business is to secure a reasonable rate of return for the investment made and the trust reposed in the corporation by the shareholder) in the same way that a government has, it has the potential of acquiring a good deal of adverse publicity (that may prove to be far more costly than giving pink slips to a few individuals) when its approaches run contrary to the wishes of the community. Thus decision-making in these circumstances is not as easy as may appear at first sight.

The decision also gives rise to ethical questions. In a pluralistic society, one man's losses are another person's gains. In a parliamentary democracy ethical issues are sought to be resolved through voting, which might also translate into situations when for the sake of majority, the minority may have to forgo some benefits. In other words, it is difficult to attain Pareto optimality as there is some section of people who may have to make greater sacrifices in order that the majority in a democracy would benefit. The trade-off in each case tends to be different from another case and any generalisation tends to suffer from severe limitations. The problems involved in these transactions were sought to be illustrated, in classes of philosophy, through a hypothetical case of what is called a trolley problem, which requires the sacrifice of a fat man to save other human lives, including those who are in the trolley and those who are working on the trolley track. This illustration has acquired considerable traction in the literature and continues to attract a good deal of discussion both in the classrooms and in the conference halls.[1] A similar case, drawn from incidents in everyday life, has been made into a movie entitled "Two Days and One Night", produced in Belgium, and has attracted the attention and critical acclaim even of a stodgy periodical like *The Economist* (22 August 2014). This case offers us considerable scope to illustrate the complex ethical dimensions and the difficulty in achieving any meaningful solution except through the process of establishing morality through numbers, viz., majority and minority.

The story of the film, like the New Age films produced in Italy and Japan during the early 1950s, is fairly simple. It is about a small company which has sixteen employees and another lady employee. The lady employee's case, in particular her continuation in her present position, is the question awaiting a decision from the management. The management says that it is willing to continue her in her job if the other employees are willing to forgo their annual bonuses. In short, their bonuses would pay her annual wage. What do her colleagues think of the choice given to them – their sacrificing the bonus so that it could finance the wages of the lady and what is their responsibility for her? An added complication is that she is the only breadwinner in the family and it would face severe difficulties if she is retrenched in her present job. On the other side, each employee, who would otherwise have received his bonus, has his own needs, commitments and personal obligations, all awaiting the payment of the bonus. If it is surrendered to pay for the wages of the lady, then they have to make a lot of adjustments in their personal lives. So, what should be their decision? Is it meaningful for the lady to expect others to forgo their bonus so that her wages could be paid? What is their obligation to her? Does the company have an ethical responsibility to maintain the existing level of employment while paying bonuses even when the company is not doing too well? These and a host of other related questions need to be answered and the ethics involved need to be examined.

The situation offers a variety of options and many of them appear reasonable and even sympathetic. These options need to be considered in some detail.

1. For a recent discussion of this highly stimulating case, see Edmonds, David, *Would You Kill the Fat Man*, Princeton, MA: Princeton University Press, 2014

(i) It may be argued that hiring and firing are within the rights and responsibilities of a company. It retrenches some workers when its production levels have been reduced owing to a weak demand for its products. Even governments that are wedded to the concept of social responsibility have been engaged in promoting voluntary retirement schemes and on occasion have even reduced the levels of their staff through retrenchment. Given this overall tendency, why should this case be treated differently? Inevitably, every measure aimed at reducing the staff levels has its own costs and in many cases, it also means changing the demographics of the workforce in that the young are retained while those that have long records are let out. All these practices are now accepted by governments and societies alike without any demur. In turn this means that the lady's case is not different from all those who have lost their jobs.

This approach does not go into the ethical implications at all as it is based on the conviction that lines have already been drawn in a clear manner, demarcating the situations where companies and governments reduce their workforce depending on their financial position. As a consequence of such an action by the employers, the affected parties make their adjustments and proceed with their altered lives. The acceptance of this approach means that society has no responsibility in these cases and each affected individual makes his own decision. From a broader angle, however, it is appropriate to consider, when the numbers of affected parties become large, whether society and the collective devices evolved by it should undertake some introspection to reduce the individual deprivation. This may appear as a political question but it is also an ethical one in that it tries to determine society's role in minimising these hardships. Indeed it is this recognition that has led to the formulation of social assistance schemes.

(ii) The problem is one but the solutions are many. The choice, in turn, poses the problem of selection for the decision-maker. The greater the number of decision-makers, the larger may be the range of solutions, as each one looks at the problem *de novo* and from his own prism, which may not be the conventional one. At the preliminary stage it is appropriate to consider *all* the available options. It is also necessary to differentiate between the decision-making approaches of the political class and the administrative class. The former class has other channels of accountability. In the day-to-day work, the task of the latter class is to present the different options available to the former group and explain the strengths and weaknesses of each option and its current and potential capacity to face the problem and its consequences.

Accordingly, another option may be considered. The proposal offered by the management may be rejected by the workers' union. Such rejection puts the workers on a confrontation path with the management, which in the new developing situation may seek the services of an adjudicator to resolve the issue. Meanwhile the problem escalates and becomes a do-or-die question for the workers' union, a situation that was not imagined by the management when it made the first offer of paying the wages of the lady from the funds earmarked for bonuses for the staff. In this developing situation, the union, depending on how it perceives its own strength, may even threaten to go on strike. The strike, when it becomes unavoidable, may be for a prolonged period and the management may declare a lock-out. General experience shows that in India a small issue between labour and management escalates into a major conflict in a short period, with even threats issued to the management. There are situations in which a distinction between what is an individual grievance and a collective grievance is blurred and the former morphs into the latter as a form of natural progression. The situation described here is not out of the ordinary. In situations of this type, the lock-out by the management may lead to the unemployment of the workforce, which stands to lose its regular earning power, let alone the bonus that was one of the original issues of the problem. In the context of a lock-out, the management also stands to lose a good deal in that it makes money only when the unit is working. The issue then morphs into a major financial crisis, with major consequences for all the participants in the conflict. If the product of the unit is of importance to the community, it also stands to lose a good deal.

The question then is that a small issue has the potential of transforming a win-win situation (i.e. when the unit is working) to a loss-loss position. The ethical issue is whether the union is correct in making an individual issue into a major issue of collective bargaining. Similarly, the question could also be raised whether the management's response is ethical if it is recognised that it also has an unspecified responsibility to the community. But is that responsibility such that it should be prepared to incur losses? Or should it resort to political arm-twisting of the union so that it is persuaded to give up its demand? These chain reactions become a part of the problem, and all of them assume serious proportions; and as such, the necessity of resolving the problem at the earliest stage becomes an obvious solution. It does not, however, resolve the underlying issue: on the other hand, the problem is exacerbated at every stage.

(iii) The foregoing discussion of the dimensions of the issue makes it clear that what is ethical is that the solution should be financially sound while also serving the interests of the community. Toward this end, other alternatives may be envisaged by the parties and by the representatives of the people, in the event that political mediation is also brought into the picture. This underlines the fact that in a democracy very few issues can be settled and ethical considerations met except with the participation of the people too.

With a view to avoiding drastic courses of action, it may be considered appropriate by the parties to explore other alternatives. (a) The workers may request the management to consider moderating the demand made by the latter in that the burden may be equally shared by the workers and the management. Under this approach the workers agree to forgo a part of their bonus and the management for its part would also be prepared to share the burden. Each party would consider its contribution as equivalent to the annual contributions made to the United Givers Fund (an autonomous fund maintained as a non-government body in the United States to which white- and blue-collar workers of all organisations contribute voluntarily and the proceeds are given to needy people). (b) The unit may be organised as a cooperative rather than as a company owned by the investors. In this proposal, the workers may become the owners and managers and in that format may be willing to share the burden for a short period. (c) The unit may be taken over by the government and the additional cost of maintaining the lady may be borne by the government: a variation of this approach is for the government to provide alternative employment for the lady. And (d) to evolve a programme under which some workers may take early retirement, making place, in the process, to the lady who would have otherwise been unemployed. Many of these approaches look to the government as a solution, which also involves socialising the costs of unemployment of a single person or a group of persons. It is important to note that once the government takes over the case, the appropriateness of socialising the costs is generally not raised again, as the assumption is that it is an obligation which the government has to discharge.

What obligations are to be assumed and what obligations are to be ignored becomes an ethical question in that those who stand to benefit and those who stand to lose out belong to different groups. For example, in the financial crisis of 2008, the financial rescue package devised by the US government primarily helped the financial industry, while thousands of people lost their homes due to foreclosure. In terms of the number of people, the former home owners were clearly in a majority. In this case, it was not the numbers but the political clout of the financial industry and the argument that in the absence of the bailout, the economy would come to a halt.[2] The ethical question becomes further muddled when politics are injected into the scene. It also means that ethical issues cannot be determined solely on ethics but will have to be considered in conjunction with the economic situation and the political context.

Changes in the levels of employment are usually the results of changes in economic activity and may also be influenced by changes in the international

---

2. In formulating this package, the meaning of the term itself has been changed to mean something different. Normally, bailout, a nautical phrase, means throwing the water over the side of the boat, while in the government parlance, it was used to mean injection of money

activity and thus go beyond the range of correction by domestic authorities. When the economic situation changes for the worse, it becomes incumbent on the government to take corrective action. In general, the responsibility for a review of the economy rests on the government but the corporate sector may also be assigned a role that complements the efforts of the government. The participants in the market become instruments for economic action. But the market itself will continue to function under the normal demand-and-supply rules, though government actions aim at manipulating the levers of market economic activity. Extending the above example, the question arises whether the corporate sector is expected to assume additional social responsibilities so that the outcome may be better. It is normally held that every individual acquires some values of public life learnt from his religion or through a process of osmosis with the elders in society. These values, which are common to all religions, include charity, compassion and piety. Are these values to dominate the approaches of corporate bodies during periods when economic activity is in a recession? No definite answers are provided by ethics. Ethics does not prescribe a particular approach. It leaves it to the participants to judge the proper course of action within the overall framework of public values. Then the task of determining the proper course of action is left to the individual or to the corporate body concerned. Such delegation of responsibility is appropriate where there are several decision-makers with diverse interests and different rates of compliance to the set of common values. In everyday activity there are several economic decisions that are made by every participant in the market. The individual enjoys total freedom to make his own decisions. Some of the participants' decisions may adversely affect some groups of individuals, and some others may enjoy the benefits. This aspect and its occurrence in daily life may be seen from the following example.

It is common experience that in the cellular age, where every consumer is viewed as an uncrowned king, many individuals receive calls on their phone (there is no direct contact between the individual and the caller except through voice) asking him to order this or that product. The sales pitch may be high-powered but the consumer is not moved as he already has one of those products and does not need a new one. The caller at the other end of the phone, however, continues her efforts to persuade the consumer, and as a final tipping point may appeal to the compassion of the consumer, saying that she is short of her assigned target for sales for the day and her failure to sell the product could lead to her getting a pink slip. So, could the gentleman please place an order for one unit and save her from joining the ranks of the unemployed? Does the consumer have a responsibility to save her? Ethically it is the responsibility of the consumer to decide one way or another. He is entitled to his fundamental right under the unwritten charter of the market. If he chooses to be compassionate, he does so at his own expense and out of his own choice. If on the other hand, he rejects the appeals of the marketing caller and if the caller would, as a consequence, be unemployed – a possibility that cannot be eliminated – then the consumer may feel a bit of remorse, and if he is very sensitive, may even seek the pardon of the gods, but would quickly reconcile to the fact that these adjustments are a part of the market functioning. The functioning of the market has an ethical issue that is always in the background and thus may not even be recognised by the participants.

Index

A

accounting standards 55, 292
agreements, contractual 120
administrative
games 48
process 48, 120, 157
appropriation, re-appropriation, misappropriation 12, 20, 21, 22, 26, 30, 47, 49, 55, 64, 104, 106, 108, 137, 144, 201, 209, 213, 214, 219, 220, 286, 293, 298
assets, natural 192, 290, 291
atomic energy 174-76, 178, 181-83, 279, 280

B

bidding 93, 128, 145
Budget, annual 13, 19, 21, 45, 49, 50, 60, 75, 87, 90 103, 108, 138, 216, 219, 286, 287-89, 293, 296
budgeting, outcome 15, 19, 58, 261, 292
bureaucracy, street-level 26

C

citizens' grievances 14, 91
colonial magisterial outlook 283
conflicts, social 253
Constitution of India 20, 23, 30, 213, 232
contractorisation 124, 126, 127, 130, 133, 134, 143, 145-149, 153, 159, 161
controls, policy, process, regulatory and performance 45
corporate sector 19, 39, 41, 43, 55, 80, 81, 85, 96, 99-117, 119, 122-25, 128, 134-37, 139, 151, 158, 173, 182, 183, 186, 188, 204, 228, 258, 268, 277, 290, 291, 303, 308
government: differences and similarities 110

D

dependency, effects of 247
development fee 120, 121

E

East India Company 12, 106, 110, 111, 208, 223, 251, 264
economy, efficiency and effectiveness 58, 87, 294
expenditure
determination of 39, 40
management, anchor of 276, 299
planning, medium term 43
reduction 75

ethics and corporate action 303-09
European Union 86, 112, 164, 224

F

Finance Commission 51, 60, 69, 91, 127, 194, 202, 228, 231, 236, 241, 242, 245-48, 281
Finance Department 12, 56, 89, 106, 107, 210, 216, 248, 288, 291
financial
  crisis, 2008 69, 104, 160, 162-64, 166, 194, 224, 307
  federalism 230, 239
  management, internal 19, 22, 24, 56, 90, 96, 103
  stability 18, 19, 71, 193
fiscal
  balance 198
  policy 13, 17, 18, 68, 84, 287
framework, ends and means 255

G

grant-in-aid 138, 204, 228, 237
government and corporate sectors, plans and operational culture 103

I

institutions, international 21

J

jugaad or Indian adjustment process 32, 163, 210
just state by just means 13

K

Kautilya 12, 51, 136, 160, 257

M

MPLADS 64, 65

N

NGOs 133, 137-41, 155, 157, 179, 203, 207, 208

P

payment/s
  process 53, 211, 214
  third party 125
performance budgeting 13
PPPs (public-private partnerships) 15, 28, 60, 62, 81, 92, 95, 96, 119, 121-23, 153, 157, 174, 203, 204, 207, 212, 221, 258, 261, 268
planning, strategic 183
political
  interference 130-33, 145, 177, 278
  markets 43
  mediation 62, 63, 117, 127, 139, 306
process controls 45, 50, 51, 69
public
  borrowing 14, 274, 281
  expenditure management, principles of 11
  management philosophy, new 44, 102, 119
purchases, bulk 93

R

Ram Rajya 257, 262
regulatory
  agencies 163, 165-68, 171
  controls 45, 54
reporting system 71, 72, 103, 155-157, 237

remunerative dependence 243
resource
allocation 37-39, 41-43, 45, 49, 254, 293, 300, 303
utilisation 37, 45, 59, 61, 69, 96, 219, 248, 300
Ricardian theory of equivalence 14
risk analysis 164
RTI (Right to Information) 120, 131, 261, 265, 277

S

services, delivery of 64, 67, 122, 143-54, 276-78
social services 81, 133
state
hollow 19, 143, 221, 261, 267, 268, 270
soft 258, 267, 269, 270

T

tax
administration 50
exemption 61
tribals, rehabilitation 65, 66

U

urban-rural divide 134